Across Great Divides

true stories of life at Sydney Cove

'First Fleet in Sydney Cove': original painting by marine artist, Frank Allen

Susan E Boyer

©Birrong Books

Published in Australia by Birrong Books
PO Box 255, Glenbrook, NSW, 2773
www.birrongbooks.com
www.susanboyer.com.au
Email: boyer@eftel.net.au

First published in Australia by Birrong Books in 2013
Reprinted in 2016

Copyright © Susan E Boyer 2013

National Library of Australia Cataloguing-in-Publication:
Author: Boyer, Susan E,

           Across Great Divides: true stories of life at Sydney Cove

ISBN: 9781877074424 (paperback)
Notes: Includes bibliographical references and index.
Subjects: Aboriginal Australians - First contact with Europeans.
           Aboriginal Australians - Social conditions - History.
           Aboriginal Australians - Biography.
           Convicts - Australia - Biography.
           Convicts - Australia - History - 1788-1821.
           First Fleet, 1787-1788.
           Penal colonies - New South Wales.
           Sydney (N.S.W.) - History, 1788-1851.
           New South Wales - History, 1788-1851.
           Australia - History, 1788-1851.

Dewey Number: 994.402

Cover design by Susan Boyer
Cover images of historical people (from left to right) are: Sarah Leadbeater, a convict who later married a soldier, marine officer Watkin Tench who kept a journal of his adventures and an unnamed Aboriginal man whose portrait was later found among the papers of Governor Macquarie.
These images were supplied by Mitchell Library, State Library New South Wales.
The harbour image is a detail from an original painting, 'First Fleet in Sydney Cove' and supplied by courtesy of its creator, Frank Allen.
Maps herein are by Susan & Leonard Boyer.

Information for Indigenous Australian communities:
Readers, please be aware that this book contains names and images of deceased persons which in some Indigenous Australian communities may offend cultural prohibitions.

This book is dedicated to my sons, Adam and Clinton Bagley whose namesake, Corporal James Bagley arrived in Sydney Cove in January 1788, with the First Fleet...and to all those who have strived since to make Australia a just and equitable place to live.

Across Great Divides

Would you cross a great divide
if you thought someone had lied
about what lay on the other side?

Would you take the long slow fight
so all could live with equal right?
Close the gap 'tween black and white?

Would you take an unknown ride
to open doors, change the tide
of ignorance so long denied?

Would you?

S. Willder

Contents

Acknowledgements   vii

A note from the author   viii

Forward by Peter Turbet   x

Maps of Sydney Cove, etc.   xi

Ships of the First Fleet   xiv

Introduction – setting the scene   xvi

1.   The end and the beginning   1

2.   First encounters   3

3.   A line in the sand   11

4.   Strange comings and goings   14

5.   Sydney Cove, 1788   17

6.   Reflections   20

7.   Different eyes - different sight   27

8.   Issues and challenges   31

9.   A night of revelry   36

10.   The governor's speech   39

11.   Strange appearances and disappearances   44

12.   Creatures, great and small   47

13.   A beating for a beating   50

14.   View from the ridge   53

15.   Beyond the boundary   59

16.   The Kable's story   65

17.   Into the wild blue yonder   70

18.   Into the unknown wilderness   74

19.   Friends and thieves   77

20.   Frustration and progress   82

21.   The rush-cutter incident   85

22.   Across the social divide   89

23.   Across the racial divide   96

24.   Rose Hill   100

25.   An opportunity not to be missed   103

Contents

26. Kidnaps and adoptions 106

27. Into the vast unknown, 1789 118

28. 'A most unpleasant service' 125

29. Teachers and students 131

30. Impatient for news 134

31. Survival tactics 136

32. Crucial decisions 139

33. The escape 146

34. Thoughts of freedom 148

35. Letters and questions 150

36. The Second Fleet, 1790 153

37. Mayhem at Manly Cove, 1790 161

38. Making amends 170

39. Pemulwuy 181

40. Retaliation 184

41. Conflict and bungles 188

42. Growth and adjustment 196

43. Life and death 200

44. Forward planning 204

45. New territory 206

46. Great escapes 217

47. Family matters 223

48. Arrivals and departures 225

49. Nanberry and Ballooderry 230

50. Maurgoran's family 236

51. More goodbyes 239

52. A time of transition 247

53. Pondering the known and the unknown 252

Illustrations of Sydney and relevant people 265

Notes on sources 270

Bibliography 301

Index 310

Acknowledgements

It is with pleasure and appreciation that I acknowledge the following people:

I am thankful for the comprehensive and thoughtful review of this book by Christopher Tobin, Aboriginal cultural consultant, writer, and artist. His comments added much to the culturally sensitive issues in this account and contributed to a more precise coverage of Aboriginal content. I also wish to thank Aboriginal researcher, Gai Marhiene for her reading of this book and her positive feedback on its attention to indigenous history. I am also very thankful that history writer Peter Turbet, whose research and writing I admire, agreed to read this work and contribute his valuable observations on its historical content.

I would like to acknowledge marine artist, Frank Allen, for allowing me to use images of his paintings *'First Fleet in Sydney Cove'* and of the transport ship, *'Lady Penhryn'*. I would also like to thank Rhona Hughes and Andrew Boyer for their thorough appraisal and constructive written feedback on the earlier versions of the book. I'd like to thank Jeanette Christian, Clinton Bagley and Ray Bonello for their editorial and proofreading work. I'd also like to thank my family, friends, and colleagues who read the manuscript at various stages and offered insightful comments: in particular, Edward and Peter Boyer, Robert Ellis and Elizabeth Hunt. Julie Ellis came up with the great idea of providing a bookmark with a list of historical characters in the book. My husband, Len knows how much I have appreciated his support throughout the project.

History lecturer, Associate Professor Carol Liston, School of Cultural Histories and Futures, University of Western Sydney, initiated my interest in Australian colonial history and I am very grateful to her for that.

I wish to recognise the research assistance provided by the staff at the Mitchell Library, State Library of New South Wales, National Library of Australia, New South Wales State Records, Penrith City Library and Blue Mountains Library.

I am thankful for the input of those mentioned above; however any errors herein are my sole responsibility. I would be grateful to know if any are found.

Notes on quotations in this book taken from original sources:

Where there are several spelling variations for Aboriginal and English names in original quotes, one variation has been adopted to avoid confusion. Minor changes have been made to direct quotations where punctuation, spelling or grammar could hinder understanding of the original. For example, 'cloathes' has been change to 'clothes'; 'musquet' to 'musket'. Full stops have been added to sentences where original paragraphs contained none.

A note from the author

It was a clear autumn morning when I sailed between the sandstone cliffs to enter Sydney Harbour for the first time. I was only seven years old but the excitement and anticipation in the crowd leaning over the deck-rail was contagious. Houses dotted the escarpment in clusters, but for the most part, the many little coves bounded by dense low forest, were deserted. Ahead, the iconic Sydney Harbour Bridge spanned the tapering waterway of the harbour. It was the early 1960s; the Opera House had been conceived, but not yet built.

I was part of a government sponsored immigration program to encourage the settling of British families in Australia. I was the child of 'ten pound poms' as we were then known. It had been difficult to leave aunts, uncles and cousins in England and the six week voyage had seemed endless, but my parents had made the journey in the hope of a better life in the 'lucky country'.

In my naivety, I had expected Sydney to look like a wild-west town such as those portrayed in American movies: timber buildings with wide verandahs lining dusty streets. My vivid imagination had pictured ladies wearing long dresses and bonnets shopping with baskets over their arms. I'd imagined koalas gazing down at the scene from the gum trees and kangaroos hopping amid the activity with joeys peering from their pouches. So, I was surprised and somewhat disappointed to see tall, modern buildings against the skyline, and to see tarred roads and noisy traffic when we disembarked. I didn't realise then how fortunate I was.

I was completely unaware of the fact that less than two hundred years earlier, children my age had sailed through the heads of Sydney Harbour as I had done, but as the children of convicts or marines on the 'First Fleet'. Had I known the history, I could have imagined their arrival on one of the small timber ships after eight long months at sea and their first view of the dense and mysterious wilderness surrounding their landing place; so different to the bustle of a crowded British city.

Had I known their stories then, I could have imagined being rowed ashore and landing on the narrow beach surrounded by nothing but virgin forest. I could have imagined their astonishment at seeing naked black people for the very first time, and the gradual realisation that *their* amazement on seeing white skin wrapped in strange body coverings was as mind-boggling as that of the new arrivals.

When I sailed into Sydney as a seven year old, I was aware that 'Aborigines' had lived in Australia 'before', but when we landed I had no expectation of seeing 'black people'. When we disembarked it was into a predominately white society as I'd expected. I didn't question the absence of Aboriginal people around the harbour; my young mind did not wonder about the transition. My ignorance of Australia's cultural journey continued far too long.

Sadly, during my continuing education, I didn't go on to learn much about Australia's early history. I learnt a few basics about Captain Cook's discovery of the east coast of Australia and Arthur Phillip as leader of the First Fleet, but that was about it. It wasn't until I was required to take compulsory units on 'Australian colonial history' at university that I began to see beyond those boring, skimpy facts.

My history lecturer, Associate Professor Carol Liston was responsible for introducing me to the fascinating world of the early colony: the lives of convicts, Aboriginal residents and their varied and dynamic encounters. It was only then that I began to grasp the unprecedented circumstances of the founding of Australia as a nation.

Fortunately, in recent years, the Australian School Curriculum has placed greater emphasis on the nation's formative years. However, it is by learning about real people's experiences that history comes to life and I want to share and spread those intriguing and vital stories. **'Across Great Divides – true stories of life at Sydney Cove'** aims to do just that. My wish is that, like me, those stories will leave you wanting to know more.

Susan Boyer, 2013

Forward

When the men and women of the First Fleet disembarked at Warran (Sydney Cove) in January and February 1788, the environment they encountered could not have been more alien. The climate was extreme, the plants and animals exotic and the culture of the indigenous people completely foreign. Similarly, when the men and women whose ancestors had lived around Warran for countless generations saw the light-skinned beings with their big canoes, strange body coverings and terrifying gooroobeera (sticks of fire) they must have felt something like we in the 21st century would feel if a multitude of extraterrestrials had landed in our neighbourhood.

This book examines the experiences of convicts, military personnel and Aboriginal people whose lives were thrown together during the seminal years of Australia's unique history. We read about the earliest inklings by some of the transported prisoners that their lives in the new land may be better than in the old but we also hear about the desperation of others who were driven to attempt escape. We learn about liaisons between soldiers and convict women as well as the tentative initial contacts between the Eora and the British. The first major punitive expedition against Aboriginal people is retold.

But we do not just read about the events in and around the new settlement, absorbing though they are. The book, very successfully, portrays how the people in our story actually felt as they confronted situations with which they had little previous exposure.

I recommend this book to all who want to know more about the fascinating and remarkable story of the human experience on the Australian continent.

Peter Turbet, 2013

Historian & author 'The Aborigines of the Sydney District before 1788' (2001) & 'The First Frontier: the occupation of the Sydney region , 1788-1816' (2011)

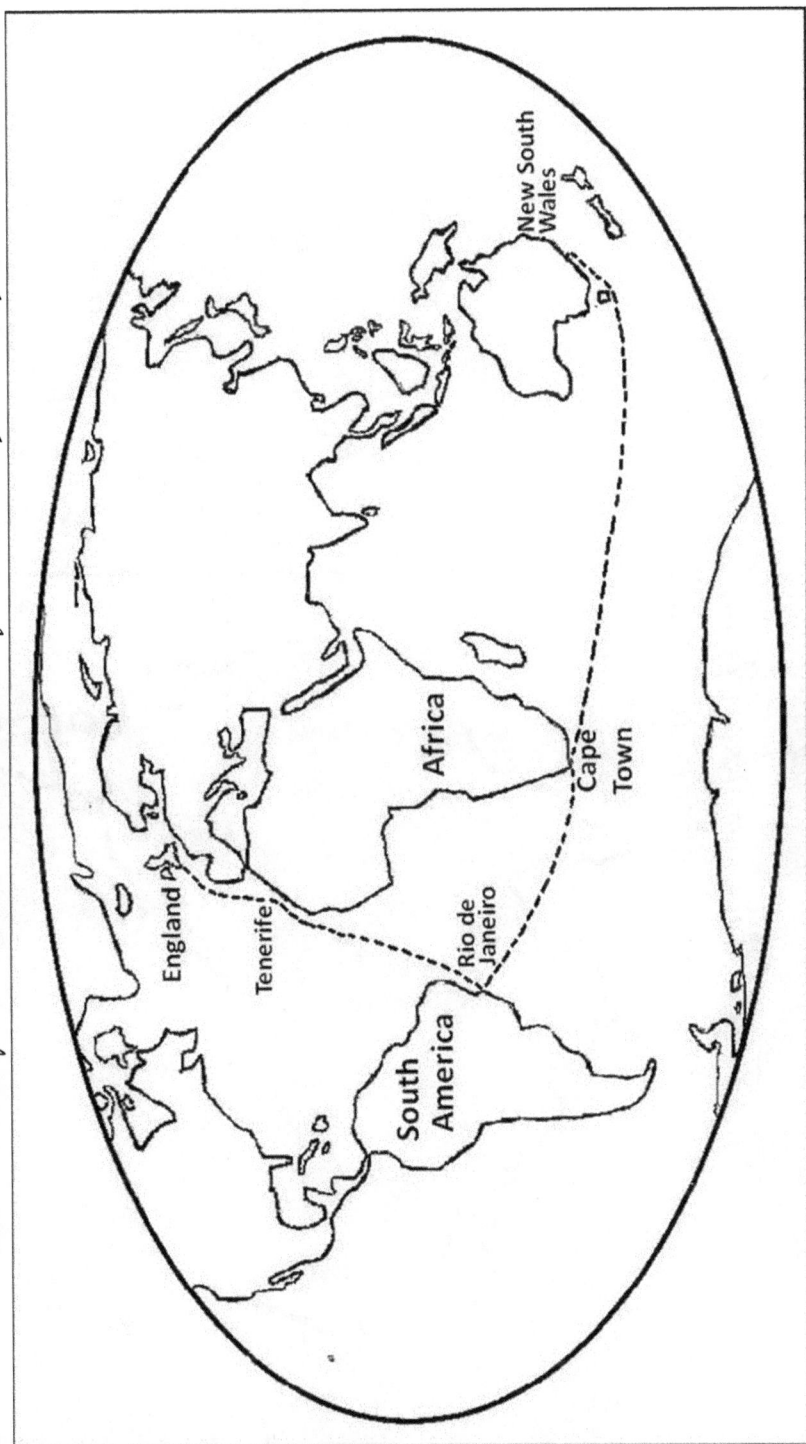

The route of the First Fleet, May 1787 – January 1788

The First Fleet's transfer from Botany Bay to
Port Jackson in January 1788

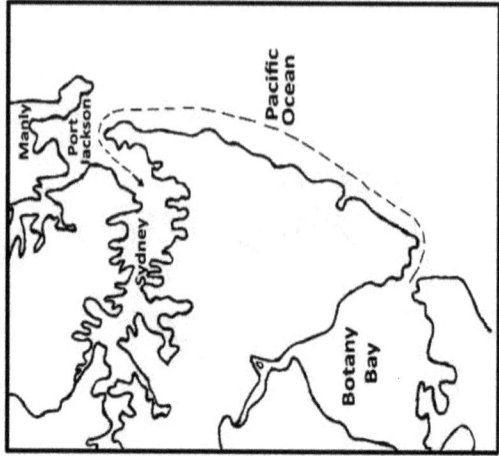

Sketch of Sydney Cove, April 1788

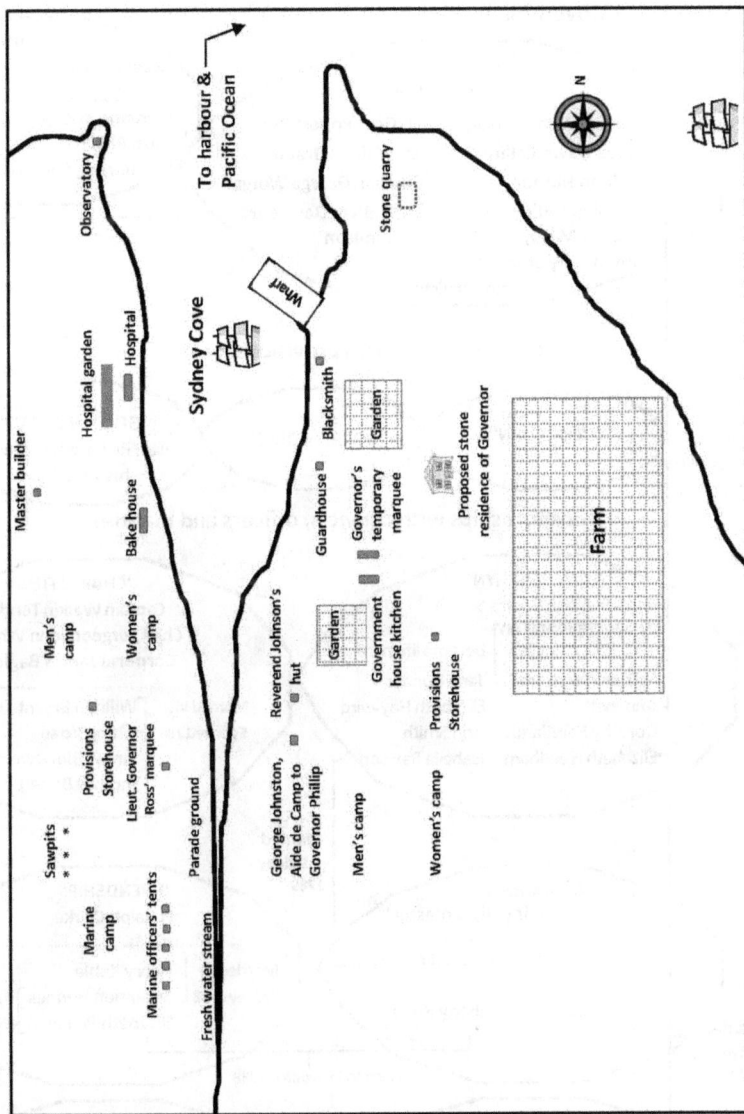

This sketch, based on the first published map of Sydney Cove, is attributed to Francis Fowkes, a convict transported for seven years for stealing a coat and boots. It depicts the marquees, storehouses and gardens of the Sydney settlement in April 1788 and shows the siting of the convict camps relative to the marines. You can see the original map at: http://nla.gov.au/nla.map-nk276. Now, the southern pylon of the Sydney Harbour Bridge stands near the original observatory. The Sydney Opera House is situated on the eastern point of the cove.

The eleven ships of the First Fleet with people related to this story:

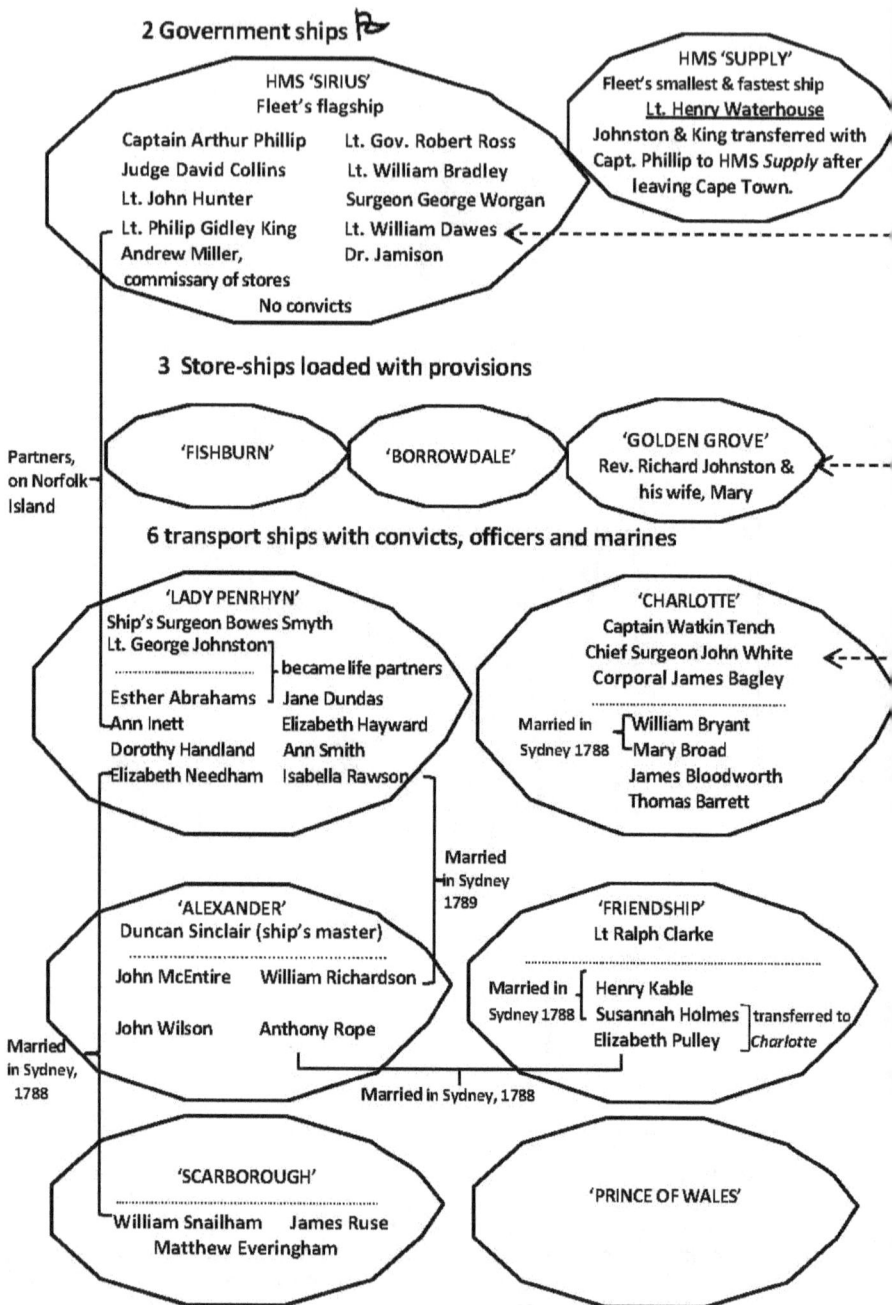

2 Government ships

HMS 'SIRIUS'
Fleet's flagship

Captain Arthur Phillip   Lt. Gov. Robert Ross
Judge David Collins   Lt. William Bradley
Lt. John Hunter   Surgeon George Worgan
Lt. Philip Gidley King   Lt. William Dawes
Andrew Miller,   Dr. Jamison
commissary of stores

No convicts

HMS 'SUPPLY'
Fleet's smallest & fastest ship
Lt. Henry Waterhouse
Johnston & King transferred with
Capt. Phillip to HMS *Supply* after
leaving Cape Town.

3 Store-ships loaded with provisions

Partners, on Norfolk Island

'FISHBURN'

'BORROWDALE'

'GOLDEN GROVE'
Rev. Richard Johnston &
his wife, Mary

6 transport ships with convicts, officers and marines

'LADY PENRHYN'
Ship's Surgeon Bowes Smyth
Lt. George Johnston

became life partners

Esther Abrahams   Jane Dundas
Ann Inett   Elizabeth Hayward
Dorothy Handland   Ann Smith
Elizabeth Needham   Isabella Rawson

'CHARLOTTE'
Captain Watkin Tench
Chief Surgeon John White
Corporal James Bagley

Married in Sydney 1788   William Bryant
                         Mary Broad
                         James Bloodworth
                         Thomas Barrett

'ALEXANDER'
Duncan Sinclair (ship's master)

John McEntire   William Richardson

John Wilson   Anthony Rope

Married in Sydney, 1788

Married in Sydney 1789

'FRIENDSHIP'
Lt Ralph Clarke

Married in Sydney 1788   Henry Kable
                         Susannah Holmes   transferred to
                         Elizabeth Pulley *Charlotte*

Married in Sydney, 1788

'SCARBOROUGH'

William Snailham   James Ruse
Matthew Everingham

'PRINCE OF WALES'

Note: Ship sizes are not to scale.

In all, there were almost 1,500 people aboard the First Fleet, including convicts, officials, marines and crew.

Aboriginal people of the Sydney region relevant to this book:

The native people of the Sydney region referred to themselves as 'Eora', meaning 'the people of this place'.

Arabanoo: the native man kidnapped and brought into Sydney in December, 1788

Pemulwuy: the native warrior who speared the convict, John McEntire

- - - - - - - - -> Pattye: young Aboriginal woman, who taught William Dawes her language

Yellomundi (also Yarramundi): a *'koradji'*, or renowned man of special healing powers, from the Hawkesbury area.

Aboriginal children, smallpox survivors, raised in the white settlement from 1789:

- - - - - - - - -> Boorong <- - - - - - - - - - - - - -> Maugaron (Boorong's father)

(13 year old girl adopted into the household of Rev & Mary Johnson) - - - - - - - -> Ballooderry (Boorong's brother)

friends

- - - - - - - - -> Nanberry <- - - - - - - -

(10 year old boy adopted by Chief Surgeon John White)

Eora (black men) kidnapped & brought into the Sydney settlement in 1789:

Colbee <- - - - -> (Daringa)
Bennelong <- - - - -> (Barangaroo)

wives of the kidnapped men after their escape from Sydney

Aboriginal men who volunteered to go to England with Governor Phillip:

Bennelong
Yemmerrawanne

Introduction

setting the scene

Imagine that one of your family or friends is about to embark on a journey across space to a proposed settlement on Mars. The event would no doubt create immense anticipation and interest. Everyone at home would want to keep track of their journey, follow their daily adventures and know the details of everything they saw and experienced in such alien surroundings. They would want to share the excitement of discovery.

Now visualise the scene of their departure under very different circumstances: imagine your friend or loved one being taken against their will, as punishment for an alleged crime, and from the day of their leaving till some unspecified time, communication between you will be cut off. An added issue is that in all likelihood the journey will be one-way; the prospect of a return passage is extremely improbable. They are in effect being banished. This unpleasant scenario - the absence of choice, lack of communication and little prospect of return - would of course completely alter feelings and reactions surrounding the impending journey.

★

In May 1787, when the 'First Fleet' of eleven ships set off from Britain to the furthest reaches of the globe to establish a colony, it would have been as unique and astounding as a journey to outer space. Almost 1,500 people, many against their will, were heading into a largely unchartered region; a vast and mysterious unknown. Captain Cook, the famous British explorer, had marked their destination on a map almost eighteen years earlier but no-one really knew what to expect. Nothing remotely similar had been attempted before and depending on the participants' involvement in the undertaking - whether they were going as prisoners, crew or appointed administrators - the experience would evoke a range of emotions: grief, fear, anticipation...

Back then, there were of course no satellites to send digital messages across the globe within seconds, so once the fleet left South Africa they were cut off from the civilized world. When the voyagers reached their destination, communication with home in the form of hand-written letters would take a turnaround time of at least twelve months, if there wasn't a ship wreck along the way. Therefore all news, whether it was an official report of great achievement or acute distress; or it was private news of a birth or a death, it would be received many months after the event.

When the letters and journals of those on the First Fleet did arrive in Britain, telling firsthand of adventure, disaster and discovery, it is not surprising that several were published and became best sellers. People in Britain were eager to know about the strange new land and speculation abounded: What kind of wild animals existed there? Had they found gold or other treasures? Were there lost civilisations? Were there the cannibals that had been hinted at in the London newspapers?

A young captain-lieutenant in the British military service by the name of Watkin Tench had volunteered for the venture, hoping it would be full of new experiences and discovery, and he kept a journal for publication. Knowing news of the isolated colony would be of great interest in Britain, his eyewitness stories gave a gripping account of the adventures he was having in his alien environment. He wrote about the plight of the convicts, his intriguing encounters with the native people and his daring excursions into the unknown interior. As it turned out, life in the colony was a rollercoaster of highs and lows and several times Watkin Tench ended up in very unenviable situations.

We have other journals too: the formal dispatches of the expedition's leader, Governor Phillip, and the private letters of officers with their mixed versions of events. We also have the observations of convicts who had been forced to take the voyage as punishment for their crimes. In fact, some of them wrote to their families before the ships even set sail from England.

Tench, as an inspector of convict letters, says they wrote about *'the impracticability of ever returning home, the dread of a sickly passage and the fearful prospect of a distant and barbarous country.'*

Their fear and distress was justified. The voyage of the First Fleet to Botany Bay, in a land known as 'Terra Australis', was unparalleled in history. They were heading to a place never before inhabited by white men. As the fleet left its last port of call at Cape Town, to cross the vast southern Indian Ocean to their mysterious destination, an officer on board wrote:

> *All communication with families and friends now cut off, we were leaving the world behind us, to enter a state unknown…*

The convicts, forced to take the journey imprisoned in dismal conditions below deck, would have been utterly miserable at their plight, not knowing what lay ahead for them.

As the ships approached their final destination after eight months at sea, another group of unsuspecting people were about to become participants in the unfolding drama of the First Fleet. They had no idea that eleven ships with over a thousand people were heading their way and about to land on their doorstep. They had no idea that their ancient and unperturbed existence was about to be shattered.

There were no journals written by those looking out from the shore in 1788; no recorded observations exist from those who watched the arrival of the pale people in their strange boats. But from accounts written by the fair-skinned visitors, we can envisage what happened. John White, Chief Surgeon of the fleet, stood on deck as his ship sailed into Botany Bay. He wrote in his journal what he saw:

> *As we sailed into the bay, some of the natives were on the shore, looking with seeming attention at such large moving bodies coming amongst them.*

So, we will begin with a view from the shoreline.

1

The end and the beginning

Picture yourself in the scene on the shoreline of Botany Bay, January 1788. It's late morning. You're at the beach with friends and family at a spot you've been coming to all your life. You've already been in for a dip and now you're sitting on a large curved boulder overlooking the bay, feeling the summer heat soak into your back.

There'll be fish for lunch – the catch is already well under way. You'll all move to the shade of the sandstone overhang in an hour or so; the sun is close to its highest point for the year. The sounds of frolicking are punctuated with the occasional shriek of a childish voice. The younger kids are busy gouging a trench around a mound of sand. You lay back on the smooth warm rock letting the sounds wash over you in a contented blur. You tilt your head slightly backwards giving an upside down view of the slope behind; the smooth pink angophora trunks against the backdrop of a brilliant blue sky.

You close your eyes, faintly aware of the chatter and the oily aroma of grilling fish mingled with wood smoke...Your daydreaming is pierced by a sharp menacing call.

'Warra, warra'! (Go away!)

You sit bolt upright. There's a buzz of alarm on the beach; someone pointing out to sea, others running toward the headland. It must be more than the childish squabble you'd initially imagined. Your curiosity turns to apprehension; your heartbeat quickens. You scramble across the rocks and follow the others to the headland. You stand in a group peering across the distant waves. Something strange is approaching; something you've never seen before.

Some of the older ones are agitated. They *have* seen this sight before. In their customary way the older men begin to relate the story, complete with vivid gestures. Like so many past events, the arrival of strangers long ago in their *murray nowee (very big canoe)* had been commemorated and incorporated into stories, song and dance. The story, though told with different words, went something like this:

> *It came in from the open sea, like a floating island with great white wings. When it reached our bay, strange beings put smaller boats over the side and came ashore. They were peculiar; their faces were as pale as sand. They offered curious implements and took our fishing spears in return.*
>
> *They tried to communicate with strange sounds but they couldn't speak properly. They needed water and we helped them. Soon they returned to their boat and left the way they came. We were relieved to see them go...they were so different...not like us at all.*[1]

That was many seasons ago now, but it seems the strange visitors are back. You watch, as the largest *nowee* you have ever seen, approaches from the sea. As it gets closer, you try to make out the creatures peering back across the water. You hear one of the older men tell the group to be wary of them. Others are following his lead, brandishing their spears and shouting,

'Warra, warra!'

But the shouting and aggressive gestures make no difference. The boats are getting closer. There is discussion now about how to deal with the visitors and not everyone agrees. You follow the others down the slope to the beach knowing something very significant is about to happen. This day will be remembered. This story will be related to your children and grandchildren and for generations to come...This day would be the end...and the beginning.

---

[1] For evidence of Aboriginal storytelling tradition, see notes for this chapter.

2

First encounters

Botany Bay, January 1788

As the white men leaned expectantly over the ship's rail, combing the shoreline for a suitable landing place, the black men in like manner, studied the huge approaching object. One of the fleet's doctors, George Worgan, an inquisitive young man who had never been so far from home before, described the scene in a letter to his brother Dick, in England:

> As we were sailing in we saw 8 or 10 of the natives, sitting on the rocks on the south shore and as the ships bordered pretty near, we could observe them talking to one another very earnestly, at the same time pointing towards the ships. They were...entirely naked, and each of them had long spears and a short stick in their hands.

Twenty-nine year old Lieutenant King, observing the natives from the deck of *HMS Supply*, tried to put himself in their situation. Considering what they must have been thinking as the ships' inhabitants became visible, he said, *'They seemed quite astonished at the figure we cut in being clothed'.* Then, further imagining himself through their eyes, he added: *'I think it very easy to conceive the ridiculous figure we must appear to these poor creatures who were perfectly naked.'*

As the British ships drew closer to the shore, the natives retreated into the forest where, according to our observer, they *'lit a fire, and sat around about it...as though nothing had occurred.'* We can only imagine the dilemma of the black men, gathered around their campfire after witnessing such a bewildering spectacle. We can only surmise the differing opinions and strategies that would have been put forward about their next move:

If we ignore the strange beings, they will go away in due course.

But no, look they are coming ashore! We must get away from here. No, we must find out their intentions...then can we decide what to do. We must go and meet them. We must show no fear.

☆

On seeing two smaller boats lowered over the side of the large ship and advancing towards the shore, the natives came out of the forest and walked along the beach at a safe distance from the water's edge. George Worgan described the incident when Governor Phillip landed on the beach:

> *The Governor held up some beads, red cloth and other baubles and made signs for them to advance... But they were still exceedingly shy and timid, and would not be enticed...*

> *The Governor...showed them his musket and then laid it on the ground, advancing singly towards them...Now seeing that he had nothing in his hands like a weapon, one of the oldest of the natives gave his spears to a younger and approached to meet the Governor...making signs for the things to be laid on the ground...*

> *At length, after various methods to impress them that we meant no harm...they began to show a confidence, and became very familiar and curious about our clothes, feeling the coat, waistcoat, and even the shirt and on seeing one of the gentlemen pull off his hat, they all set up a loud whoop.*

Eventually one of the natives was curious and confident enough to grasp at one of the officer's hair-braids, plaited at the back of his neck in the customary fashion. The daring young fellow, called to his companions to come and look at it, prompting *'another loud whoop, accompanied with other emotions of astonishment'.* In the same letter to his brother, Worgan painted the scene: *'In a word, they seemed pretty well divested of their fears, and became very funny fellows.'*

The natives, however, weren't the only ones who were curious. As Worgan describes the natives' body decorations, we can sense his awe and astonishment. The black men, he said, were decorated with *'red and white clay, and in such lines and circles as to resemble the belts, sashes, and ornaments of soldiers';* they had raised scars across their chests which *'seem to have been cut in particular lines by way of ornament.'* Most intriguingly, almost all the black men they met had an upper front tooth missing. The white men were at a loss to know what the custom signified among the natives, but it was obviously important to them because Worgan said the black men *'sometimes thrust their fingers into our mouths to see if we have parted with this tooth.'*

By an amazing coincidence Governor Phillip had exactly the same tooth missing in his mouth, and when the natives noticed this, they were *'somewhat pleased and surprised'.* The white men later learnt that the upper front incisor was deliberately removed as part of an initiation ceremony when a native boy reached the stage of becoming a warrior. The natives must have been intrigued that the leader of the white men had the same distinguishing feature.

Worgan also noted that some of the men had *'a bone thrust through the bottom division of their nose.'* Elaborating on nose piercing and decoration in his letter to his brother, he wrote:

> They likewise want to know if we have the hole in that part, so a fellow picked up a quill…and was trying to see whether he could poke it through my nose and two or three other gentlemen's, who were with me…

> Animal's teeth and bones, stuck in their hair with gum, is another of their elegant ornaments. When we took hold of these decorations to admire them, several good-natured fellows immediately pulled them off, and presented them to us.

At this early intercultural meeting, all participants seemed to be having a ball; the natives were *'laughing heartily and jumping extravagantly'*, as they allowed the white men to put caps on their heads and drape coloured cloth over their shoulders. But later, when each party regrouped, there would naturally be discussion about the peculiarities of the other culture and debate about how best to proceed.

Over the following few days, when all the ships of the fleet were anchored in Botany Bay, other 'first encounters' took place which helped to clarify some unresolved questions for each side of the cultural gulf. Watkin Tench, eager for interaction with the intriguing native inhabitants, devised a somewhat risky plan for opening communication with them in another area of the expansive bay; he hoped it would be the perfect ice-breaker...

☆

The natives stood in the shade that bounded the beach watching as a small boat drew closer to the water's edge. The figures wading ashore from the longboat were strange indeed. The only parts of their bodies to be seen were their odd-coloured faces; the rest was entirely covered, even their feet and the tops of their heads were hidden.

The white visitors approached cautiously up the beach, one of them holding the hand of a child of about seven, whose small, thin face was also as pale as sand. With the other hand the man gestured in a reassuring manner but the little one appeared unafraid as the group slowly moved forward. Both parties, the black natives within the fringe of trees and the white men venturing from the boats, carried weapons but the presence of a child had a calming effect; it seemed unlikely weapons would be needed after all. The initial apprehension of both parties faded; shoulders relaxed a little, replaced now by anticipation. The natives pointed at the child and spoke animatedly to each other as they came within a few paces of the strangers. The child, who still seemed unperturbed, was gently led forward and the white man holding his hand, gently pulled back the covering on the top half of his body to reveal the whiteness of his chest. The black natives gasped in amazement.

One of the black men, an older man with a long beard, edged closer. He leaned forward and put his hand tenderly on the child's head, muttering to himself. Others moved forward now to scrutinise the child's clothing. The young boy, by now becoming a little agitated, was taken back to the boat amid gestures of apology. But the black men weren't offended – they understood completely; they too had kept their own youngsters at a safe distance. Other white people came from the boat now carrying a heavy object up the beach and from it they took out a number of things which they offered to the natives.

What are they? Are they edible?

One of the natives put an object to his tongue but it was tasteless. It seemed a strange, pointless gift. The natives looked at each other; they must try to be tolerant. The black man allowed the white stranger to take the mirror from his hand, hold it up and demonstrate that the black man should look into it like water. But it still seemed of little value, worthless compared to his small stock of necessary implements and weapons. A white man now gestured to one of the spears. It hardly seemed a fair swap but the natives decided, after a mumbled discussion between themselves, that the white men would be offered a wooden club. That was all. Several more of the natives had by now come forward. Something had been bothering them.

What kind of creatures are these strangers? Are they men or women?

It was impossible to tell. Their cheeks were as smooth as girls' and their bodies were completely covered but they weren't behaving like women. They tried to question the white strangers who didn't seem to understand the simplest of questions.

Are you men or women? They tried using signs and gestures to ask.

At last one of the strangers grasped their meaning but seemed unsure how to respond. After some hesitation, one of the white men dropped his trousers and the truth was revealed, causing loud exclamations and embarrassed fits of laughter all around. The ice seemed to be broken.

The natives now attempted to teach the white men some basic words but though they repeated themselves patiently many times, the white men couldn't pronounce them properly, and after an hour, the natives gave up. The meeting was over.

Whurra, they called over their shoulders. The white men got the gist, interpreting the word to mean, *'be gone'.*

Despite the communication obstacles, restraint on both side of the cultural divide seemed to be relaxing and the white men, as they returned to their ship, were feeling positive; the natives however were still unsure of the newcomers' intentions. As they walked away, they wondered about the appearance of the mysterious strangers; close up they were very odd. Their noses were thin like fingers; their eyes pale; the odour of them was strange.

Who were the peculiar white beings?
Could they be spirits returned from death?

☆

Watkin Tench, the man who had led the little boy forward, had enjoyed his encounter with the natives. His assessment of meetings with the people of Botany Bay was optimistic and made the British intention clear:

> *...after several more interviews with the natives, which ended in so friendly a manner, we began to entertain some hopes of bringing about a connection with them. Our first object was to win their affections and our next to convince them of the superiority we possessed...*

However, not all the meetings between black and white at Botany Bay, ended on the high note assumed by Tench. Late one afternoon, a group of native men who were accustomed to spearing fish one at a time, watched with interest as the British threw a large net, called a seine, over the side of their boat. Their amazement was apparent when the white fishermen hauled up a great shimmering mass of fish in one clean swoop. Eagerly they paddled alongside the boat in anticipation. John

White, chief surgeon on the British fleet and a keen fisherman himself, wrote his version of the incident:

> *One evening while the seine was hauling, some of them were present, and expressed great surprise at what they saw, giving a shout expressive of astonishment and joy when they perceived the quantity that was caught. No sooner were the fish out of the water than they began to lay hold of them, as if they had a right to them, or that they were their own; upon which the officer of the boat, I think very properly, restrained them giving however to each of them a part. They did not at first seem very well pleased with this mode of procedure, but on observing with what justice the fish was distributed they appeared content.*

John White, seeing the episode through British eyes, believed the natives were 'content' with the fact that the white men decided who got what. The black residents however, in light of the fact that the harbour was their ancestral domain, may have been questioning the visitors' ignorance of established ways.

Did the strangers not understand that food caught or gathered, was traditionally shared among all?

The natives considered the issue but did not act in haste; they would wait and observe some more. They had already witnessed the white men's weapons of great power. In a previous meeting onshore, two groups of men, black and white, had engaged in sociable banter but in the actions of each, there had been an ominous message. John White described the encounter:

> *They were friendly... though each of them was armed with a spear or long dart and had a stick, with a shell at the end, used by them in throwing their weapons. Besides these, some few had shields made of the bark of the cork tree...sufficient to ward off their own weapons, some of which were pointed and barbed with the bones of fish, fastened on with some kind of adhesive gum.*

The white men, obviously keen to demonstrate their superior weapons, set the scene up for target practice by urging a native to place his shield at a distance. John White continues:

> One of the men who appeared to be the most confident, on signs being made to him, stuck the end of his shield in the sand, but could not be persuaded to throw his spear at it. So I fired a pistol ball through it. The explosion frightened him, as well as his companions a little; but they soon got over it, and on my putting the pistol into my pocket he took up his shield, and appeared to be very surprised at finding it perforated.

Not to be outdone however, the black man took the opportunity to 'caution' the white visitors:

> He then, by signs and gestures, seemed to ask if the pistol would make a hole through him, and on being told that it would, he didn't show the smallest signs of fear; on the contrary he tried to impress us with an idea of the superiority of his own arms, which... by staggering, and a show of falling wanted us to understand that the force and effect of them was mortal...

John White's later remarks provide a clue as to how the natives may have felt after that meeting:

> I am well convinced that they know and dread the superiority of our weapons... as they, on all occasions, have discovered a dislike to a musket and so very soon did they understand the nature of our military dress, that, from the first, they carefully avoided a soldier or any person wearing a red coat.

News of this demonstration of the stranger's 'gooroobeera' (sticks of fire) would have travelled overland in a short space of time. Many of the natives began to hope that, like last time, the white aliens would soon be gone.

3

A line in the sand

Meanwhile Arthur Phillip, the expedition's leader, had taken a small party of officers and select convicts in open boats further north along the coast, in search of a better settlement site.

Captain Cook, during the first-ever survey of the east coast of the great southern land eighteen years earlier, had declared Botany Bay a suitable place for a settlement. But Phillip disagreed with his assessment and decided to investigate a place marked 'Port Jackson' on Cook's map. It was an inlet named by Cook as he had sailed north past its entrance, without stopping to explore its interior shores. Now as Phillip and his men came level with the imposing cliffs of Port Jackson and turned between its huge stone citadels, they saw opened before them *'a capricious harbour, equal if not superior to any in the world'.*

This was much better than Botany Bay!

Phillip soon realised that the harbour offered so many possibilities that they would have to camp overnight in order to investigate all their options. As they explored the many bays and inlets, natives came to meet them. News of the arrival of white men may have travelled overland already. One of the explorers recorded their reception by the black men:

> *...twenty waded into the water unarmed, received what was offered them, and examined the boat with curiosity... This confidence, and manly behaviour, induced Governor Phillip, who was highly pleased with it, to give the place the name of Manly Cove.*

However, when the white men landed and began preparing a meal, the mood gradually changed. The natives, as was their custom, assumed that the food being prepared by the white men would be shared among everyone present and hung around, socialising and trying through signs and gestures to learn more about the visitors. But the white expedition leader and his men had obviously had enough cultural exchange for one day. They were tired of the sign language, noisy enjoyment and inquisitiveness of their visitors; it was becoming inconvenient and they just wanted to be left alone. The explorers' account describes the scene:

> *During the preparation for dinner the curiosity of these visitors rendered them very troublesome, but...Governor Phillip drew a circle round the place where the English were, and without much difficulty made the natives understand that they were not to pass that line; after which they sat down in perfect quietness. Another proof how tractable these people are, when no insult or injury is offered.*

The white men believed the quiet co-operation of the natives meant they understood that 'no insult or injury' was intended. The black men, on the other hand, may have been thinking something quite different as they sat subdued and silent outside that circle in the sand, watching as the white men turned their backs to them and wolfed down all the food.

What did the line in the sand really mean? Why did the white men insist they stay outside the circle? Was it a bad omen, meant as a warning?

☆

The next day, after more exploring, Phillip's group found a '*small snug cove on the southern side*' of the harbour. They were delighted to see it had a stream of fresh water flowing into it and its proportions were perfect for a settlement:

> *Ships can anchor so close to the shore that at very small expense quays may be constructed at which the largest vessels may unload...*

Without consideration that the little cove had already been given the name *'Warran'* by its long established caretakers, Phillip proudly declared: *'We will call the place Sydney Cove.'*

Governor Phillip returned to Botany Bay with his party, to announce their magnificent find and to order an immediate transfer of the whole fleet northward to Sydney Cove. Phillip was pleased with his efforts, but the following day he was even more impressed with his timing.

Astonishingly, given the odds, the First Fleet had arrived safely from the other side of the world with relatively few deaths. He had found, and claimed, a protected site on which to build the British settlement. And even more astoundingly, he had managed to achieve this only days before other alien ships arrived unexpectedly in the same bay as the British fleet.

History may have been very different, had he been only days later.

4

Strange comings and goings

In such a vastly remote corner of the globe, the appearance of any other large vessels, besides that of the British fleet, was a bizarre co-incidence. Watkin Tench describes his shock at seeing strange ships appear out of the blue at the entrance to Botany Bay at precisely the same time as the British ships were preparing to leave to head north to Sydney Cove:

> *Judge my surprise on hearing from a sergeant, who ran down almost breathless to my cabin where I was dressing, that a ship was seen off the harbour's mouth.*

He laughed at first, thinking it was a practical joke but the sergeant, hastily repeating his information, assured him with all seriousness that 'another sail' had indeed been seen trying to enter the bay. By the time Tench had dashed up to the deck, two ships had been sighted. Questions flashed through his mind as he struggled to make sense of the inexplicable report.

Who on earth could it be? Were they Dutch ships, there to dispossess them? Perhaps they were store-ships from England with supplies for the settlement already? No, that wasn't possible.

The mystery and cause of the alarm was unravelled when the governor recalled a voyage of discovery to the southern hemisphere announced by the French several years earlier. On investigation by a lieutenant sent in a long boat, this theory was confirmed and their message of peaceful intent was reciprocated. As the French dropped anchor to do repairs to their vessels in Botany Bay, the British ships made their way into the open sea and north along the coast. The important thing for Governor Phillip was that they had arrived first, establishing their claim on the land as part of the 'British Empire'. He would send a representative to visit the French in Botany Bay once his fleet was settled at Sydney Cove.

Governor Phillip had good reason to feel satisfied. He had secured a suitable site for the settlement in Port Jackson, a very pleasing harbour, and just as importantly, the native inhabitants of the country, it seemed, were going to be co-operative. They had not appeared to view the newcomers as trespassers and Phillip envisaged that soon he and his officers would be introducing the civilising influence of the British into their lives. As one of the officers wrote in his journal:

> ...the natives had conducted themselves socially and peacefully toward all the parties of our officers and people with whom they had met, and by no means seemed to regard them as enemies or invaders of their country and tranquillity.

So far, so good as far as the new arrivals were concerned.

☆

The native clans living around the bay they called 'Kamay' (Botany Bay) watched the white strangers packing up and leaving their territory.

When they had arrived several days earlier, the ghostly pale people had come ashore in their bizarre body coverings, speaking an unintelligible language, and looking as if they may stay for a while. They had cut down trees and set up peculiar shelters, then suddenly they had decided to move on, and the black families were relieved. The uninvited strangers had seemed friendly at first, offering their amusing, though impractical gifts; but they were unpredictable creatures. The natives who had interacted with them would send cautionary messages northward, to those related to them through marriage, warning the 'Cadigal' and 'Wangal' clans that they may receive a visit from a large number of white aliens.

The two remaining *nowee (ships)* - the ones that had arrived as the others were leaving the bay - would hopefully be gone soon too. With all the unusual comings and goings it had been a very strange time indeed.

★

5

Sydney Cove

January, 1788

The natives watched from a safe distance as the biggest *nowee* they'd ever seen entered the quiet cove of *'Warran'*, not far from the special place reserved for ceremonial gatherings. Soon after, smaller boats were lowered over its side, bringing the white men close enough to wade ashore.

Now, one of the white strangers splashed towards the bank carrying another man on his back. The man being carried wore a bright red coat which, the natives had already learnt, signified a superior one. As the men reached the water's edge, the man in the red jacket jumped into the shallows, lost his footing, and as he stumbled and splashed about, his hat floated across the water out of reach. The white men watching from the boat laughed and cheered, and the natives hidden within the circle of trees rimming the cove couldn't help smiling to themselves.

Maybe they are just young men like us, and not so strange after all.

But unbeknown to the black observers, the camaraderie shown between the white men in that incident *was* strange; very strange indeed. The two white men coming ashore were in fact at opposite ends of a huge social divide; one was a convicted felon, James Ruse, and on his back had been Lieutenant George Johnston of the British marines. The good-natured taunting coming from the boat would, in 'normal circumstances', be highly inappropriate. The black onlookers could not have known that the white men were from a distant country with a social system in which people were divided into strict levels of importance; the lines of which could not be crossed. The higher classes of British society strongly believed in the fixed superiority of a privileged few; a concept unfamiliar to the black men.

The scene the natives had nodded and smiled at would be highly unlikely in Britain. Yet in this isolated cove, far away from the stratums of British society, the frivolity the black men had observed was a sign that the rigid lines of that social order were already beginning to blur.

Lieutenant Johnston, the cause of the amusement, had sensed it too, but it hadn't irked him. In fact, it would suit him. As he walked up the slope of the thickly wooded cove feeling his legs adapt to solid ground, he thought about Esther Abrahams, the young convict he would take as his housekeeper. She wasn't rough like many of the other women. In fact she was lovely. He pictured her long black hair, her almond shaped eyes and slender face.

It had been a difficult voyage for her, trying to look after her small baby, who'd been born in prison only a few months before the ships sailed from England. It wouldn't have been easy, keeping a baby clean and healthy in the unhygienic conditions of the ship, but she was devoted to her daughter.

Accused of stealing a roll of black lace, she'd been lucky to escape death by hanging. She'd only been a teenager at the time and swore in court that she was innocent. She said that the lace had fallen to the ground from the counter but another customer had sworn the roll had dropped from beneath Esther's coat as she tried to leave the store with it concealed. Although three character witnesses had vouched for her good reputation, she'd been sentenced to transportation to Botany Bay for seven years.

Well, he'd look after them both, Esther and her daughter, from now on. When they came ashore, he'd give them the protection his superior rank allowed; he'd provide a decent hut for them to live in as soon as it was possible.

'Lieutenant Johnston!'

Hearing his name brought Johnston back to reality. The tall, fair-haired young Scotsman squared his broad shoulders and braced himself for the task ahead. There was so much work and planning to do!

★

A day prior to the main fleet's arrival from Botany Bay, Governor Phillip had already started setting things in motion at Sydney Cove. A priority was to officially claim the territory for Britain:

> *In the evening of the 26th the colours were displayed on shore, and the Governor, with several of his principal officers and others, assembled round the flag-staff, drank the king's health, and success to the settlement...*

That day, 26th January 1788, would be remembered in future years, as a historic occasion. The following day the governor lost no time in disembarking the troops and a number of male convicts. The prisoners were immediately put to work clearing ground for the officer's tents. The sooner a camp was established, the better.

★

6

Reflections

In the pristine bay of Sydney Cove, the officers, marines and a select group of male convicts gazed around the landing area, not knowing what to think, wondering where to begin. David Collins, a thirty-one year old officer, whose dual role would be judge advocate to the colony and government secretary, describes the scene just before, and just after, clearing began for their campsite:

> *The spot chosen for this purpose was at the head of a cove, near the run of fresh water, which stole silently through a very thick wood, the stillness of which had then, for the first time since creation, been interrupted by the rude sound of the labourer's axe...a stillness and tranquility which from that day were to give place to the voice of labour, the confusion of camps and towns, and the busy hum of its new possessors.*

The quiet little cove would never be the same again. As the clearing work began, the female convicts and children were kept confined to the decks of the ships, awaiting the preliminary formation of a settlement. As they waited anxiously to step onto dry land for the first time in more than eight months, many of the women felt apprehensive about their new surroundings.

Esther Abrahams, nursing her baby daughter, Rosanna, looked around trying to adjust to the bright sunlight. She had come from the bustling city of London; she was not accustomed to eerie, empty places like this. She looked toward the forest wondering what was lurking in there; looking for signs of the black savages she'd heard about. She'd heard the rumours of enormous snakes, and spiders the size of dinner plates. Terrifying stories of wild, flesh-eating animals and fierce venomous reptiles had abounded on the voyage but she was an intelligent young woman and would put those ideas out of her head. How would they know what was there, when no-one had been out there yet? She held her baby daughter closer; they had already endured so much. The voyage had not been easy for them and at times Esther thought it would never end.

None of the hundred or so women on board the convict transport *Lady Penrhyn* had been prepared for the horrors of the grueling journey. None had been on a lengthy sea voyage before and though they had heard they would be going 'thousands of miles', the figure held no meaning for people who rarely ventured outside their immediate locality.

What they *had* understood was that their journey, in all likelihood, would be a one-way trip – they would probably never see their families again. Even if they survived the voyage and their years of confinement in the world's strangest 'prison', they knew no provision had been made for them to return to England and the realisation caused great anguish. Some had left elderly parents, and some like Esther's fellow voyager Ann Inett, had left young children behind. Very few women had been allowed to take their children; only nursing infants had been reluctantly permitted onboard, and only after an appeal on their behalf had been made by someone of influence. There had been no alternative for Ann but to leave her nine year old son and six year old daughter behind and the other women felt for her. Who was caring for them in the absence of their mother wasn't known and some things were too painful to discuss. In the semi-darkness of the female convict quarters, a collective hopelessness permeated the overcrowded lower decks where the women shared their anxiety and heartache.

Once the voyage got underway, however, the endless crashing of waves and creaking of timbers filled them all with a far more tangible and immediate fear; the huge heaving ocean brought on gut-wrenching seasickness making them weak and lethargic. The female convicts were confined below the waterline of the vessel where their cramped accommodation was dimly lit and poorly ventilated. The body odour and smell of open toilet buckets was constant and overpowering.

When they hit the tropics, Esther feared her baby would die of heat exhaustion; the air was so humid and stifling in the claustrophobic, airless confines of the ship's hold. There was no privacy and very little room to move. Governor Phillip had stipulated that those who behaved well would be allowed to exercise on deck for set periods when the weather allowed it, but the decks were cluttered with equipment, stores and animals of all kinds – cattle, pigs, goats and hens – so movement was restricted there too. Most of the women's clothes were threadbare and in tatters when they boarded and though Phillip had requested the government to provide some, the fleet eventually sailed without enough clothing for the women. They didn't receive an outfit of clothes until just before they landed at Sydney Cove.

In the clammy, crowded conditions bullying, squabbles and fighting were inevitable. Arthur Bowes Smyth, the ship's doctor, complained that the women were *'perpetually thieving the clothes from each other'* and that it frequently became *'necessary to inflict corporal punishment upon them'*.

One or two had been flogged with the 'cat of nine tails' on the naked buttocks but the 'decency' issue made it a last resort. The doctor recorded in his journal the punishment at times inflicted on female convicts:

> *Upon occasion such as thieving, fighting with each other or making use of abusive language to the officers, they have thumb screws put on or iron fetters on their wrists...and sometimes their hair has been cut off and their head shaved, which they seemed to dislike more than any other punishment they underwent...They were also whilst under punishment so very abusive that there was a necessity for gagging them.*

Even before sailing some women had already landed themselves in serious trouble. Lieutenants George Johnston and David Collins had come on board to do a roll-call and found five women missing from their quarters and with crew members. The sailors were punished and the offending women 'put in irons'; an uncomfortable restriction on a swaying ship. Some of the women were hardened prostitutes and experienced tricksters who bartered sex for extra rations and bits of cloth for blankets but other women were preyed on by the marines and felt they had little choice about submitting to their sexual demands.

Some of the quieter women like Esther thought it unfair that the doctor, Mr Bowes Smyth, lumped them all together, saying *'there was never a more abandoned set of wretches collected in one place'*, and at other times referring to them collectively as *'abandoned prostitutes'*. What did he know of their lives and circumstances? Elizabeth Needham, condemned to a seven year sentence for shoplifting, hadn't relished the advances of a particularly persistent marine but had been reluctant to refuse a 'connection' with him. To her female companions however she made clear she would be finished with him once they were out of the ship.

There were over a hundred female convicts on board *Lady Penrhyn* and during the eight month voyage the women no doubt heard each other's stories. Thirteen year old Elizabeth Hayward was the youngest convict. She had been accused by her factory employer of stealing clothes to the value of seven shillings and though she had pleaded for mercy, she had received none.

The oldest female on board was Dorothy Handland, listed on the ship's records as eighty-two years old, a 'dealer in old clothes' and sentenced to seven years for perjury. Her pallid, wrinkly complexion, stringy hair and decaying teeth no doubt bespoke her tough life, making her appear older than her true years. Old Dorothy could certainly spin a yarn; in fact it was her 'tall tales' that had landed her in trouble. She had apparently concocted a story of theft from her lodgings, saying *'it had cost her dearly'* and that as a result, she would be obliged to rely on charity.

'I was crying, and breaking my heart', she had told the court.

But in the end, the judge was convinced that not only had she fabricated the story, but she had also persuaded a young man in her debt to give false evidence. Despite her deviousness, one and all had shaken their heads at the decision to send old Dot on such an arduous journey across the globe. Nevertheless, Dorothy was unwavering in her determination to get herself back to England 'when her time was done'. There were more than a few onboard however who doubted Dot would ever see her homeland again.

Esther knew that some of the women on board *Lady Penrhyn* had suffered greatly. Isabella Rawson, for example, has been plagued with guilt at the circumstances of her conviction and was one of the few who insisted her banishment was justified. She had stolen household linen from her employer's trunk when she had gone to the cellar to collect coal and when confronted by her mistress she had immediately admitted her guilt. In court her mistress, a London barrister's wife, retold the incident:

> *...the prisoner on seeing me advance up to the trunks to open them, immediately fell on her knees, and cried out, 'Madam, I have robbed you...Madam, do what you will with me, kill me, I deserve it...*
>
> *I told her she had no reason for mercy, because she had behaved ungrateful.*

Isabella was pronounced guilty and sentenced to seven years transportation. Esther and the other women learnt that Isabella had been a school-mistress before going into service in the barrister's London home and had been pregnant when she boarded the *Lady Penrhyn*. Poor Isabella had gone into pre-mature labour on a thin straw mattress in the dingy surrounds below deck two weeks after the fleet sailed. She had struggled to keep her baby alive but the tiny girl died a week later. The other women tried to console her but to no avail; she had been overcome with grief.

Later in the voyage however the women each became so preoccupied with the real possibility of their own imminent death that they were too consumed with private terror to respond to the fears of others. If they thought the earlier months of the voyage had been bad, they were in for a shock. The unpredictability of the weather made the final and longest leg of their journey the most precarious. Soon after leaving Cape Town, the ships ran into a fierce headwind, impeding their progress to the extent that Captain Phillip, believing they may run out of water before reaching their destination, reduced everyone's daily ration. The livestock they had taken on board at Cape Town began to die of cold and disease; then an epidemic of dysentery took hold among the convicts. To make matters more uncomfortable, the wind changed direction and the ships were tossed erratically by gale-force winds.

They were in unchartered waters when, even more unpredictably, the wind dropped and a dense, murky fog engulfed them. There was no wind power to drive them forward, and for some of the women shut in below deck, the eerie stillness was more nerve-racking than the violent pitching of the ship they had experienced days before; it felt as if they were trapped in a floating coffin.

As they drifted through unfamiliar seas, low visibility made sailing conditions hazardous; they could not predict what lay immediately in advance of the ships. Lieutenant King aboard *HMS Supply* revealed his apprehension by recording that the thick fog, which lasted for twenty-four hours *'...renders our present situation rather perilous as no ship ever ran in this parallel of latitude before.'* They were in a vast unknown with no idea what danger may lie ahead. At one point, crew on the lookout yelled urgently that they could see the outline of an enormous rock almost directly ahead of their ship's course.

> *...but upon a second view it proved to be a dead whale of a most enormous size. In all probability it had been dead some time as it was prodigiously swelled... its back was a great height out of the water and at first sight had very much the appearance of a rock, especially as it was covered over with a variety of sea birds.*

At various times, huge whales came perilously close to the ships. In fact, when two enormous creatures swam under the bow of one of the ships during the night, those confined below deck reported feeling *'the vessel going over their tails'.* Some locked in the bowels of each ship imagined they would meet their death being swallowed alive by the sea monsters.

Midway across the southern Indian Ocean, the air turned icy. The freezing winds caught even experienced sailors like Lieutenant King by surprise. On Christmas Eve, 1787 he wrote:

> *...squalls very violent...great quantities of rain, sleet and large hail stones...the cold is in the extreme here as it is in England at this time of the year, although it is the height of summer here.*

They were close to the southernmost point of their voyage, at Latitude 41° South, and were still over a thousand miles from their destination. But by the first week of January 1788 they had rounded the south-east cape of 'Terra-Australis' and were heading north along the coast of New South Wales. Then, just as they were beginning to feel they had endured the worst, they were hit by truly horrific storms. Only weeks before arriving in Botany Bay they suffered a terrifying night as torrential rain and hail lashed the ship so violently that the women's quarters began filling with sea water. Expecting to drown as the swirling water washed them from their beds, the women aboard *Lady Penrhyn* fell down on their knees to pray as the ship was surrounded by incessant lightening and gale-force winds that ripped some of the ship's sails to pieces...but they had survived. All that was behind them at last.

Now that they had anchored safely in the small cove, they were facing another challenge, another transition. They were again cast into a state of strangeness and uncertainty as they prepared to leave the ship and enter the vast unknown of a new land. In the scene before Esther, there was not a single familiar sight. No roads, no fences, no buildings...just wilderness.

Image courtesy of marine artist, Frank Allen

The transport ship, Lady Penrhyn (pictured) was just over one hundred feet (thirty metres) in length and had two decks. The vessel carried over a hundred female convicts and eight children, as well as marines and officers, including Lt. George Johnston.

7

Different eyes – different sights

Esther's attention was abruptly brought back to the deck of the *Lady Penrhyn* as a commotion broke out. She watched as Ann Smith, a convict woman in her early thirties, put on another of her typically outspoken performances.

'You can keep your slops. I won't be needing 'em. I won't be staying long enough to put 'em to use.'

The other women exchanged knowing glances. The commissionaire of stores had just come on board to issue clothing, commonly referred to as 'slops', in preparation for their going ashore after tents had been erected. The commissionaire glanced at the pile of rough clothing Ann had flung in defiance on the deck. The ship's doctor mumbled that this particular woman had *'always behaved amiss during the voyage'* and Mr. Miller, of the commissary, taking note of her *'very indifferent character'* decided she didn't merit the slops anyway. They were short of provisions as things were, and at this early stage no-one had any idea when more would arrive. He ignored the insolence of the woman, but his expression spoke his thoughts.

The convicts witnessing the outburst recalled Ann's threats of escape during the voyage and began to suspect that she may actually follow through. When she'd announced her intention to abscond at the earliest opportunity, the other women had thought it was bravado. She had declared openly that she would flee the settlement once they were landed and now, it seemed she was serious. She was a confident, resourceful woman with nursing experience but still...

Where on earth would she go?
What would she live on out there in the wild?

As the doling out of clothing continued, Ann Smith looked to the shore and took in the panorama. She was weighing up the options and she could see her daring plan coming to fruition.

★

Across the bay, from the deck of their ship *Charlotte*, another group of female convicts looked to the shoreline, at the mish mash of tents dotting the clearing amid fallen trees, boxes, piles of provisions and equipment. Marines in their red jackets and black hats paraded around the place trying to look busy, as groups of male convicts were bullied and browbeaten into dragging felled trees. The still hot air was stifling and muggy. The grey-green forest, as it met the narrow beach appeared alien, motionless, menacing.

The stillness was suddenly shattered by a weird cackling noise coming from somewhere among trees. The strange chortling increased and intensified to a chorus of raucous laughter; it seemed as if hidden observers were mocking the work-in-progress from the fringe of the forest.

Haha, hoohoo, kaka, kookoo haha...

The workers stopped and looked around, baffled. Someone pointed to a line of plump brown and white birds perched high on a branch warbling out the most outlandish sounds the visitors had ever heard. The birdcall was so like raucous laughter it was uncanny and someone proffered the name 'laughing jackasses' for them. No sooner had the cackling faded away, leaving the newcomers to resume their unpacking, than the stillness was again pierced by a series of high-pitched, blood-curdling screeches from a large white bird swooping low across the clearing. The place was baffling; full of unexpected contrasts and contradictions.

We're in the middle of nowhere amid who knows what.
How will we ever survive this God-forsaken place?

Others however, gazed at the clear blue sky and felt optimistic. The shrieking birds had startled them initially, but when they'd realised what they were, the birdcalls had symbolised freedom. The forest beyond the little cove held a placid, serene quality; the air was laced with an aromatic yet undefinable scent. Speckled shafts of sunlight, angling through the tall forest trees, enhanced its unspoiled beauty.

Susannah Holmes, a young mother convicted for burglary, felt a flicker of hope as she took in her surroundings. After years of confinement in prison, then on the voyage, this strange place held promise. Soon, after the landing of all the convicts, there would be a marriage service and she would marry Henry, her baby's father, as they had pledged to do. She was hopeful that her circumstances would be better from here on. She thought back to the time, almost a year before, when things had become so unbearable that she had not wanted to live and had sworn she would take her own life. She was glad she had not had the opportunity to go through with her threat. She breathed in the fresh air.

There's no filth; there are no slums. There's space...This could be a new start.

Some of the convicts seeing the same scene were not so optimistic. Some were downright lazy; some were tired and depressed. Some were sick and weakened by scurvy or dysentery; they were beyond caring where they were.

Amongst the officers were equally varied responses to the new surroundings. Many had embarked on the expedition as a 'tour of duty' for a set period of time, as a way to improve their career prospects. Some had volunteered with a sense of adventure and couldn't wait to go exploring. There were people who, trying to adjust to the unique surroundings couldn't make up their minds.

Lieutenant Clark for example, aboard *Friendship* was feeling positive as the ship entered Port Jackson and made its way toward the little cove, named Sydney. He described the scene before him in a letter to his wife Betsy as *'one of the finest harbours in the world...I never saw anything like it...Port Jackson is the most beautiful place.'*

The following day, with the ships anchored in the cove, he felt just as optimistic: '*I am quite charmed with the place...the tents look pretty amongst the trees...*'

The next day however, as barrels and crates were taken ashore, his view began to change: '*I never saw so much confusion in all the course of my life as there was in the three companies of marines disembarking.*'

Two days later, sleeping ashore in a tent, he saw things very differently:

> *What a terrible night it was last night... thunder, lightning and rain. I was obliged to get out of my tent with nothing on but my shirt to (fix) the tent poles...it's remarkably hot; I've nothing to sleep in but a poor tent and a little grass to sleep on.*

Within days of setting up camp, Lieutenant Clark was regretting his three year 'tour of duty' in New South Wales. He was wishing he'd never set foot in the place, as is evident in excerpts of letters to his wife back in England:

> *My God, how it did thunder and lightning. I was very much frightened; above all the places in the world, this is the most terrible for thunder and lightning...in all the course of my life I never slept worse my dear wife, than I did last night what with the hard cold ground, spiders, ants and every vermin that you can think of was crawling over me, I was glad when the morning came...I could not stay longer than three years for the world...I wish I could get home now...*

And so, with such a varied collection of people, each with their own views, attitudes and agendas, Governor Phillip had to build a settlement. The adventure, toil and mystery of a new world had begun.

☆

8

Issues and challenges

By the last week of January the work of clearing the area for storehouses, tents and other buildings was well underway. However, the effort of clearing a place for the campsite can't easily be imagined. The whole area was covered with magnificently tall trees so the chopping and removal of them was an enormous job. David Collins, secretary to the governor, described the scene:

> *The confusion that ensued will not be wondered at when it is considered that every man stepped from the boat literally into a wood. Parties of people were everywhere heard and seen variously employed; some in clearing ground for the different encampments; others in pitching tents, or bringing up such stores…and the spot which had so recently been the abode of silence and tranquility was now changed to that of noise, clamour and confusion.*

They soon found that the timber of the enormous trees was extremely hard. When the men lifted their axes and swung them at the tree trunks, they just bounced off. When they tried to push their spades into the ground, the surface was rock hard. Axe handles were breaking; spades and saws were blunt and ineffective. They weren't used to this sort of exertion; they'd been cooped up on a ship for months and their muscles had become scrawny, their legs feeble, their backs weak. They weren't used to the stifling heat and humidity. But the clearing work had to be done and some sort of plan for the settlement had to be devised.

They were starting from scratch and Governor Phillip walked around pointing and giving directions. This was a project like no other. The colony would be built with convict labour under a system of compulsory community service. The scene before him in the camp was 'all hurry and exertion' as he strode around surveying the progress and defining the layout: the government farm, storehouse and his headquarters on the east side of the cove; the marine camp, portable canvas hospital and main area of convicts' tents on the west with the freshwater stream running between. His official dispatch states:

> *The plan of the encampment was quickly formed, and places were marked out for every different purpose, so as to introduce, as much as possible, strict order and regularity.*

The erection of canvas hospital tents was given priority as many convicts, after the long and trying conditions of the voyage, were showing signs of dysentery and scurvy. Both were extremely unpleasant and potentially deadly conditions. Dysentery (also known then as 'flux') brought symptoms of fever, dreadful griping pains in the gut and severe diarrhoea.

As the colony's chief doctor, John White was relieved and delighted when a remedy of *'the red gum of trees found in the area'*, had been pointed out by natives and had proven helpful in treating dysentery. During the voyage he had worked diligently, being rowed between the ships when weather permitted to check on and treat sick convicts. Now that they were landed, he was determined to keep the colony as healthy as circumstances allowed.

Scurvy, a common problem in the days of long sea voyages without fresh food, could be equally nasty and deadly. The first symptoms of overwhelming exhaustion and depression were followed by sores, mainly on the legs and thighs, which turned weepy and pus-filled. Fever took hold and the mouth and gums became sore, spongy and bleeding as teeth loosened and fell out. It was not a nice way to die and could be avoided with a diet of fresh fruit and vegetables. John White knew they needed food to supplement what they'd brought with them in wooden casks from England, so supervised groups were sent to scour the area and collect what wild greens they could find.

Another priority was the setting up of a tent for the governor's temporary dwelling and headquarters. The framework for a prefabricated canvas house for the governor, brought from England, was being put together with as much speed as the circumstances allowed, on the eastern side of the cove. Gradually, the settlement was taking shape. Watkin Tench however, thought that to an onlooker, the scene would be amusing:

> *In one place a party cutting down the woods; a second setting up a blacksmith's forge, a third dragging along a load of stones or provisions; here an officer pitching his marquee, with a detachment of troops parading on one side of him, and a cook's fire blazing up on the other.*

So, despite the lack of tools and experience, the little cove that had sat quietly beside the bay, its unspoiled stream flowing beneath a tranquil forest for thousands of years, had become a hubbub of noisy activity.

★

From the escarpment, native eyes were looking on with a mixture of shock, dismay and amazement. They were puzzled too.

Why are they cutting down trees? And why so many?
Don't they understand it will affect the hunting?
Can't they see that shade will be lost for the edible plants and ferns?
Don't they know trees are needed to make bark canoes, spears and shields?

They had been mystified to watch men struggle half the day to bring down a tall, straight, slender tree, remove all its branches, haul it across the clearing and after digging a deep hole, plant it again.

Why were these strange beings, huffing and puffing in the heat to drag trees from one place to another? What was the point? Was it part of a ritual?

They had watched, transfixed, as a piece of the same stuff they used to cover their bodies, was attached to the tree and hoisted to the top. Men had then stood around it, looking up and shouting in unison the strange words:

Health...Majesty...Colony.

There seemed to be divisions between the people too. Some men were being forced to work by others who were striking them; some had come from the ships tied together while others shouted:

'Hurry along! Get moving!'

It didn't seem right that some men had no freedom. Why did they not fight back? The natives looked on, feeling both intrigued and perplexed, and the question asked most often was:

'How long will they stay?'

In the meantime, they decided, it was a place for them and their children to avoid.

☆

Governor Phillip, aware that the French ships they'd encountered at Botany Bay were still anchored there, was also wondering how long the foreigners intended to stay. In early February he sent Lieutenant King to investigate and offer whatever assistance could be afforded. King, conversant with French, learnt that the ships under the command of Monsieur La Pérouse had been on a voyage of discovery for two and a half years, most recently snaking their way around the Pacific islands before reaching the east coast of Terra Australis. The French commander informed the Englishman that after completing the necessary repairs to their ships, they would head homeward and hoped to be back in France within fifteen months.[2] Being well-supplied, the Frenchman offered to leave whatever provisions they could spare with Governor Phillip. They furthermore told King that several convicts had already made their way

---

[2] When, in early March 1788, the French ships sailed from Botany Bay into the Pacific Ocean, they vanished and were never heard from again by their countrymen. See notes for this chapter.

34

across country, along a native track between Sydney Cove and Botany Bay, to plead a passage to Europe but had been sent on their way with severe warnings. The natives, they added, had also been 'troublesome' and there had been cause to shoot at them.

Lieutenant King returned to Sydney Cove with his report. The governor would deal harshly with the convicts that had caused 'trouble and embarrassment'. However, the concern the French had encountered with the natives was surprising. So far they had kept their distance from the Sydney settlement.

★

9

A night of revelry

Arthur Phillip took in the scene of his tent settlement. It had been only weeks since he'd found the cove and decided it would be the starting place for the British colony. It was certainly a relief that the convicts were all finally landed. The women and children had initially been restricted to their respective ships until land had been cleared and tents set up for them, apart from the main men's camp.

On reflection that had been a good move because, on the evening after all the female convicts had been brought ashore, there had been an unleashing of pent up desire that in hindsight, may have been predictable. According to Arthur Bowes Smyth, the doctor aboard *Lady Penrhyn,* it turned out to be an uncomfortable and chaotic night in more ways than one:

> The men convicts got to them (the convict women) very soon after they landed and it is beyond my abilities to give a just description of the scene of debauchery and riot that ensued during the night.

The severe electrical storm and torrential rain that fell that night, drenching the bodies of the revellers, apparently did nothing to dampen their ardour:

> They had not been landed more than an hour before... there came on the most violent storm of thunder, lightning and rain I ever saw. The lightning was incessant during the whole night and I never heard it rain faster. About 12 o'clock in the

night one severe flash of lightning struck a very large tree in the centre of the camp... it split the tree from top to bottom...

The sailors in our ship requested to have some grog to make merry with upon the women quitting the ship; indeed the captain himself had reason to rejoice upon their being all safely landed and given into the care of the governor... for which reason he complied with the sailor's request...

The scene which presented itself during the greater part of the night beggars every description; some swearing, others quarrelling, others singing...I never before experienced so uncomfortable a night, expecting every moment the ship would be struck with the lightning. The sailors, almost all drunk and incapable of rendering much assistance had an accident happened, and the heat was almost suffocating.

Bowes Smyth, obviously quite shaken by the storm and observing the on-shore scene from across the water, may have exaggerated the 'debauchery'. Watkin Tench, pondering the convicts' circumstances, gave a more philosophical summary of events in his journal:

...a candid and humane mind (will not) fail to consider and allow for the situation these unfortunate beings so peculiarly stood in. While they were on board ship the two sexes had been kept most rigorously apart, but when landed their separation became impractical, and would have been, perhaps, wrong. Licentiousness was the unavoidable consequence ...What was to be attempted?

Whatever the governor and his officers thought of the goings-on that night, an official 'blind eye' was turned. Some of the women probably participated in the carousing as readily as the men; however, it seems likely that those who sought to avoid it were given the option. On the other hand, there may have been convicts who were caught up in the scene against their will, with nowhere to escape.

★

Twenty two year old Elizabeth Pulley and twenty year old Anthony Rope apparently had a liaison that night because nine months later, by then dutifully married, their first child Robert was born. Elizabeth had apparently tarnished her name during the voyage aboard *Friendship* where, according to Lieutenant Ralph Clark, she had been put in leg irons and hand cuffs on more than one occasion for secreting herself into the marines' quarters and for fighting with a group of equally notorious females, all of whom he labelled, *'damned whores...a disgrace to their whole sex'*. Whatever truth there was in Clark's opinion of Elizabeth Pulley, it was her past. In the early months of the colony, she became Mrs Anthony Rope and mother-to-be of one of the first colonial born children of the British settlement.

Anthony and Elizabeth were not the only couple to formalise their relationship soon after the landing of the fleet. Before the end of February 1788, fifty eight convicts were married in open-air services performed beside the harbour by the Reverend Johnson, the First Fleet's only clergyman.

★

10

The governor's speech

The intense storm and carrying-on described by Arthur Bowes Smyth during the night of February 6th 1788 must have left the camp area, and some of its inhabitants, looking rather disheveled. However, the following day, Governor Phillip promptly established discipline and authority. The convicts were assembled into the clearing with guards surrounding them. The marines and officers stood to attention in full military dress, their rows of polished buttons gleaming on bright red woollen jackets, their muskets at the ready. The governor stood before them all, his smart blue jacket signifying his status in the Royal Navy and with as much pomp and ceremony as a small isolated group on the edge of a wilderness could muster he attended to all the necessary administrative business. Surgeon Bowes Smyth, probably rather blurry eyed after experiencing such a stressful night, nevertheless recorded the details in his journal:

> *...the soldiers marched with their drums and fifes and formed a circle round the whole of the convict men and women who were collected together...A camp table was fixed before them and two red leather cases...containing the commissions were opened and unsealed in the sight of all present...*

As the marching band formed into lines and paraded through the clearing, blasting military music into the humid summer air, some of the convicts must have been confounded by the proceedings. The native inhabitants of the area, unable to ignore the commotion, must have been baffled.

David Collins, in his position as secretary to the governor and judge advocate for the colony, stood beside his superior. It was his job to read out the many orders and instructions prepared by the officials in Britain, giving directives on all aspects of the new government. The governor was officially 'sworn in' and his extensive powers were outlined. He was to appoint magistrates to sit in court but it was his prerogative to grant degrees of freedom as reward for good conduct and administer grades of punishment as he thought fit.

Much of this 'official talk' with its legal jargon would have been dreary, irrelevant and beyond the comprehension of some convicts but when the governor addressed them directly, it was a different matter. He surveyed the motley crowd before him and '*distinctly explained to them the nature of their present situation*'. In a firm voice he assured them he would:

> *...show encouragement to those who showed themselves worthy by good conduct and attention to orders; while on the other hand, such as were determined to act in opposition... and observe a contrary conduct, would inevitably meet with the punishment which they deserved.*

He warned that stealing would be punished by death; with such limited supplies, he could not afford to be lenient. At the end of his address, the military band played 'God Save the King' and three volleys were fired into the air by the troops to mark the importance of the occasion. As the soldiers marched off, and the convicts were ordered to resume their various activities, some of them were likely thinking: *What a load of codswallop.* Others, though comparatively few, were mulling over the possibilities:

This place could offer opportunities never thought possible back home.

James Ruse and John Wilson were among the convicts herded into assembly that day to witness the 'swearing in' ceremony. Both men had been convicted for seven years for theft: James Ruse for stealing two watches and John Wilson for pilfering 'nine yards of cotton cloth... to the value of ten pence'. Both men had heard the governor's speech and both could see possibilities for themselves in this strange land. Both had a plan brewing, but each man's thinking was at opposite ends of the spectrum.

James Ruse, the convict who had carried Lieutenant Johnston ashore two weeks earlier, had listened attentively as the governor promised 'encouragement' for good conduct. He understood the governor's motive completely. From where Ruse sat, the governor was holding out more than mere encouragement; he was offering incentive. As he cast his eyes over the disgruntled mob of resentful faces around him, he saw how few of them could be relied upon. As he looked across the higgledy-piggledy clearing, the need for incentive was glaringly obvious. He saw the slothful, apathetic expressions around him and knew he was different. The governor needed men with farming experience; he needed men with motivation and drive, and James Ruse believed he would fit the bill. But he would wait for the right time before approaching the governor. He had been convicted in 1782 so he didn't have long before his seven year sentence was over.

Yes, the place held possibilities. Maybe, one day, a plot of ground... perhaps even a farm?

John Wilson, in his late teens, had also heard the governor utter the word 'encouragement' and knew it was probably wasted on the crowd around him. Most of the convicts were too lethargic to be concerned with inspiration. Most of them just wanted to get back to England, although John Wilson could not understand why. *Had they forgotten what England thought of them?*

As John toiled in the work gang, clearing and digging and as the men around him cursed the rock hard ground and the blazing sun, he didn't say much. He was taking everything in; focusing on his surroundings and the skills he was learning. He was storing the pieces of information away for the future.

Unlike James Ruse, Wilson didn't have a background in farming, and cultivation didn't appeal to him. He was attracted to the wilderness beyond the settlement; enticed by its unruliness. He was noting the weather, the bush and the native people he'd seen on various excursions when sent to collect timber, vines and reeds for the thatching of huts. The natives were watching the settlers... but he was observing them too. He knew there were bush survival skills he could learn from them and he was already picking up snippets of their language – a word here and there. His sights were set on the wild forests and mountains. That's where he'd be heading when the time was right.

☆

Although the British authorities had provided lengthy instructions on the governance of the penal settlement, the formation of courts and provision for the British East India Company's monopoly on trade in Asia and the Pacific, the convicts' indent papers had not arrived with them in the colony. They had no proof of the expiry date of their sentences. Almost half the prisoners had been convicted and held in British prisons since 1784, and a few (like James Ruse) had been sentenced as early as 1782, so soon after arrival in New South Wales, some were already anticipating the end of their seven year stint. Judge Collins recorded the governor's dilemma:

> *Unfortunately, by some unaccountable oversight, the papers necessary to ascertain these particulars had been left...in England, instead of being brought out and deposited in the colony and thus situated, it was impossible to admit or to deny the truth of their (the convicts') assertions ...It must be acknowledged, that these people were most peculiarly and unpleasantly situated...*

Governor Phillip knew it could become a serious problem when convicts began claiming they had 'served their time', yet could not prove it. In their remote community potentially volatile situations must be avoided and he accordingly devised a solution for when the issue arose:

> *The governor, however, terminated this business...by directing the judge-advocate to take the affidavits of such persons as would make oath that they had served the term prescribed by the law, and by recommending them to work for the public until some information was received from government...*

☆

The British government had chosen wisely in assigning Arthur Phillip as Governor to the first colony of New South Wales. The experiences of his early life had set him up well for the job.

While still in his mid-teens, he had been apprenticed to the master of a whaling ship who had promised not to *'immoderately beat or abuse him.'* As one of the youngest on board, he sailed with a fleet to the freezing waters of Greenland with the perilous task of bringing back highly prized whale blubber and where, as one of the junior crew members, he would have been given the most disagreeable jobs.

By the age of seventeen he had joined the Royal Navy and almost immediately saw action with enemy forces when the ship on which he was an 'able bodied seaman', captured and sank a French warship. The following year, again in battle with the French but this time massively outnumbered, the British fleet suffered many casualties. On returning to Britain, the Admiral in command of young Phillip's squadron was court-martialed, convicted and executed for 'neglect of duty'. Young Phillip, in a letter to his sister, strongly condemned the Admiral's actions as 'downright cowardice'. He had witnessed the devastating effects of poor leadership.

Over the ensuing years Phillip gained broad experience on long sea voyages, sailing on various naval assignments to the Caribbean, the North Sea, the Mediterranean, South America, India and South Africa, at the same time working his way up through the ranks. As well as the thousands of fatalities witnessed in battle, he saw first-hand the countless unnecessary deaths of his comrades caused by malnutrition and disease, as a direct result of insufficient food, water, and appalling conditions. He had seen what life could be like below decks and what it was like to be the victim of negligent supervisors. He had witnessed the hardening of seamen brutally punished with the lash for seemingly trivial offences. All this had put him in good stead for his command of the First Fleet and his governance of New South Wales.

By 1788 he was fifty years old and had developed a cool, controlled disposition balanced with fair-mindedness; he was a humane man but he could mete out harsh justice when necessary.

★

11

Strange appearances and disappearances

Governor Phillip had been profoundly aware from the outset that the penal settlement under his control could be no ordinary prison with the usual high stone walls and metal bars to confine criminals. The convicts that couldn't be rehabilitated through incentive would have to be restricted and controlled in other ways: public flogging, the denial of food, and solitary confinement... He'd seen a small rocky island in the harbour that could be used to isolate a convict if needed... and hanging would be a last resort.

To the governor's advantage, during their first weeks at Sydney Cove, an unexpected but effective deterrent against escape presented itself. Only days after the female convicts had landed, someone came stammering into camp with the report of a terrifying creature seen lurking in the bushes near the edge of the camp. One of the doctors recorded its appearance:

> *An alligator, 8 feet long, has several times been seen near the camp and among the shrubs behind the camp near the run of water...*

Added to this, around the same time, one of the sailors went missing. He had last been seen, just before dark, standing near the edge of the encampment; then he had vanished into thin air. Several days later, another alligator sighting was reported near the tents; this time the creature was said to be fourteen feet long. To English city dwellers, the thought of huge man-eating reptiles waiting in the undergrowth near their tents would have been petrifying. And that was not all. George Worgan, in a letter to his brother, wrote with a hint of disbelief of another 'sighting' which had caused alarm:

Some of the convicts reported that they saw a tiger one evening, but we believe it was one pictured by their own creative imaginations. You know, to a timorous man, a bush in the dark might be easily mistaken for a tiger.

A week after the sailor's disappearance, he was found in the forest near the coast, eight miles from the camp. He hadn't been eaten by an alligator or a tiger; he had wandered into the wilderness and lost his way. But he was half-starved and completely naked when he was found. He said that in the whole time he'd been absent, he had eaten only a handful of periwinkles (small shellfish) picked from the rocks. He said the natives had chased him, taken his clothes and pelted him with stones and that he had been so afraid that he'd waded into a swamp where he'd hidden neck-deep in water among the reeds until hunger had forced him to keep walking in search of food and the campsite, which by then had become 'home'. At least his arrival back at camp had extinguished talk of 'death by alligator'.

With time, the newcomers learnt that alligators and tigers did not exist around Sydney. The 'alligators' they thought they'd seen were actually large goannas which despite their menacing appearance, were harmless. They soon learnt however, that equally intimidating creatures certainly did exist in the area surrounding the camp. One of the men reported seeing the ground near the settlement 'covered with red and black ants of the most enormous size'. On another occasion a large and frightening reptile was caught and brought into camp:

...a very large snake among some rushes in a swampy place... was nearly as big as my arm, upwards of 8 feet long, a wide mouth with 2 rows of very sharp pointed teeth in the upper jaw and 2 in the under one – the teeth were ½ inch long. It was of a very dark colour, approaching to black with large bright yellow spots regularly dispersed over the whole body.

The snake was a slow-moving, non-venomous diamond python, but to novice campers the sight of it would be nerve-racking just the same. As well as the reptiles, the newcomers had to get used to the sudden, raucous shrieks of unfamiliar birds throughout the day and the eerie appearance of bats swarming above the camp at dusk. And there were the strange night noises: the breathy, blood-curdling growl of competing male possums heard around the tents would be terrifying to the inexperienced settlers. The sudden unanticipated sensation of sticky spider webs strung between trees at face level would be equally disconcerting.

However, considering his limited man-power, the governor was prepared to use fear of the unknown – strange intimidating creatures, 'savage' natives, and a mysterious wilderness – to keep most of his charges confined to the limits of the campsite. There was so much they didn't know about their new environment but it was their home now. They had to focus on setting up a permanent settlement and it was still early days.

★

12

Creatures, great and small

From the escarpment the black families had watched wide-eyed as many of the felled trees from the clearing were carried and laid over a frame to form a type of track that protruded into the water. Along this construction the white men carried boxes and rolled barrels between their boats and the shore.

But more astounding and formidable were the four-footed creatures that were led from the boats onto land, making the most peculiar bleating, bellowing and oinking noises that had ever pierced the tranquility of the cove. They were outlandish, alien looking beasts, the like of which the natives had never imagined. Some were short, stocky animals with stiff, squiggly tails and bizarre features, covered with an almost hairless skin of a similar shade to the strange men who herded them ashore. There were other pale, squat animals with even stranger body coverings; they were wrapped in a thick layer of 'something' and made dismal bleating sounds, like a chorus of crying children. There were larger fearsome looking beasts too; bigger than any animal the black men had ever seen, each with two pointed bones protruding from its head. These ominous creatures stamped their feet and made the most menacing bellowing sounds. Even the smaller two-legged feathered creatures were peculiar; some extended their necks to hiss at passers-by; some produced penetrating, far-reaching cries of 'cock-a-doodle-doo...'

★

Governor Phillip assessed the progress around the campsite. On the east side of the cove a wharf had been constructed and near the landing area, fenced areas for the animals. Seeing the farm animals in their makeshift enclosures brought memories of the voyage. At Cape Town, the ships had stocked up on provisions, including plants, seeds and animals needed for the establishment of the settlement; some being bought by officers for their own stock.

That stopover had been their last port of call before heading into the virtually unchartered waters of the southern Indian Ocean. As the ships were loaded, remarks had been made about the large number of animals going aboard:

> ...the ships, having on board not less than five hundred animals of different kinds, but chiefly poultry, put on an appearance which naturally enough excited the idea of Noah's ark.

The comments had been made in jest but Phillip hoped the settlement, the animals, the people clearing the ground, would be the foundation of a new agricultural society. It was obvious some of the officers were already pessimistic about the prospect but he believed the colony held possibilities. If only the British government, the planners of the settlement, had included more skilled men in the fleet. And if only there were more willing workers.

As he neared his makeshift canvas house, supervised convicts were planting the trees that had been bought and shipped with them from Rio de Janeiro. The grape vines they'd brought from the Cape of Good Hope weren't wilting, which was a good sign. But they needed to get all the corn, wheat and cotton seeds in the ground as soon as possible. And they needed a sheltered spot for the apple and pear saplings. There were still huge tree stumps littering the open area; they would have to be dug out if an orchard was to flourish.

☆

And it had all eventually got underway. There had been setbacks: six sheep, two lambs and a pig had been killed in a violent storm as lightening shattered the tree they'd been fenced beneath; a number of convicts had already succeeded in escape, and the marines (some, not all) were grumbling and objecting to directives. But all in all, progress was visible.

The ground was still damp from another massive storm that had raged earlier in the week and the governor pictured the fig, pear, and apple trees taking root and establishing themselves in the soil of this new land. Yes, with time, perseverance and patience something could be made of the place.

☆

13

A beating for a beating

The governor considered the security measures he had implemented as he walked the perimeter of the settlement. The outer boundaries had been set and guards had been ordered to patrol the outer limits to stop the more daring convicts from escaping. The male convicts had been banned from entering the women's tents and any male found in the women's encampment, they were warned, would be fired upon.

The governor's order, however, hadn't stopped one of the marines trying to force Elizabeth Needham, a convict from the *Lady Penrhyn*, to go into the woods with him. He was sure she would comply because she had never refused him during the voyage. Once landed though, in light of the governor's recent orders, Elizabeth felt it was safe to reject the marine's sexual demands and flatly refused to go with him. Her refusal, however, resulted in a severe beating from the enraged marine.

When charges were laid against him, some of the officers felt the marine's penalty of two hundred lashes was too harsh. The woman involved, in the biased opinion of the doctor aboard *Lady Penrhyn*, was a *'most infamous hussy'* with whom the marine had *'had connections'* on the voyage anyway. Elizabeth, on the other hand, felt exonerated by the sentence though she was aware how differently things could have turned out had a different man been governing the colony. She resolved then and there to overcome her reputation and make something of herself. It wouldn't be easy but she would show them her worth. The first step was to become a respectable married woman so the following week Elizabeth Needham married William Snailham, a convict also transported for seven years for theft.

☆

The punishment of Elizabeth Needham's attacker, who on the day of his punishment, received only a hundred of his two hundred lashes, '*excited great murmuring and discontent*' against the governor, because on the same day, a convict had received only a hundred and fifty strokes for striking a sentry. Arthur Bowes Smyth, a man already shown to be hasty in his judgement, reported:

> *...an evident discontent prevails among the different officers throughout the settlement; the marines and sailors are punished with the utmost severity for the most trivial offences, whilst the convicts are pardoned (or at most punished in a very slight manner) for crimes of the blackest die.*

The population soon learnt however, that the governor had his own ideas about the administration of justice in the new penal settlement. He had expected the support of his second in command, Major Robert Ross, in urging the marines to provide a good example to the convict population. But instead of backing the governor, Ross began a campaign to undermine his authority. He told the men under his leadership it was not their job to supervise convicts. He argued that they were the colony's defence force; they had been sent to do garrison duty, to guard against invasion by a foreign army (such as the French) or an attack by the natives. Their job was to prevent civil unrest but they were not prison wardens. It was clear that Ross, under the circumstances, was being unreasonable but in theory he was correct. The British government should have sent designated overseers for the convicts. However, in the secluded camp, thousands of miles from Britain, the governor could not quickly seek advice or re-check directives. In their very isolated situation, the buck stopped with Phillip. He had to re-think his strategy.

This supervisory nightmare left the governor with no option but to use convicts to oversee their comrades – not an ideal formula for building a workable society. Disunity in the officer ranks was an equally undesirable situation but it was evident to the marines. Lieutenant Ralph Clark wrote of it in his journal:

*I am sorry to say that the Governor and Major Ross are not
on very good terms or is the latter with several of us.*

As well as being disruptive, Ross was already pessimistic about the
colony's future and did not keep his negative opinions to himself. His
view, that *'in the whole world there is not a worse country...'* became
generally known.

Fortunately for the governor, not all the marines were as uncooperative
as Major Ross but it was obvious that many were not interested in the
long-term future of the colony and spent their time fault-finding and
quarrelling. They didn't want to be there; they just wanted to go home.

The main detachment of marines was stationed next to the parade
ground on the western side of the cove. From there they could guard the
central campsite where most of the convicts' tents had been erected and
had specific orders in the case of escapees:

*The patrols are to bring in all stragglers and to fire on any
that attempt to escape or any convicts that are seen out of
camp at night.*

Apparently, this task was considered by Major Ross as part of the marine
detachment's brief. The governor was aware that in some cases there
was a thin line between the characters of the convicts and the men
who had volunteered as marines for a three year 'tour of duty' with the
First Fleet. He knew many of the military men were there in the colony
because it was better than the no pay (or very little pay) they would
receive in peacetime Britain. However, as members of His Majesty's
forces, he had assumed he could rely on them as convict supervisors.

Unfortunately for Governor Phillip, convict management was not the
only issue weighing on his mind. The amicable association he'd hoped to
establish with the natives of the area was not happening as quickly as
he'd originally envisaged.

★

14

View from the ridge

The Aboriginal people around Sydney Cove, after another passing of the moon, suspected that the strangers were not just travelling through. They had denuded the little cove of trees and littered the place with their strange equipment. Their camp looked very much like a permanent arrangement now. At first they'd been intrigued by the newcomers' peculiar dwellings, their cooking pots, the cutting and hammering tools, as well as the unfamiliar animals of various shapes and sizes that had been herded along the ingenious wooden structure across the water and onto the shore. But the novelty of the strangers had worn off.

During February, two elders had visited the white man's site to investigate and report on the goings-on of the foreigners' camp. Entering the place of the aliens was a mission that no doubt involved great apprehension and courage on the part of the scouts. They had however returned to their people unharmed, with gifts of iron hatchets and an account of what they'd seen. The white leader, the one with the missing front tooth, had welcomed them with seeming pride at the changes he and his people had brought to the site.

But what the emissaries had observed had been mystifying and perplexing. The white men and women were still all wrapped in their strange body coverings despite the heat of summer. The strange smelling food that was offered to the black men came from the wooden containers that had been brought from their boats; apparently it was the foreigners' main source of sustenance. When the white leader offered some spongy white matter he called 'bread' and a portion of unappealing dried meat he called 'pork', the black men were wary.

The black men also found the social structure of the white settlement baffling. The assumed superiority of the men clad in bright red body coverings was evident; they carried the *'gooroobeera' (weapons, or fire sticks)*. But what was particularly disconcerting was the fact that some of the other men in the camp reacted like ill-treated animals to the directives of the 'red coats.' A mood of brooding resentment pervaded the strangers' camp.

Since that visit, buildings had continued going up across the cleared area. Some of the structures appeared to be for storing the white men's peculiar food, another with a fire burning before it, was apparently a place for repairing the white men's implements. In yet another structure, many of the strangers lay sick and dying. Another area of the camp seemed to be for the exclusive use of the 'redcoats'. On a well-trodden, dusty plot of ground they carried on strange ceremonies; amid calls and commands they marched and paced with their weapons to their shoulders. The scene was perplexing.

☆

Given all the activity in the area and the immense changes that they had brought to the place, Governor Phillip and his officers couldn't understand why the natives weren't showing more curiosity and returning to the settlement for a closer look. In fact the opposite had happened; the natives seemed to be consciously avoiding the place. David Collins, secretary to the governor, complained in his journal:

> *During the first six weeks, we received only one visit, two old men strolling into the camp one evening, and remaining in it for about half an hour. They appeared to admire whatever they saw, and after receiving a hatchet each... they left, apparently well pleased with their reception.*

That token of interest was little enough, but then nothing.

What was keeping them away?

Governor Phillip was growing impatient. His instructions from England had been to build an amicable relationship with the natives and he wanted and needed to know how *they* lived. He had hoped for a mutually beneficial exchange of information. He wanted to learn about the surrounding district and hoped they would act as guides.

Why weren't they coming to visit in scores? Couldn't they see the advantages the British could offer them? Couldn't they see the superior mode of living demonstrated in the settlement?

★

The busy goings-on in Sydney Cove had, of course, been impossible to ignore. The native people, standing in the fringe of trees on the ridges had over the weeks observed the mode of living in the settlement; and it had been enough to show them that the white 'boat people' were indeed very different. The settlement continued to make them uneasy.

Black women from their canoes had witnessed the devastation of the site that had once given shade and solace. The trees, where birds and honey bees had once flourished, were now only ugly stumps. The sweet fragrant bushes that blossomed with fluffy golden clusters of sugar treats were already becoming sparse around the settlement.

Where was their respect for the land, their forethought for future seasons?

But that wasn't all they'd observed. They had several times witnessed men stripped to the waist, tied to a specially made frame and beaten relentlessly with an implement designed to inflict great pain. The whipping device was made from thick, rigid animal skins of many cords, on which hard knots were seen at intervals. The lashing had continued long after deep, bloody gashes criss-crossed the white flesh and the black men had turned away, not because they were troubled at the sight of blood, but because of the humiliation inflicted on a man who could not shield his body. Their warrior code required that a guilty one face his opponent and bravely defend himself; otherwise it was not fair play.

Then to their bewilderment, not long before sunset one late-summer afternoon, the natives had been drawn by the sound of drums and looked on horrified as they'd viewed, from a safe distance, the punishment inflicted on one of the subservient ones in the white settlement. They watched as a young man was led, bound and trembling to a tree, under which a platform had been built; from the tree hung a rope. The young person had been prodded to climb what they later learnt was a 'ladder' and there the rope had been pulled over his head. The red-coats, armed and rigid, surrounded the whole assembly of white men and women who also stood motionless facing the platform; no-one made an attempt to intervene as the victim stood quivering and helpless. No-one rushed forward in his defense; and later, when the young body dangled limply, they had just lowered their heads, turned and slowly walked away.

The natives seeing the event must certainly have been disturbed by it, yet they could not have known how disagreeable the execution of Thomas Barrett had been to the white leader, nor sensed his regret and disappointment that the leniency shown thus far had so blatantly been abused. The young culprit had been hung for stealing a quantity of food - butter, peas and pork - on the very day that he had received his week's allowance. The offence, not Barrett's first, could not go unpunished.

Even if the governor had been given an opportunity to explain to the black observers his reasons for the execution, it would still have been implausible to them. The necessity for a leader to dole out stored, stale food once a week to a line of hungry dependents would have been unfathomable. It was obvious to the natives that there was wild food to be found all around the white men's camp. The whole situation was baffling.

In addition to the punishment and suffering deliberately inflicted, many of the white people had died of sickness or weakness in the first weeks and had been buried near the settlement. Pain and death breathed in the white men's camp; bad things were happening there. As they'd skirted the area, they'd seen the white men toil all day, many of them in chains which weighed them down and restricted their movement; the drudgery appeared never-ending and for no apparent purpose. The strangers rarely laughed – their days seemed to pass in utter misery. They would stay away from the place – it did not have a good aura.

☆

Despite the set-backs and discontent among some, Governor Phillip, was feeling optimistic about the settlement's progress. He had finished inspecting the structure being erected on high ground on the western point of the cove. A team of marines, under the direction of Lieutenant Dawes, were building an observatory with a cone shaped roof made of whitewashed canvas and a specifically designed flap that opened to view the stars. Dawes, with his deep interest and expertise in astronomy, had explained to his colleagues that he was expecting a comet to appear in the southern hemisphere during 1788. Phillip had listened with quiet courtesy, but as always, a myriad of thoughts was buzzing in his brain. Not least was the dilemma of the natives. He sensed them watching from their canoes, or from the escarpment.

Surely they wanted to know more?

Returning to the camp along the elevated path above the bay, he approached the settlement from a vantage point and surveyed his project: the first white settlement on the 'great southern land'. He couldn't help admiring it and recorded his thoughts:

> *There are few things more pleasing than the contemplation of order and useful arrangement, gradually arising out of confusion...where a settlement of civilised people is fixing itself upon a newly discovered or savage coast.*

The campsite huddled in the cleared space contrasted starkly with its wild surroundings. The disparity presented by the scene made him realise his vision:

> *But by degrees large spaces are opened, plans are formed, lines marked, and a prospect of future regularity is clearly discerned.*

Yes, he thought, something will be made of this place; order will be brought to the wilderness.

★

The natives, as they paddled past, had also observed the large spaces being opened up in the forest, the strange structure going up on the western point of the cove and the gradual flattening of the wild flowers and fragrant shrubs along the escarpment. But they didn't know what to do about it...not yet.

★

15

Beyond the boundary

Watkin Tench sat on a tree stump on the edge of the forest. The day was particularly fine. The sky was so blue it seemed tangible, as if he could reach up, press his finger into it and leave an indent. He could feel the sun piercing his back and thought about the huge canopy that, only weeks before, had sheltered the area.

He was aware of being one of the most educated officers in the young colony; after all, his parents were the proprietors of 'a most respectable boarding school' in the north-west of England. When writing his journal, he enjoyed quoting lines from Shakespeare, and inserting a French phrase here and there and in his free time, he looked forward to wandering down to the observatory, where he knew his friend William Dawes would welcome a session of intellectual debate.

Yet, despite his relatively comfortable background, Tench had seen his share of the harsher side of life. He had joined the Marine Corps at the age of sixteen and had almost immediately been involved in military action in the American War of Independence. In fact he had been captured by American forces and spent three months as a prisoner of war. With the end of the war however, he had been put on half-pay and in his late twenties he had decided to volunteer for service with the First Fleet.

As far as he was concerned, his time in New South Wales would be temporary; his 'tour of duty' was for the first few years of establishment of the colony. So for him, the expedition was a grand adventure. He gazed around, thinking about the progress that had been etched out of the wilderness beside him, and what still lay ahead.

From where he now sat, he had a view of the native canoes bobbing and dipping in the bay and pondered the resourcefulness of their makers. They were skillful, the way they balanced in such lightweight craft; the way they maneuvered them in squally seas though they sat scarcely above the water. To have a fire burning on a pad of clay inside the canoe in order to cook and eat the fish as they were caught was ingenious. They were patient and persistent people too; the women, often with a child on their lap, sat fishing in their flimsy canoes hour after hour. Most native women he'd noticed had the top joint of their little finger removed and he'd surmised it was done purposely to enable them more easily to wind their fishing lines over their hand. He made notes about their fishing techniques in his journal:

> *Fishing indeed, seems to engross nearly the whole of their time...The canoes in which they fish are...nothing more than a large piece of bark tied up at both ends with vines. Their dexterous management of them, added to the swiftness with which they paddle, and the boldness that leads them several miles in the open sea, are highly deserving of admiration. A canoe is seldom seen without a fire in it, to dress the fish by, as soon as caught.*

He looked beyond the fishing craft pleasantly aware of the sounds of native women laughing and singing in unison as they paddled. The sun reflecting on the bay, cast shimmery patches of light across the silvery green of the opposite shore. There were so many intriguing little inlets still to explore in the harbour. Lieutenants John Hunter and William Bradley, both of *HMS Sirius,* had already surveyed the main body of water and reported that it extended much further west than originally anticipated.

What was out there yet to be discovered?

While charting the harbour in the early weeks of February, Hunter and Bradley had met groups of inquisitive, friendly natives who had '*danced and sung*' with them. According to Hunter, they had expressed 'utmost astonishment' at the layers of clothing worn by the white men, believing them to be '*so many different skins, and the hat as part of the head*'.

There had been mutual curiosity in the early days and Tench wondered what had changed.

He peered over his shoulder, squinting against the intensity of light thrown in shafts between the nearby trees. There was such a vast unknown out there in the forests too. He had to concur with the governor's recent comment that *'as far as the eye can reach to the westward, the country is one continued wood.'* And yet here they were, perched on the edge of it - between the ocean and that seemingly endless wilderness - huddled into a camp space only a few hundred yards across.

What lay westward, in the interior? He was itching to know... and hoped he would soon have an opportunity to go exploring. His attention was brought back to his immediate surroundings by a sharp, angry bellow from a convict guard:

'Keep going you good-for-nothing, lazy, scoundrel! Dig!'

Watkin Tench contemplated the convict cargo that had been under his charge aboard the ship *Charlotte*. Although other officers had complained about the 'abandoned wretches' on other transports, for the most part he had disagreed with their assessment. He had been relieved when early in the journey, Phillip had issued a directive that when appropriate, the officers *'were at liberty to release the convicts from the fetters in which they had been confined'*. Tench had written with pride:

> *In complying with these directions I had great pleasure in being able to extend this humane order to the whole of those under my charge without a single exception.*

Later in the voyage however, he had been made acutely aware that his compassion had been undeserved in certain cases. While just outside Rio de Janeiro harbour, a Portuguese trading vessel had come alongside *Charlotte* to sell fruit, and through dealings with the merchants, it had come to light that one of the convicts, Thomas Barrett, had been involved in a ploy to pass off counterfeit coins produced from old buckles, metal buttons and pewter spoons during the journey. Surgeon

John White had voiced his astonishment at the convicts' feat in producing the currency:

> *How they managed this business without discovery, or how they could effect it at all, is a matter of inexpressible surprise to me...The impression, milling, character, in a word, the whole, was so inimitably executed that had their metal been a little better the fraud, I am convinced, would have passed undetected...*

The British officers, not wanting the Portuguese traders to have an 'unfavourable opinion of Englishmen' from the conduct of the rascal prisoners, explained that the perpetrators were convicted felons, doomed to exile. It was evident however that the counterfeit was remarkable, particularly given the circumstances of its manufacture. Yet, despite a thorough search of the convict quarters, none of the equipment necessary for the melding of metals was found. How they had managed the forgery no-one could fathom until it was discovered that a marine had been involved. For his part in the scheme, the marine was court-martialled and punished with two hundred lashes. John White, still staggered by the incident and the convicts' talent had remarked in his journal:

> *A business that required so complicated a process, gave me a high opinion of their ingenuity.*[3]

With hindsight, Tench realised his trust had been seriously abused but he had tried to put the episode behind him. In fact, he had chosen not to mention it in his journal at all. However, at the colony's first execution, as he had stood straight faced and solemn witnessing Barrett's life snuffed from his body as a consequence of stealing food, memories of the onboard scam had been unpleasantly rekindled. He could not help wishing that Thomas Barrett had put his brilliant and exceptional skill to better use.

---

[3] Thomas Barrett has been credited as the engraver of the 'Charlotte Medal' a beautifully inscribed metal disk, allegedly commissioned by Surgeon John White in January 1788 and made from a surgeon's metal kidney bowl. The artwork is now held in the Australian National Maritime Museum, Sydney. See notes for this chapter.

It was true that since landing, other convicts had also shown themselves to be dishonest, unreliable rogues; they would have to be watched...and pushed, forced and beaten...to get any work out of them. On the other hand, a good percentage of them were decent men and women. His mind went to two convict men in particular.

There was the builder, James Bloodworth with a seven year sentence, who was already making an impression on the governor. He'd shown himself to be a cut above the useless 'workers' who scratched at the surface of the soil with as little effort as possible. Many of them didn't know a shovel from an axe and didn't want to learn. The governor suspected that some of them had deliberately broken or 'lost' their tools.

But Bloodworth had shown initiative. He'd demonstrated to convicts and marines how simple huts could be built with the raw materials found nearby. He had shown them how walls could be framed up with straight timber or palm poles as vertical supports; then lighter branches from cabbage palms or acacia saplings threaded sideways through the uprights. A woven mat of thinner branches and reeds was covered inside and out with thick mud, and a roof added by laying reeds, long grass and rushes over a frame so that the rain naturally ran off. The floors were merely stamped earth and windows were openings covered with a mesh of thinner twigs. They were rough and ready dwellings and leaked in torrential rain, but they would do for now.

Within a short time, Bloodworth had started talking about a design for the governor's house; a two-storey dwelling to be made of bricks and stone. It had seemed an ambitious project, thinking about a permanent official residence amid the mish-mash of tents and mud huts dotting the cleared ground and the doubters had shaken their heads. Some, like Major Ross, had openly expressed the view that there was no future for Sydney Cove and therefore no point starting long term ventures. Besides, so far, despite an extensive search, no lime had been found to use as mortar. A small amount had been brought from England, but that wouldn't go far.

How on earth, given the lack of bricks and mortar, could a sizable building of any kind be considered at this stage? Even if they had bricks, what would hold them together and who had the skills to do the building work?

But Bloodworth had considered that.

He could teach men to make bricks and how to lay them. They had already located a place with suitable clay; as for mortar, there was an abundance of shells that could be collected, burned and turned into lime mortar for cementing the bricks.

The governor was impressed with Bloodworth and had put him in charge of brickmaking and assigned him as building supervisor of his official government residence. Soon the officers wanted Bloodworth's input on plans for their permanent barracks – down the track of course. It was almost as if this man, a convict, was becoming indispensable to the settlement.

Then there was the young fisherman, William Bryant. He'd been convicted for resisting inspectors as they'd searched for smuggled goods in his possession. On the voyage however he'd shown himself to be trustworthy to the degree that Tench had given him the job of issuing food rations to the other convicts. A short time after landing in Sydney Cove, William had married Mary, a young woman from the same English fishing coast as him. She had been transported for stealing but had also behaved well during their passage from England. Governor Phillip, keen to reward good behaviour, had given permission for the young couple, and baby Charlotte, born to Mary during the voyage, to live in a small hut near the water. With William's fishing experience, his capacity to supply the colony with additional food was invaluable and the governor had already put him in charge of the fishing boats.

Life would not be too bad at Sydney Cove for the Bryants, but all William could talk about was serving his time and getting back to his village on the south-west coast of England. His sentence, however, wouldn't expire until 1791; he wouldn't be free to return to his homeland for another three years, even if he had the means. Mary had two years longer than William to serve, but that didn't stop them talking about it...and making secret plans.

★

16

The Kable's story

On the same day in February 1788 that Mary and William Bryant were married, several other couples had exchanged wedding vows.

The marriages had been conducted outside, under the canopy of a huge tree beside the harbour. One of the couples getting married that summer morning had waited for over two years for such a day. Henry Kable and his bride Susannah had fallen in love in an English prison but when they'd asked for permission to marry then, it had been repeatedly denied them despite that fact that they had already had a child together.

Henry and Susannah's poignant and intriguing saga had become widely known and the Reverend Johnson, who had conducted their marriage service, hoped their wedding day would signal a more positive phase for the young couple. Their story, which had appeared in the London Chronicle newspaper prior to the sailing of the fleet for Botany Bay, goes like this:

Henry, a strongly built, red-haired youth had been convicted with his father and another labourer for burglary. All three had been sentenced to death by hanging but young Henry had been shown mercy on account of his age and was to be transported to New South Wales instead. His father and friend, however, were hanged just outside Norwich prison where young Henry was confined.

The only consolation for Henry at this terrible time of his life was meeting Susannah, who had been imprisoned for a similar crime. They fell in love and before their baby, Henry junior was born in the prison, they repeatedly asked the prison authorities for permission to marry, but it was refused each time.

A few months after baby Henry's birth, prisoners started being gathered from various prisons throughout England to sail with the First Fleet to the planned penal colony at Botany Bay. The order came from London to transfer female convicts from Norwich prison onto hulks, or disused ships, to await transportation. One of these unfortunate women was Susannah, and at the time her little baby was only five months old. As soon as Henry Kable heard that Susannah and little Henry were being taken away he appealed to go with them but his pleas were ignored.

One wintery day, the women prisoners, including Susannah and her baby, under the guard of a prison warden named John Simpson, set out on the bitterly cold 300 mile journey by coach to Plymouth where they would be put in a prison hulk until the fleet was ready to sail. Susannah huddled her baby close to keep him warm and cushion his little body against the rough ride. Saying goodbye to Henry, the man she already considered her husband had been agonising, however as the women sped southward in the coach, little did Susannah know that there was so much worse to come.

After waiting in an open boat for hours in the freezing November air, Susannah and the other women were ordered aboard the prison hulk. However, when the captain of the prison hulk saw the baby in Susannah's arms he refused to allow the infant on board on the grounds that there were no papers listing his name. Despite Susannah's pleas and the added attempts of the prison warden who had brought them, the captain remained unwavering in his refusal. Finally, baby Henry was pulled from his mother's arms and she was dragged away crying uncontrollably and threatening to kill herself. She was grief-stricken:

I can't live without my baby! she cried as the captain turned his back and walked away.

The prison guard, Simpson, intensely affected by the scene was forced to return ashore with the child. Fortunately for Susannah, he was a compassionate man of strong principles. He couldn't stand by and allow such a deplorable situation so he decided to directly petition Lord Sydney, the man responsible at the time for all issues relating to convict transportation. Simpson left immediately for London.

On arrival there, he went straight to the office of Lord Sydney where he, on being told that His Lordship was very busy, waited patiently in the hall until the Lord finally came down the stairs and noticed him. Simpson immediately took the opportunity to explain the situation and begged him to sign an order for the baby boy to be re-united with his mother. To his acclaim, Lord Sydney, listened and was 'deeply affected' by the story. He not only signed the order, but gave instructions that the mother was to be informed without delay that her baby would be returned to her. He then went a step further: he ordered that the father, Henry Kable, was to be transported in the same fleet. Simpson hurried away to share Lord Sydney's ordinance with the distressed mother and father. He must have felt pleasure in delivering that news, and seeing the family reunited after what must have been an agonising ten days separation.

Simpson's humane intervention attracted the attention of the British media and London news-readers were captivated by the story. The account consequently came to the attention of an influential lady who, in turn, organised public donations for the couple. Contributions amounted to the substantial sum of twenty pounds - about four times the value of the goods Susannah had stolen and enough money to buy things that would make a real difference to their life in New South Wales. It had been an unbelievable turn-around for Susannah and Henry.

A crate with their donations of practical goods was loaded onto the transport ship, *Alexander*, and the young family, Henry, Susannah and their baby, sailed together on *Friendship*. Later in the voyage, at Cape Town, Susannah and her baby were transferred to the ship, *Charlotte*, to make way for livestock needed for the new settlement in New South Wales. That was when Watkin Tench had become aware of the young mother, Susannah, and her devotion to her baby.

After the fleets' arrival at Sydney Cove, Henry Kable gained the governor's attention and trust. As a level-headed young man, clearly devoted to his partner and child, he was assigned as overseer of the women's encampment; he being more dependable in that role, the governor suspected, than many of the marines. As a consequence, the couple lived near the governor's canvas marquee, on the eastern side of the cove where a select group of reliable male and female convicts were sited to act as his domestic servants. Some were entrusted as supervisors and watchmen over the small government farm being established.

☆

As Henry and Susannah put their few possessions into their makeshift dwelling, they must have envisaged a far more promising future for themselves and baby Henry than they had ever thought possible in England. There was no doubt that adjustment to their new environment still had to be made; so many aspects of life in Sydney Cove contrasted starkly with life in England. The strange insects and animals were unnerving at times and the extreme weather, particularly the violent thunder storms, could be daunting.

Another necessary adjustment was to a new diet. As far as they knew, the only edible plants growing naturally in the vicinity of their new home were a few leafy herbs, a leafy vine the convicts dubbed 'sweet tea' and some tart red berries which had to be stewed. The sterility of the soil was discouraging but Henry would attempt to grow turnips and cabbages to supplement their otherwise monotonous rations of rice, flour and salt-pork. There was the occasional treat of fish or game, but that addition was unreliable. Everything, including cooking pots, was in short supply, so Susannah had to bake bread on the end of a shovel held into an open fire. Like everyone else, the Kables would improvise for furniture, and cooking and eating utensils.

Despite the challenges, they knew that once they'd adjusted to their surroundings and to the fact that separation from their families in England was most likely permanent, they would find contentment in their new circumstances. They were together, that was the main thing.

☆

The drama of the Kable's story hadn't ended with their arrival, marriage and homebuilding in Sydney. Another incident, a twist to the tale, was to cloud their early months in the colony.

The Reverend Johnson, the minister who'd officiated at their wedding, had been asked before setting sail from England, to ensure that their crate of donated goods was delivered safely to them on arrival in New South Wales. At the time of their marriage ceremony, it was assumed that the box was still on board the *Alexander* as most of the ships were still to be unloaded. However, on that warm summer day no-one involved with their wedding, including the happy couple themselves, could have known that their legacy had gone missing.

☆

17

Into the wild blue yonder

Meanwhile, as the fledgling colony in Sydney Cove took on signs of permanency - the building of timber storehouses and the digging of gardens - Governor Phillip, as per his instructions from England, had sent Lieutenant King on a very important mission. He was to set up a small British outpost on a tiny island about one thousand miles (1,600 km) from Sydney Cove, way out in the Pacific Ocean. The Lieutenant was instructed to command a settlement '*to be formed in Norfolk Island*' in order to '*prevent it being occupied by the subjects of any other European power*' and hopefully to begin cultivating a flax plant reportedly in abundance on the island. Under the governance of the young officer would be a small party of about twenty people. He had taken with him a naval doctor, Thomas Jamison, a couple of skilled men, a handful of marines and a small group of convicts: nine males and six females. It was an enormous undertaking for a young man of only twenty-nine years. There were few places on earth as isolated as the island he was to settle and very little was known about it.

During his discussions with the French commander Monsieur La Perouse, while anchored in Botany Bay, King had learnt that during their expedition across the Pacific, the French had intended landing on Norfolk Island in search of fresh water, but the dangerously rocky approach had prevented them. The Frenchman's opinion of the small island was that it appeared to be 'fit only for eagles'. Although Lieutenant King was an experienced naval officer, this new undertaking was something very different. Careful planning was essential.

His lack of information about the island and his lack of experience in administering an isolated penal colony meant he'd had to choose his convict population wisely. So he had boarded *Lady Penrhyn* before the women disembarked to consult with Bowes Smyth, the ship's doctor, and Lieutenant Johnston about which women they would recommend as participants for the proposed community of Norfolk Island. They would, like the convict men chosen, have to be of good character as there would only be a few marines going to the outpost to maintain order. Among the women recommended was Ann Inett, a level-headed young woman who, like Esther Abrahams, had stayed out of trouble on the voyage. Also like Esther, Ann Inett had been a needle-worker and garment maker, convicted for stealing and sentenced to seven years transportation.

Surprisingly, the selected convicts had been given a choice about whether they wanted to go to Norfolk Island or stay in the Sydney settlement. King had assembled the chosen group and informed them they would be rewarded for their co-operation and promised to return them to England when their convictions expired (an arrangement not available to convicts generally). Ann Inett, after weighing her options and assessing Lieutenant King to be a fair and honest man, had 'volunteered' to be part of the small outpost on Norfolk Island.

The departure of the Norfolk Island assemblage had been a difficult farewell for the convicts. They had shared cramped quarters on their respective ships for over eight trying months of the voyage to New South Wales. No-one knew what dangers lay ahead or if they would ever meet again. The group bound for Norfolk Island had left Sydney Cove in mid-February 1788 on *HMS Supply*, the smallest ship of the fleet, taking two weeks to reach their remote Pacific destination through rough seas. They had been given provisions for only six months which, King was told, they would have to supplement by 'procuring fish and vegetables' around the island.

Once the party landed, *HMS Supply* was to return to Sydney so the settlers on Norfolk Island would be completely marooned and, as the island had no previous inhabitants, the group would be entirely alone. Lieutenant King was supplied with only one four-oared boat and had specific instructions from the British government on the matter of boat building:

It is our Royal will and pleasure that you do not on any account allow craft of any sort to be built for the use of private individuals.

It was a safeguard against convict escapes but there was also a political motive to the ban of vessels over a certain size. It was a known fact that the 'British East India Company' wanted to keep its monopoly on trade with China, India, and the islands of the South Seas; they didn't want the new settlements of New South Wales to jeopodise that lucrative operation. The instructions went on to specify that if any vessel appeared on the island 'by accident', it was to be 'rendered unserviceable' until further instructions were received.

In such an isolated situation, the small band of settlers on Norfolk Island formed a close-knit farming community. Like Governor Phillip, King's vision for the island settlement was to rule by incentive and reward, rather than punishment. From the outset, the young Lieutenant was attracted to Ann Inett and she was soon assigned as his 'housekeeper'. She would, no doubt have realised, given the loneliness and seclusion of their circumstances, that before long her role would involve more than housekeeping. Within a short time, the couple became aware that Ann was pregnant with their first child.

☆

On the mainland, while most of the settlement had been preoccupied with the departure of a small number of their group to Norfolk Island, Ann Smith, the outspoken convict who had continually sworn she would escape, took the opportunity to quietly sneak out of the Sydney campsite. The other women from *Lady Penrhyn*, who had listened to her ranting throughout the voyage, were astounded that she had actually gone through with her plan. Given the evidence they had already seen of fearsome creatures lurking in the wilderness, they were stunned that she would attempt life alone in unfamiliar and apparently hostile territory. Like Esther Abrahams, Ann Smith was a Londoner, a city girl who had been arrested for stealing in the same year and tried in the same courthouse as Esther. But she was almost twice Esther's age, didn't have the care of a child and was obviously a risk-taker. She was never seen in the settlement again and it was assumed that she had died soon after absconding. As 'evidence' of her wretched end, a piece of linen petticoat was found miles from the settlement some time later and it was presumed to have belonged to her. But rumours about Ann Smith's fate would circulate for years.

★

With the sailing of the small band to Norfolk Island, Governor Phillip set his attention to the future of the Sydney Cove settlement. He had plans drawn for a 'proper' town and its area surveyed and 'streets' marked out. He was also looking beyond the limits of the settlement. The ground around Sydney was not as fertile as it had at first appeared. They needed to look further afield.

What was out there to the west, toward those hazy blue hills, and beyond?

It was time to find out.

★

18

Into an unknown wilderness

From the first weeks of their arrival at Sydney Cove, exploration had taken place around the harbour and its environs and to a limited degree, along the coastline. Governor Phillip had set off with groups of officers on various tours of discovery which were restricted in duration by the provisions they could carry.

During April 1788, one of the most promising and challenging excursions was attempted westward. The governor and a group of officers including George Johnston, David Collins and Surgeon John White, with some soldiers, headed into the unknown interior, toward the hazy mountain range, already being referred to as the 'blue' mountains. Watkin Tench gives some background and explains what they hoped to accomplish:

> At the distance of 60 miles inland, a prodigious chain of lofty mountains runs nearly in a north and south direction, further than the eye can trace them. Should nothing intervene to prevent it, the Governor intends, shortly, to explore their summits… If large rivers do exist in the country…their sources must arise amidst these hills.

So the intention was to reach the mountains and hopefully find an inland river. The party headed westward, first by boat along the narrowing harbour to reach its source; then on foot across country. They took supplies for only seven days, as everything they needed for the trek, their tents, weapons, clothes, food and cooking pots, had to be carried on their backs. They also had to carry water, not knowing if they would come across a river. In addition they took spare shoes, as the rugged terrain on a previous trip had completely demolished the men's footwear.

Only a day's journey from Sydney, John White wrote of the remoteness he felt in the bush:

> *Here in the most wild and solitary seclusion that the imagination can form any idea of...we washed our shirts and stockings and took up our abode for the night...*

Watkin Tench didn't go on that particular expedition, but made sure he got the details on their return:

> *With unwearied industry they continued to penetrate the country for four days; but at the end of that time, finding the base of the mountains to be yet at the distance...and provisions growing scarce, it was judged prudent to return...*

They had found that the mountains were deceptively far-away and a longer expedition would be needed to reach them. But their exploration had revealed areas of good land westward *'capable of everything, which a happy soil and good climate'* could produce. The area they were most impressed with was at the head of the harbour. It appeared to be an excellent place for a second mainland settlement. Their excursions that month had been very worthwhile but one aspect had mystified them; though they had seen the *'indisputable tracks of the natives having been there'*, on the whole journey *'none of them were to be seen'*. There had been a conspicuous absence of black people. They had however, seen samples of native artworks which particularly impressed John White:

> *We saw, however, some proofs of their ingenuity in various figures cut on the smooth surface of some large stones. They consisted chiefly of representations of themselves in different attitudes, of their canoes, of several sorts of fish and animals; and, considering the instruments with which the figures must have been made, they seemed to exhibit tolerably strong likenesses.*

Besides being baffled by the fact that they had not met any inhabitants of the forests, they were also mystified about what foodstuff the natives survived on away from the coast; the white men hadn't seen anything edible since leaving Sydney. They had, however, found the forest less dense and the soil promising for farming. The governor later named the area, near the head of the harbour, 'Rose Hill'.

★

Out in the hinterland it had been easy for the natives to avoid the explorers. They had watched the white men trudging through the undergrowth, heard them cursing at the prickly vegetation, and huffing and puffing up the rocky inclines and wondered at the heavy burdens on their backs. They had observed their conspicuous red jackets, the body-hugging material restricting their movement and the heavy coverings on their feet but they couldn't fathom why men would encumber themselves in such a way. In the wilderness, it had not been difficult for the black people to keep a comfortable distance between themselves and the white men.

★

19

Friends and thieves

On the coast, however, it was a different story. In the area immediately surrounding Sydney Cove, it was becoming more and more difficult for the black families to avoid the white strangers and their expanding campsite. So, in their determination to shun the mysterious goings-on at the encampment, the natives took the long way around the whole settlement area. It meant they had to go further to gather food and find the raw material needed to produce their utensils and fishing equipment. But it was necessary, they told their children, to be wary of the pale foreigners.

However, as the weeks turned to months, through various observations and meetings with white people *outside* the encampment, some of the natives began adjusting their outlook. It had become apparent that not all white skinned people were the same. It seemed unreasonable to generalise about a whole race because of their observations at the main settlement.

The man they'd heard called 'Dawes', who lived alone near his strange construction on the secluded western point, behaved differently to the 'red coats' in the central camp. As they'd paddled past his isolated dwelling on the headland, they had observed the quiet stranger's interest in the plants and shrubs growing in the bush around his hut. They'd seen him observing the stars move across the night sky and they had seen him, from his vantage point, studying them as they fished from the rocks. It seemed apparent that he wanted to connect with them, but they were not yet ready to pay him a visit.

Later, when they did make contact, Dawes was to learn that the families on whose land he had built his hut, referred to themselves as 'Eora', meaning 'the people'; Sydney Cove had been named *'Warran'* by them long before the white men arrived, and its western peninsular where his observatory stood, they called *'Tarra'*. Dawes had faithfully recorded each word with its meaning in his language journal.

The natives also encountered other inoffensive white men and women outside the main camp, collecting oysters on the rocky shoreline, or in the forest looking for edible greens. Seeing the stranger's lack of basic knowledge of bush skills, they had shown those willing to listen which plants were suitable and palatable. Out in the bay, interaction between the black and white men remained co-operative. When the fishing nets were hauling in big catches the natives *'often assisted with cheerfulness, and in return were generally rewarded with part of the fish taken.'*

Some of the convicts, once their fear of the bush had lessened, ventured a little further afield where they found, and subsequently visited, a local native campsite:

> *In the adjoining cove resided a family of them, who were visited by large parties of convicts of both sexes...where they danced and sang with apparent good humour, and received such presents as they could afford to make them; but none of them would venture back with their visitors.*

Some natives were apparently happy to interact with the whites in the security of their own domain, but they were not interested in becoming part of the white man's world. Of course, the convicts who were received into the campsite of the black families didn't carry guns; they brought only the simple offering of open-minded friendship and visited for the down-to-earth pleasure of song and dance. Unknowingly, these groups were demonstrating, at a micro level, what could have been possible on a broader scale.

As these types of alliances were forming outside the main settlement, individuals from among each race began seeing positive and negative aspects of the other. Some natives saw the opportunity to exchange kangaroo meat or fish for the white men's metal axes or bread, and for some, the white men's delicious mind-numbing liquor became an irresistible enticement for trade. On the other hand, white men who were willing to listen, learnt valuable bush survival skills, such as finding wild food and water in places they would never have thought to look. During scouting or hunting excursions white men were impressed by native implements such as the *woomera,* a short timber extension from which a spear could be *'discharged with considerable force'*. Through these limited interactions, various amicable connections emerged. However, while some groups were building good relationships, others were tearing down any trust that had been established.

It had not taken long before the natives realised that they could no longer leave their property unattended as they had been accustomed to do before the white people arrived. Unscrupulous convicts had quickly seen the value of the native implements as souvenirs back in England. They could make money by selling spears, shields and fishing equipment to sailors of the ships that would eventually be returning to Europe. They knew there was a good market for these items as 'collectables' in Britain. Previously, the natives had been accustomed to leaving their belongings in their campsites and on rocks and beaches with no doubt that they'd be there when they returned. Now, their patience was being tested; their weapons were essential to fish and hunt food, and they were constantly going missing.

It wasn't long before it became obvious that competition for food would be one of the main ongoing issues. When the boat loads of white people had arrived in Sydney Cove at the beginning of 1788, the population around the harbour had nearly doubled overnight. At Governor Phillip's estimation, the native residents of the vicinity were about the same in number as the English that had arrived in the ships. The quantity of fish and other food sources, that had once sustained the native people of the area, soon became strained.

As the white population's first southern winter approached, the natives, who had generously assisted the white fishermen to drag in the heavy fishing nets, became tired of hauling in the big catches only to receive a small portion of the proceeds. They were becoming indignant and angry, and one day, a group of native men took matters into their own hands:

The natives...either driven by hunger or moved by some other cause, came down to the cove where they were fishing and... took by force about half of what had been brought ashore.

They were all armed with spears and other weapons, and made their attack with some show of method, having a party stationed in the rear with their spears poised, in readiness to throw, if any resistance had been made.

Governor Phillip acknowledged their response in his report back to England, stating the episode:

...seems to indicate that they were still distressed for provisions, or that they very highly resent the encroachments made upon their fishing places.

This is the only instance in which these people have attempted any unprovoked act of violence, and to this they probably were driven by necessity.

But what was to be done about it? If only they could be persuaded to come into the settlement. The governor, in his report to England, mulled over the natives' actions and continued avoidance:

They think perhaps that we cannot teach them anything of sufficient value to make amends for our encroachments upon their fishing places.

They seem to be among themselves perfectly honest, and often leave their spears and other implements upon the beach, in full confidence of finding them untouched. But the convicts too frequently carry them off and dispose of them to vessels going to England.

The governor was exasperated. He wanted to show the natives that the theft of their belongings was not condoned by him. He wanted to explain to the natives, to make them understand, that the men who injured them were 'convicts', and already a disgraced class of people. He wanted to show them that the white people who stole and harmed them would be punished severely. He had to find a way to bring the natives into the camp, to demonstrate the advantages to them of the 'white man's world'. He had to find a way to bridge the great cultural divide that was hindering the 'amicable relationship' that he hoped to foster. He began formulating a daring strategy; he knew his scheme had its risks, so he would bide his time.

★

20

Frustration and progress

In the meantime, life within the settlement continued to have its ups and downs. Judge Advocate, David Collins was exasperated by the bold conduct of some convicts. Thefts had become so blatant that *'scarcely a day passes without some of these miserable delinquents being punished'* and, as a consequence, flogging and hangings continued. He recorded one in particular:

> *The month of May opened with the trial, conviction, and execution of James Bennett, a youth of seventeen years of age, for breaking into a tent...and stealing property...He was executed immediately on receiving his sentence, in the hope of making a greater impression on the convicts than if it had been delayed for a day or two.*

For stealing food and clothing, Bennett was hung by the neck at the 'fatal tree' as it was called, as a lesson to others that stealing could not be tolerated in a place where there was already too little. Despite the punishments, as the weather grew colder and the days shorter, overnight thefts from vegetable gardens continued without letup. Many convicts were too lazy or inept to grow their own food even though the governor had introduced a shorter working day for that purpose. By allowing two hours each afternoon for convicts to work in small garden plots he had hoped to encourage them to grow food independently, alleviating the colony's growing food shortage. For the most part, the incentive hadn't worked; many would rather steal than work.

Yet, amid the negativity, positive developments were evident. When marines had refused to supervise convict work, the governor had been forced to appoint the better behaved convicts as overseers of work-gangs.

This had provided unparalleled opportunities for some, like the builder James Bloodworth, who had shown initiative in supervising and undertaking construction projects. Referring to this, the governor's secretary had recorded with satisfaction:

> *There having been found among the convicts a person qualified to conduct the business of a bricklayer, a gang of labourers was put under his direction, and most of the huts which grew up in different parts of the cleared ground were erected by them.*

On the 15th of May, a milestone took place in the colony's development. The first stone of the governor's residence was laid on the east side of the cove. To mark the importance of the occasion, an engraved copper plaque was placed in the foundation of the building.

After an extensive area of clay had been discovered south of the settlement, in the early weeks of the colony, brickworks had been set up and by mid-May, between 20,000 and 30,000 bricks had been made in a firing kiln that had been built on site.

The process for making bricks wasn't easy: after clay of the right quality had been located and excavated, it had to be made into the right consistency for bricks. The brick-makers had to knead the clay with their feet, then the clay had to be packed into prepared frames and left to dry before the bricks were fired in the kiln to make them rock-hard. Despite the very basic equipment, a visitor to the site commented that the bricks were *'as good as those made in England'.*

Most of the men working at the brickfield had no previous experience of their task; they had to be trained and it was backbreaking work. But it was necessary for the construction of barracks and storehouses, and all the other buildings essential for a civilised society. There were no horses or bullocks available to transport the heavy piles of bricks, so convicts were harnessed eight, ten or twelve to a cart to drag the hefty loads for miles up and down hills, along the rough, bumpy tracks to the main site where the bricks were used in construction. However, those with sense and foresight obeyed orders, worked hard and learnt the trade knowing that in the long run they would be better off than their equals who languished in filthy crowded prisons in England awaiting their execution by hanging.

Other groups of convicts were learning the art of stone-cutting while others worked in the saw pits, preparing the local timber for building. Some, with varying levels of carpentry skill, worked under the supervision of an overseer to prepare wooden shingles for covering the hospital and storehouses; the slats being fastened to the roof with wooden pegs made by female convicts.

So, depending on their character, while some convicts were causing havoc and being punished, others were proving they could knuckle down and apply themselves to whatever work was assigned to them. Many had to be closely watched and pushed but others - those who proved trustworthy - were put in supervisory roles and treated liberally.

Outside the main camp, equally significant positive and negative interactions continued to occur.

☆

21

The rush-cutter incident

One day in May 1788, Lieutenant Bradley came across a native man and two children gathering some kind of fruit on the headland; it was a wild sugary treat which they soaked in water before eating. When the white men approached, the black man and the children were friendly and unafraid:

> ...where we landed, we found a native in a tree gathering a fruit of the size of a small pine, and of a beautiful pale yellow. He got it by fixing a four pronged spear over the stalk and twisting them off. It had a sweet taste.

> We found two children, a boy and a girl, near the tree in which the man was. The children did not appear frightened when we approached them... When the man had got a good quantity of this spongy fruit, he, with the children, walked along the beach and sat down by the side of a pool of fresh water, to which place we followed him. They ate or rather sucked the whole of what they had gathered, frequently dipping them in the water. They then returned to the place where we first met with them. They eagerly accepted a gull which we gave them.

On the same day however, possibly while this pleasant interaction was taking place, violence and bloodshed was occurring in another part of the harbour. When an officer went around the bay with boats later that afternoon to collect some reeds for thatching his house, he discovered the dead bodies. The story continues:

*...on landing at the place where two convicts had been
left with a tent for the purpose of cutting those rushes, he
found the tent but not the men. Finding some blood near
the tent, they followed it to the mangrove bushes, where
they found both men dead and laying at some distance
from each other.*

As the rush-cutters had been speared and their tools taken, the governor
felt the incident couldn't be ignored and that by catching the culprits
with the tools, it might be possible to discover why the deed had been
done. So the next day he set out with a small party of twelve armed men,
including George Johnston and chief surgeon John White, for the place
where the men had been killed. After walking across country for several
hours they arrived at the north shore of Botany Bay, without coming
across any natives.

Eventually, they saw about twenty fishing canoes in the bay and decided
to camp for the night, fully expecting a visit from the native fishermen,
but not one appeared. The next morning although more canoes were
drawn up on the beach, their owners were nowhere to be seen. The
natives were apparently not ready for a meeting.

Governor Phillip decided it was pointless staying any longer – it had
been a freezing night and the morning frost still crackled beneath their
frozen feet. The men began the trek back to Sydney Cove and had hiked
for some time when all of a sudden a great number of natives, hundreds
in fact, came into view. The natives were assembled at the mouth of a
huge cave and were only ten paces away when the governor spotted
them. In fact, everything happened so suddenly that the governor hardly
had time to call a halt before a number of armed warriors appeared in
their track.

A man, who appeared to be their leader, advanced making signs for the
English to back off, but according to the British version of events, when
he saw Governor Phillip approach *'alone, unarmed, and in a friendly
manner, he gave his spear away and met him with perfect confidence'*.
Governor Phillip tells the story in his report to England:

In less than three minutes the English party found itself surrounded by two hundred men; but nothing occurred in this transaction which could in the least confirm the idea that the natives were accustomed to act with treachery, or inclined to take any cruel advantage of superiority in numbers. The moment the offered friendship was accepted on their side, they laid down their spears and stone hatchets, and joined the party in the most amicable manner.

Numbers of women and children remained at a small distance, some of whom the men afterwards brought down to receive the little articles which were offered as presents. Nothing was seen among these people that could prove that any of them had been engaged in the affray with the rush-cutters; and the governor parted with them on the most friendly terms, more convinced than ever of the necessity of treating them with a proper degree of confidence, in order to prevent disagreement.

When it was time for the governor and his men to leave, an old man made signs that he would lead the way. The governor understood his motive when the native climbed a hill ahead of them and called out, holding up both his hands, to signify to a group of forty natives in the next cove that the white men, who were coming through, were friends.

On his return to Sydney, the governor was informed of fresh evidence. Before the attack on the rush-cutters, one of the natives had been murdered and several wounded, and the investigators came to the conclusion that the deaths were related. Lieutenant Bradley gave his forthright opinion of the connection between the deaths of the convicts and earlier killing of a native:

I have no doubt that this native, having been murdered, brought about their seeking revenge and which proved fatal to those who were not concerned. They have attacked our people when they have met them unarmed, but that did not happen until they had been very ill treated by us in the lower part of the harbour and fired upon at Botany Bay...

The white men had not yet come to understand the black man's rules of justice and reprisal. They were ignorant of the process of ritual punishment which demanded 'payback' for loss of life. The black man's law demanded that the guilty one, or ones, must accept the penalty from the family and friends of the victim.

David Collins, as the governor's secretary and judge for the colony, wanted to understand the complexities of the black man's justice system. He did eventually learn and record the customs and decrees of the Aboriginal people; but too late, in this matter, for the enlightenment of Governor Phillip and the early settlers:

> *Among other customs which these people practise, is one that is highly deserving of notice, as it carries with it some idea of retributive justice. The shedding of blood is always followed by punishment...*

The natives thought it 'right, necessary and inevitable' that a deliberate death should be compensated. The 'payback' could be inflicted on another member of the guilty party's clan, especially if the real culprit wasn't known. Once justice was done however, and the wrong had been righted, grudges were generally forgotten and opponents became friends again.

The British were as yet unaware of this vital information and the gulf of misunderstanding lay conspicuously wide between the two cultures. Around the autumn campfires of both black and white communities, puzzled individuals shook their heads in bewilderment and wondered if they would ever understand the other's strange ways.

★

22

Across the social divide

The arrival of the white population's first southern winter brought a welcome break from the drudgery of work in the form of a celebration; their first 'public holiday'. As June 4th marked King George of England's birthday, the governor saw it as an opportunity to spread some cheer. He allowed 'a pint of grog', from his own supply, to every convict and soldier to drink to His Majesty's health. He issued pardons to convicts who had been restricted to bread and water and confined on the small rocky island they had nicknamed '*Pinchgut*'. And all work was suspended for the day to allow everyone to participate in the occasion. The military band paraded and played *'God Save the King'*; volleys were fired from the ships' cannons and the officers ate a hearty meal with the governor consisting of *'mutton, pork, ducks, fowls, fish, kangaroo, salads, pies and preserved fruits'.*

There were toasts to 'The King' and the officers gave a toast to 'the Governor and the settlement'. Everyone, according to an eyewitness, was in a cheery mood. George Worgan, one of the doctors, after enjoying a meal with the governor, described the evening celebrations in his journal:

> *About 5 o'clock we walked out to visit the bonfires; the fuel of one a number of convicts had been two days collecting, was really a noble sight. It was piled up for several yards high round a large tree. Here, the convicts were assembled, singing.*

He related how a group of convicts gave three cheers and joined in singing *'God Save the King'* as the governor approached their bonfire. In many ways the event must have felt surreal. They were marooned on the edge of a wilderness, a speck on the edge of a vast and alien land, as far from their home as they could imagine. Yet, here they were - singing and cheering their distant King... standing around a bonfire with Governor Phillip in their midst. Some must have felt more liberated than ever before in their lives.

Despite the governor's leniency, he was soon reminded that some people would never change. George Worgan continued in his journal:

June 5th

> *Notwithstanding the Governor's indulgence yesterday, it was found that while many of the convicts were rejoicing at the bonfire, there were others practising their old custom of thieving, and many of the officer's tents and huts had been robbed. One fellow was detected as he was making off, for the officer happened to be in bed, and jumping out knocked the fellow down. His head is cut very much, but it is to be hoped that he will live to be tried & hung...Did you ever hear of such a set of reprobates!*

To add to the governor's worries, the colony's small stock of cattle went missing during the same month. Through the inattention of their caretaker they had wandered off into the wilderness and vanished without trace:

> *By some strange and unpardonable neglect in the convict who had been entrusted with the care of the cattle, the two bulls and four cows were lost.*

It was a serious blow. The cattle were needed as breeding stock, and as a backup if other food sources became low. And though parties of men searched the surrounding countryside for days after their disappearance, the cattle seemed to have vanished into thin air or rather, into the vast unknown. It seemed highly unlikely they would survive any length of time in the wilderness that had been described by those who had ventured any distance inland, as 'impenetrable country'. The fate of the missing cattle became 'a riddle' as Watkin Tench put it.

★

During the following month, July 1788, the last of the ships that had been contracted to transport them all to New South Wales began final preparation to return to England; that is, all but two government ships, *HMS Sirius* and *HMS Supply*, which would stay for the use of the colony.

The imminent departure of the ships motivated a flurry of letter writing to family and friends back home. Some letters described the generally agreeable weather and the possibilities the new land offered. However, many accounts painted a negative impression of the settlement as writers off-loaded their feelings of isolation and despondency to their loved ones so very far away.

Major Ross believed he summarised the feeling of all colonists when he wrote: *'there is not a man in this place that does not wish to return home'* and that the government *'will surely not think of sending any more people here.'* In a private letter to England he unleashed his negative opinions:

> *I do not scruple to pronounce that in the whole world there*
> *is not a worse country than what we have yet seen of this.*
> *All...is so very barren and forbidding that it may with truth*
> *be said, here nature is reversed...*

Others sent descriptions of the astonishing animals and birds they were encountering in their strange new home: flying squirrels[4] that hung upside down in the trees, seven-foot tall birds that could outrun a man but could not fly and of course the emblematic kangaroo, which Lieutenant Clark described in a letter to his wife as, *'the most extraordinary animal that I ever saw for they have a pocket...where they carry their young'.* He promised to have the next one he caught, stuffed and sent home for her.

As well as accounts of snakes, spiders, bats and sharks, others wrote about the lack of everyday comforts such as a decent cup of tea. One

---

[4] Flying squirrels were large fur-covered bats, now known as flying foxes.

female convict, whose letter was later printed anonymously in a British newspaper, gave her perspective on the difficulties faced by the women:

> *I take the first opportunity to acquaint you with our disconsolate situation in this solitary waste of the creation… Windows we have none; so that lattices of twigs are made by our people (in) their place.*
>
> *As for the distresses of the women, they are past description…as they are totally deprived of clothes; those who have young children are quite wretched. Besides this, though a number of marriages have taken place, several women, who became pregnant on the voyage, are since left by their partners, who have returned to England…*
>
> *In short, everyone is so taken up with their own misfortune that they have no pity to bestow on others. All our letters are examined by an officer but a friend takes this for me privately.*

The Reverend Johnson also sent an account to his friend in England of an unusual case involving two convicts and a ship's master. The convicts, Henry Kable and his wife Susannah, had complained to him that most of the crate of goods, which had been donated to them by well-meaning people in England, had not been delivered to them. At the time of their complaint, all the ships had supposedly been unloaded but most of the Kable's belongings had gone missing. Henry wanted to know what could be done about it and the governor decided to convene a court hearing to investigate. The accusation was that the master of the ship, *Alexander* had not delivered the property as he had been hired to do. John White, the chief surgeon, who formed part of the court, also wrote what happened:

> *A civil court was convened to hear a complaint made against Duncan Sinclair, master of the Alexander transport, by Henry Kable and Susannah his wife (the Norwich convicts who excited so much public attention), for the non-delivery of a parcel sent on board the Alexander…containing wearing apparel, books, and other things, to the value of*

*twenty pounds. The parcel was proved (and this even by the
acknowledgment of the master) to have been received on
board; and it likewise appeared in evidence that, on moving
it from one part of the ship to another, the package had
broken and the books had fallen out, which books the convict
said had been delivered to him.*

*The court, after deducting five pounds (the value of the
books received), gave a verdict in favour of the couple…
and in consequence of the authority granted them by Act of
Parliament…they judged the master of the transport fully
to compensate the loss of the convicts, amounting to fifteen
pounds. Sinclair considered it as oppressive to be obliged to
pay…but this objection had no weight with the court, as the
ship was in the service of government and paid for the sole
purpose of conveying these people, and the little property
which they possessed, to this country.*

This was the first civil court case ever held in Australia and it was
ground-breaking. In Britain, at that time in history, the property rights of
convicted lawbreakers were non-existent.

According to British law of the day, convicts had no rights whatsoever;
they were considered to be 'deserving of death' and as such, 'already dead
in law'. They were not allowed to own property, unable to make contracts
and certainly unable to sue in court; they were considered the scum of
the earth. But on the other side of the world from Britain, it was deemed
necessity to approach things differently… and a precedent had been set.

For Henry and Susannah, the future was encouraging. Henry, in a letter
sent to his mother in England, expressed his contentment:

*I am, thank God, very easily situated…some officers have
been so pleased with my conduct that they continue me in the
office of an overseer over the women.*

The Kables were indeed in a unique position but they knew uncertainty
still lay ahead for them and for the settlement. They were trying to raise

a few vegetables in the garden adjoining their hut but the ground was hard and infertile, the weather was unpredictable. Susannah knew there was still a lot of adjusting to do if they were to make a successful life for themselves in such alien surroundings. They were not only building a future for themselves, but for little Henry junior, to whom Henry referred to in his letter as *'our boy Harry...a promising little fellow'*. They were also thinking of the future for their second child, already well on the way. The young couple knew, above everything else, they must stay on the right side of the law.

★

Ironically, around the same time, a devious group of marines, some of whom had guarded the Kables on the voyage, were devising a scam to improve their own lot at the expense of the public store. Collins, the judge advocate recorded the details:

> *Having formed their party, seven in number, and sworn each other to secrecy...they altered keys to fit the different locks on the three doors of the provision store; and it was agreed, that whenever any one of the seven should be posted there as sentinel during the night,...by means of their keys, and sheltered in the security afforded them (by betraying in so flagrant a manner the trust and confidence put in him as a sentinel), they should open a passage into the store, where they should remain shut up until they had as much liquor or provisions as they could take off.*

The idea was that if the genuine guards, during their patrols, visited the store while the thieving marines were inside, the door would be found locked and secure, and so everything would be assumed to be in order.

Their trickery was eventually discovered many months later, when early one morning, the commissary found a key broken in the lock of the main storehouse. On entering, he found a container opened and provisions taken. The broken key was immediately taken to a convict blacksmith who identified the soldier who had 'some time back' brought the key in to be altered.

Apparently, on the night in question, the thief had been standing with the key in the lock and about to leave, when he heard the patrol guard advancing. Knowing the lock would be examined by the corporal, he panicked and *'in his fright and haste...finding that he could not get the key out of the lock, he broke it; the other part of the key he threw away.'*

Evidence at the enquiry suggested that *'the store had been broken into and robbed by them at various times for upwards of eight months'*. At the trial the men were 'unanimously found guilty', and sentenced to death. As Judge Advocate Collins wrote, *'a crime of such magnitude called for a severe example'*. Gallows were erected between the two main storehouses and the marines were hung in a public execution soon after the trial.

A witness to the awful occasion wrote that *'there was hardly a marine present, officers and men'*, who did not *'shed a tear'* at the execution. The emotion stimulated by the event may have been due to feelings of shock and betrayal that men they'd thought of as friends could be so devious. It may also have been empathy with the circumstances that had seduced their comrades into such low actions - maybe they too had considered syphoning off a little extra for themselves.

Whatever sentiment the executions provoked, the episode was also clear evidence of the blurred lines that were developing between convicts and marines. They were all isolated in their remote coastal outpost, all feeling the effects of diminishing supplies and all susceptible to the same temptations.

★

23

Across the racial divide

In the meantime, adjustment and acceptance between the black and white races around the harbour continued to have varying degrees of success.

Surgeon White, being a keen fisherman and botanist, was often on the harbour away from the main camp exploring. During the course of several days in the month of July, he recorded four very different reactions from groups of natives toward the various intrusions into their activities. In the first situation the apprehension of a female native turned to apparent relief. Over the following days intruders were met with open aggression, and in the final account, a mutual sharing of information and friendship:

21ˢᵗ July:

> *I went down the harbour, to look for a cabbage tree as a covering for my hut. On our return we fell in with three canoes that had been out fishing. We rowed towards them, when the natives in them suddenly appeared intimidated, and paddled away with all possible dispatch. Willing to convince them that they had nothing to dread from us, we rowed after them, in order to present them with some trifles which we had about us.*
>
> *When we approached the canoes, an old woman in one of them began to cast her fish overboard, in great haste; whether it was for fear that we should take them from her, or whether*

she threw them to us, we could not ascertain. However, when we came along-side, our conduct soon convinced her that her alarms, with respect to us, were groundless.

She had in the canoe a young girl...who did not betray the least sign of apprehension, but rather seemed pleased at the interview. She laughed immoderately, either at us or at the petulance shown by the old woman, who I believe was more terrified on the girl's account than on her own. After this we left them fully satisfied that we did not mean to offer them any injury.

The following day John White reported quite a different reaction from some natives to a group of convicts some distance from the Sydney camp:

A party of convicts, who had crossed the country to Botany Bay to gather a kind of plant resembling balm, which we found to be a pleasant vegetable, were met by a superior number of the natives, armed with spears and clubs, who chased them for two miles without being able to overtake them.

The convicts believed the natives would have 'put them to death' if they had been caught, as the white men were unarmed and fewer in number. It seems probable however that if the natives had really wanted to, they would have easily overtaken the fleeing white men; they were generally far more agile in the bush. A few days later there was a far more serious incident:

One of the convicts was met by some natives, who wounded him very severely in the breast and head with their spears... When he was brought to the hospital he was very faint from the loss of blood, which had flowed plentifully from his wounds. A piece of a broken spear had entered through the scalp and under his ear, so that the extraction gave him great pain.

Then, less than a week later John White reports:

This day, three canoes, with a man and woman in each, came behind the point on which the hospital is built, to fish.

I went over to them, as did two other gentlemen, without their showing any fear at our coming; on the contrary, they manifested a friendly confidence. We gave them some bread, which they received with apparent pleasure, but did not eat any of it while in our presence. We likewise presented them with a looking-glass, but this they received with indifference, and seemed to hold in no kind of estimation.

I gave one of the women a pocket handkerchief, which she immediately tied round her head, and showed great satisfaction...She would not come out of the canoe, though alongside the rocks; but the man quitted it and showed us some wild figs that grew near at hand ...He ate (one) with apparent relish, and smacked his lips after he had swallowed it, to convince us how good it was.

During the encounter, both parties were apparently educated and entertained by each other. We can sense their mutual interest through John White's account:

At some little distance from the place where we were, a sheep lay dead. As soon as he discovered it, (as well as we could understand him) he was extremely inquisitive and anxious to know what it was. When his curiosity was satisfied, he went into the canoe where the woman had been waiting for him.

About ten or twenty yards from the shore, among the long grass, in the shallow water, he struck and took with his fish-gig several good fish... While he was engaged in watching for them, both he and the woman chewed something which they frequently spat into the water; and which appeared to us, from his immediately striking a fish, to be a lure.

While they were thus employed, one of the gentlemen with me sang some songs; and when he had done, the females in the canoes either sung one of their own songs, or imitated him, in which they succeeded beyond conception. Anything spoken by us they most accurately recited, and this in a manner of which we fell greatly short in our attempts to repeat their language after them.

Then, amid the happy scene, something happened nearby to abruptly change the mood:

While we were thus amicably engaged, all of a sudden they paddled away from us. On looking about to discover the cause, we perceived the gunner of the Supply at a distance, with a gun in his hand, an instrument of death, against which they entertain an aversion. As soon as I discovered him, I called to him to stay where he was and not make a nearer approach; or, if he did, to lay down his gun.

The latter request he immediately complied with; and when the natives saw him unarmed they showed no further fear, but, returning to their employment, continued alternately to sing songs and to mimic the gentlemen who accompanied me.

It seemed that the dealings between blacks and whites depended a lot on who, where and how the interaction took place.

★

24

Rose Hill

With the departure of the chartered First Fleet ships to England, the settlers became ever more conscious of their isolation and vulnerability. Their only access to the outside world was by the remaining two government ships, *Sirius* and *Supply*.

As the colony's first winter progressed to spring the governor also became increasingly convinced that the coastal soil would not support their farming needs. Acutely aware of their dwindling food supplies Arthur Phillip decided to send Captain John Hunter to Africa in *HMS Sirius* to buy supplementary provisions in September 1788.

He knew at the same time, that the colony must aim for self-sufficiency if they were to ward off serious food shortage. His mind went to the necessity of a second settlement in a more fertile area. Further west, at the head of the harbour, the soil had appeared superior.

So, toward the end of their first year at Sydney Cove, the governor sent a hundred convicts, guarded by a captain and twenty marines to begin construction on a wharf, a store house for provisions and huts for accommodation at the place he had named 'Rose Hill'. The instructions for the new settlement were that *'the convicts were to be employed in putting the land into cultivation'* and a small fortification was to be built with a captain's detachment posted in it.

Construction of a flat bottomed launch capable of conveying provisions up the harbour to Rose Hill was soon begun. The vessel, nicknamed 'The Lump' due to its cumbersome appearance and bulky construction, became invaluable in transporting provisions up the harbour to the ancillary settlement near the banks of the river. As yet, there were no suitable roads leading inland from Sydney Cove.

☆

The existing inhabitants at the head of the river, the Burramatta people, were of course troubled by the influx of so many new residents. With the clearing of timber from the land, the material used for their weapons and for the making of their canoes was removed. The places they regularly visited to dig for tasty yams were tilled over and the fern used for medicine was ripped out to make way for the white men's crops. Their hunting grounds were wiped out as animals' habitats were destroyed. No consultation had been sought and no consideration given to their existing land rights. It was now obvious the white people were not going to share resources; they had come to take over. The white settlers had appropriated the most fertile land adjacent to the river for themselves, making it effectively inaccessible to the local people. As a consequence, it became increasingly difficult for them to catch eels and other fish along the tidal limits of the river.

Yet what could they do?

This kind of dilemma was completely new to the original residents at the harbour's upper reaches. Their ancestors had lived undisturbed on the riverbank for thousands of years and never faced an upheaval of this kind. They had no structured armies or military strategies for dealing with the overpowering strength of the British battalion. Though they regularly engaged in ritualised battles with neighbouring warriors, the rules of engagement were familiar...and fair. Their inter-tribal rivals were recognisable beings; they knew what to expect from them. They shared the same respect for country. They shared equivalent warrior codes and had the same commitment to ancient tribal law.

And though the methods of food gathering differed from territory to territory, they shared the same understanding of seasons; of the necessity to take only what was needed and live in a sustainable way with their environment. The methods of the white people, on the other hand, they viewed as unsound. To tear up the land with no apparent consideration for what they were destroying was irrational. How would they cater for future needs? The white men's ways were unfathomable.

Yet the white men, self-assured of the superiority of their food growing technology, wasted no time in clearing and preparing the ground for corn, wheat and potatoes as the Burramatta people quietly looked on. Phillip, of course, assumed that the natives would see the benefits of what was happening, and with time, come to live in the new town, work with (or for) the white men and earn the comforts of 'civilisation'. It was with evident relief, some months after the founding of Rose Hill that Collins, the governor's secretary, reported there had been no trouble from the natives in the newly settled area. They had, for the most part, kept their distance. Later, after trouble had developed, he said of the original inhabitants:

> ...and had they never been ill treated by our people, instead
> of hostility, it is more than probable that...friendship would
> have subsisted.

The people of 'Parramatta', as the area of Rose Hill later became known, were being pushed to the limit of their patience. A settlement on the edge of the harbour was one thing, but expansion into other regions was something different. But they would bide their time; they would wait for an opportunity to let the white leader know they were far from happy.

Some of the Burramatta people would later, with time and growing awareness of their options, develop strong ties with the white population and go on to become significant figures in the history of the colony. But with the sudden disruption to their way of life, their immediate concern was finding enough food to survive.

☆

25

An opportunity not to be missed

When the convict, James Ruse heard about arrangements for a farming settlement at Rose Hill, he thought again of the governor's first speech at Sydney Cove and his assurance of *'encouragement for good conduct'*. He knew it was time to put forward his proposal; he believed he could do it and just hoped the governor would give him a chance. He had already served most of his seven year sentence before arriving in Sydney, so his prison term was about to expire. He approached the governor with his plan.

'I was bred to the business of farming, in Cornwall, Sir', he told the governor, hat in hand.

He went on to suggest that, with the provision of a plot of ground, labour to clear land and a supply of seed and animal stock, he believed he could become self-sufficient within a given period of time. It was a bold scheme for a convict to put to a governor but it appealed to Governor Phillip, who needed men with motivation. He agreed to the trial and the plot of ground that Ruse was allowed to plant and cultivate eventually became known as 'Experiment Farm'. Later the governor's secretary recorded the account of Ruse:

> *One of the convicts whose sentence of transportation had expired... signified a wish of becoming a settler, and had been sent up to Rose Hill by the governor; where his excellency, caused two acres of ground to be cleared of the timber which stood on them, and a small hut to be built for him. This man had been bred to the business of a farmer,*

and during his residence in this country had shown a strong inclination to be industrious and to return to honest habits and pursuits. Rewarding him, therefore, was but holding out encouragement to such good dispositions.

The success of the project was as important to the governor as it was to Ruse. Phillip wanted and needed to prove the cynics wrong:

The governor had, however, another object in view, beside a wish to hold him up as a deserving character. He was desirous of trying what time an industrious active man, with certain assistance, would be enabled to support himself in this country as a settler; and for that purpose, he furnished him with the tools and implements of husbandry necessary for cultivating his ground, with a proportion of grain to sow it, and a small quantity of livestock to begin with... An opinion had prevailed, and had been pretty generally disseminated, that a man could not live in this country... The man himself, however, resolved to be industrious, and to surmount as well as he was able whatever difficulties might lie in his way.

James Ruse was about to embark on an undertaking that would not have been possible for him in England, in his lifetime.

☆

The settling of Rose Hill inevitably led to the displacement of the Burramatta people; some families soon began relocating along the creeks which fed into the river to the north-west; others moved to land known as 'the flats' between the head of the river and Sydney harbour. And although the British officers later acknowledged that *'wherever our colonists fix themselves, the natives are obliged to leave that part of the country'*, at the time the governor seemed astoundingly unresponsive, even oblivious to the impact Rose Hill was having on the affected families. He resolutely kept to his plan of showing the natives the advantages of 'civilisation' by bringing them into the settlements. He wanted to show them that the intrusions into their territory would be more than compensated for when they saw the benefits the British could offer them. He began re-considering the daring plan he had contemplated months earlier.

Some natives must be brought into the settlement, against their will if necessary. They must be detained long enough to demonstrate how good life could be for them, living amid the white settlers.

So far he had been unwilling to try this method, but race relations were continuing to deteriorate and he was anxious for the impasse to end. The natives must be forced to see the benefits of life in the white man's domain. He could show them so much, but only if they were in the settlement, where they could see for themselves. In his dispatch to England, he pondered his intention of kidnapping some natives:

> *If it can be done in such a manner as not to create any general alarm among them, it will probably turn out to be the kindest piece of violence that could be used.*

> *Whenever it shall be practicable, by any means, to explain to them the friendly disposition of the governor and his people towards them...they will then perhaps acquire sufficient confidence in their new countrymen to mix with them, to enrich themselves with some of their implements, and to learn and adopt some of the most useful and necessary of their arts.*

By the end of 1788, he'd convinced himself of the wisdom of this strategy and on the last day of the year he sent his men to do the job for him.

★

26

Kidnaps and adoptions

Lieutenant George Johnston was the man the governor charged with implementing his plan to 'seize and carry off some of the natives'. Johnston, described as 'a very able officer and a very gentlemanlike man' who would accomplish his appointment to the satisfaction of the governor, had been appointed as the governors 'aide-de-camp' or executive officer, within the first month of the colony's settlement. We can only imagine how Lieutenant Johnston felt as he set off on his mission to kidnap, by force if necessary, some of the natives for the governor's cross-cultural project. He was by now living between the army camp and the small dwelling he'd had erected for the love of his life, convict Esther Abrahams and her little daughter, Roseanna. Whether he disclosed his day's mission to Esther that morning, we will never know.

Fortunately for us Watkin Tench, who wasn't involved in the kidnapping, made sure he got all the details for his journal. He tells us that on the 31st December, the last day of 1788, Lieutenant Johnston, with a party of armed men, left in two boats with instructions to seize and carry off some of the natives. They headed across the harbour where they could see a group gathered on the beach. He says that the natives trustingly waded out from the beach, oblivious to the deception and treachery that was about to happen.

Coaxed by the well-mannered and apparently friendly behaviour of the white men who held up gifts, they came closer and became absorbed in friendly banter with the officers. When they'd been lulled into a false sense of security, the white men rushed at them and seized two men, who were wrestled toward the boat. One of the victims, however, by dragging his attacker into water beyond his depth, managed to struggle from his grasp.

The other unfortunate man was dragged into the boat, kicking and screaming. Their friends, initially overtaken by shock had taken off back to the beach, but on realising that their countrymen were being detained, began an attack with whatever missiles they could put their hands on. Tench relates the details of what occurred, when those safely back on the beach, realised what was happening:

> ...the cries of the captives soon brought them back, with many others, to their rescue, and so desperate were their struggles that in spite of every effort on our side, only one of them was secured; the other escaped. The boats put off without delay and an attack from the shore instantly commenced. They threw spears, stones, sticks and whatever else presented itself at the boats.

Surrounded and jostled by clamouring white strangers, the sole captive must have been in pure terror. The prisoner was held down and fastened by ropes to the inside of the boat. When he saw he was irretrievably separated from his friends and relatives, Tench tells us the native began 'the most piercing and lamentable cries of distress.'

On the journey back across the harbour, he must have been wondering what the white men intended to do with him. But when they offered him some fish, it served to assure him that he was not, at least in the immediate future, going to be murdered and we are told, he 'sullenly submitted to his destiny'.

At Sydney Cove, everyone, including Watkin Tench, was extremely excited to hear the news that at last one of the natives had been brought into the settlement:

> When the news of his arrival at Sydney was announced I went with every other person to see him... His agitation was excessive and the clamorous crowds who flocked around him did not lessen it.

As the captive was brought ashore, and led through the white men's camp, the place he and his people had taken great pains to avoid, his legs must have been weak with panic. While crossing the harbour, he had also traversed an immense cultural boundary. In stepping into the foreigners' camp, he had entered another world. He was now in the domain of the aliens and he didn't know what was expected of him or what was planned for him.

But every assurance was given to him, through words and gestures that he had nothing to fear and eventually he calmed down enough to take in his surroundings. Things were pointed out and named as he was steered, still restrained with ropes, through the inquisitive crowd and up to the governor's house. Tench describes his initial impression of the man:

> He appeared to be about thirty years old, not tall, but robustly built...Though broken and interrupted with dismay, his voice was soft and musical, when its natural tone could be heard and he readily pronounced with tolerable accuracy the names of things which were taught him.

As the Aboriginal man was entering the governor's temporary house someone touched a small bell which hung over the door. He jumped with horror and astonishment at the sound it made, but as soon as the cause of the sound was shown him, he laughed at the source of his alarm. Once inside the house, various pictures of people, animals and birds were shown to him. When he saw a painting of an English lady, he immediately said 'woman' which impressed everyone as he'd only minutes earlier heard the word for the first time.

Next he was led to the governor's new two-storey house which was still under construction. As he went to enter the house, he looked up to see people leaning out of a window on the upper level and loudly exclaimed his astonishment at the possibility of such a thing. Inside he was awestruck with the dimensions of the shelter. Later, on seeing all the officers gathering to dine at the governor's house, one eyewitness said he was *'vastly frightened, so much so that his appetite failed him. After dinner he appeared more cheerful and it was afterward learnt he supposed it was intended to eat him.'*

It is not difficult to imagine the relief he must have felt when a meal of fish and duck was served to him, after believing that *he* was on the menu. Watkin Tench, enjoying the novelty of the occasion, recorded the details of the dining experience:

> *Bread and salt meat he smelled at, but would not taste; all our liquors he treated in the same manner, and could drink nothing but water. On being shown that he was not to wipe his hands on the chair which he sat upon, he used a towel which was given to him with great cleanliness and decency.*

He was regaining his composure and adjusting to the circumstances with courage, given the distress he had endured earlier. But there were more ordeals to come:

> *In the afternoon his hair was closely cut, his head combed and his beard shaved; but he would not submit to these operations until he had seen them performed on another person...To this succeeded his immersion in a tub of water and soap, where he was completely washed and scrubbed from head to foot; after which a shirt, a jacket and a pair of trousers were put upon him...*

> *To prevent his escape, a handcuff with rope attached to it was fastened around his left wrist, which at first highly delighted him. He called it 'bengadee' (ornament) but his delight turned to rage and hatred when he discovered its use...*

At first the Aboriginal man withheld his name but eventually the white men learnt that it was Arabanoo. A trusted convict was selected to guard him wherever he went. A small building, which had been built close to the guardhouse in anticipation of his arrival, was locked at night with him and his convict keeper inside.

The following morning Arabanoo appeared very dejected, and in an effort to lift his spirits, he was shown around the settlement and taken along the escarpment to Mr Dawes' observatory on the western peninsula. But from that vantage point he looked across the harbour, where he saw the smoke from the distant campfires of his countrymen on the far shore, and with several deep sighs of grief he spoke a single word: *'gweeun' (the fires of my people).*

As the following day was New Year's Day, all the officers were invited to the governor's table. Watkin Tench was there, and noted that, although earlier Arabanoo had been in a despondent mood, it hadn't affected his appetite. He *'ate heartily on fish and fresh roasted pork'* and then, to Watkin's surprise when one of the officers began singing *'in a soft and superior style',* Arabanoo stretched out, and *'putting his hat under his head, he fell asleep.'* Maybe the governor's plan was going to work after all.

Early in the New Year, the governor took Arabanoo in a boat down the harbour, hoping to convince his countrymen that he wasn't in any harm and to see if they would come and talk with him. When the governor's boat approached one of the coves, the natives quickly retreated but on seeing Arabanoo, they returned to the shoreline and a conversation took place between Arabanoo and his friends over the distance between the boat and the shore. Tench tells us that when he caught sight of his friends, Arabanoo was 'greatly affected and shed tears'.

> *At length the men began to converse. Our ignorance of their language prevented us from knowing much of what passed; it was however, easily understood that his friends asked him why he did not jump overboard and re-join them. He only sighed and pointed to the fetter on his leg, by which he was bound.*

Two days later, the governor took him on a similar boat trip but on reaching the same beach, none of the natives could be seen. However, Arabanoo displayed what Watkin Tench came to describe as his characteristic *'gentleness and humanity'* by leaving a gift of food for his countrymen.

> *Seeing a basket made of bark, which they used to carry water, he put into it two hawks and another bird which the people in the boat had shot, and carefully covering them, left them as a present to his old friends.*

Within a few weeks, Arabanoo began to settle down and quickly gained popularity with everyone at Sydney Cove, especially the children who flocked around him excitedly wherever he went. He never excluded them but drew them toward him and treated them with great gentleness; and if he happened to be eating at the time, he would *'offer the little ones the choicest part of whatever he had'*. Tench, who obviously had great affection for him, described him as good-natured and noted that his loyalty, *'particularly to his friend the governor, was constant and undeviating, and deserves to be recorded.'* However, he noticed certain behaviour that Arabanoo would not abide:

> *Although of a gentle and easy-going temper, we early discovered that he was impatient of indignity, and allowed no superiority on our part. He knew that he was in our power; but the independence of his mind never forsook him. If the slightest insult were offered to him, he would return it with interest.*

Arabanoo was apparently happy to be the butt of a joke but would not tolerate being treated in a condescending manner; he wanted respect. He soon became accustomed to eating bread and drinking tea, but always refused alcohol of any kind, showing complete disgust at the taste. A favourite evening pastime for him and his hosts was language teaching. They would sit around the governor's table taking turns at pointing and saying the names of things in each language and patiently repeating the correct pronunciation when someone got it wrong.

In autumn 1789, five months after Arabanoo had been brought into the settlement, Captain John Hunter returned in the *Sirius* from his mission to Cape Town to buy urgently needed food for the colony. On visiting the governor to make his report, he was surprised to see an addition to the governor's circle:

> *As soon as the ship was secured, I went on shore to wait on the governor... he was sitting by the fire, drinking tea with a few friends; among whom I observed a native man of this country, who was decently clothed and seemed to be as much at his ease at the tea-table as any person there; he managed*

his cup and saucer as well, as though he had been long accustomed to such entertainment.

Governor Phillip's inter-cultural experiment was going very well with Arabanoo. But so far, not one of his countrymen had shown any inclination to follow him into the settlement. What occurred next did not help matters.

With the intention of stealing native spears and fishing tackle, sixteen convicts left their work at the brickfield without permission, and armed with their working tools, marched to Botany Bay. When the convicts were almost at the bay, a large body of natives, who had obviously been given advance notice that trouble was coming their way, was waiting for them. As a result of the skirmish that occurred, one white man was killed and seven were seriously wounded. The governor was, of course, infuriated and questioned the convicts involved about the cause of the conflict. At first the convicts unanimously declared:

'We were picking leaves to make tea when, without provocation, we were attacked by the natives!'

Eventually, however, someone admitted the truth and the whole bunch were ordered a severe flogging. Governor Phillip, wanting the native man to know that he didn't condone any attacks on his countrymen, wanted Arabanoo to witness the punishment of the culprits:

> *...the whole were ordered to be severely flogged. Arabanoo was present at the infliction of the punishment, and was made to comprehend the cause and the necessity of it, but he displayed on the occasion symptoms of disgust and terror only.*

In the eyes of Arabanoo, seeing men beaten while bound by the hands and unable to defend themselves was not justice and didn't sit well with the black man. Governor Phillip however, hoped the floggings had sent a message to the convicts: the natives were not to be provoked. After such an appalling display of disregard for the natives' property by the convicts he needed to begin building trust all over again. But the *'extraordinary catastrophe'* that occurred next would only make matters worse. David Collins, the governor's secretary, tells us what happened:

In the year 1789, the natives were visited by a disorder which raged among them with all the appearance and virulence of the small-pox. The number that it swept off, by their own accounts, was incredible.

On visiting Broken Bay, we found that it had not confined its effects to Port Jackson, for in many places our path was covered with skeletons, and the same spectacles were to be met with in the hollows of most of the rocks of that harbour.

Dead bodies, and lots of them, were being seen around the harbour, on the beaches and in shelters along the coastal escarpments. Upon examining the corpses, the perplexed surgeon John White diagnosed the cause of death as small-pox; a highly contagious virus distinguished by fever and painful pus-filled blisters covering the body. It was a mystery how and from where the disease had originated, as none of the white population were affected. Governor Phillip sent parties of men down the harbour to scour the area for survivors; if they could treat the casualties, their act of humanity would be evidence of their good intentions, but all they found were corpses.

Then in mid-April a marine, while gathering building material for Lieutenant Johnston on the harbour foreshore, came rushing into the settlement with news that natives were laying in distress in a nearby cove; they were obviously very sick, but at least they were still alive.

The governor, with the doctor and Arabanoo hurried to the spot. They found an elderly black man lying feverish beside a small fire, and a boy of about nine pouring water from a shell onto the old man's forehead. Close by lay the dead body of a little girl. Tench was moved by the devotion of the little child, the frailty of the older man and the pitiable condition of both:

Eruptions covered the poor boy from head to foot; and the old man was so reduced, that he was with difficulty put into the boat. Their situation rendered them incapable of escape, and they quietly submitted to be led away.

Before leaving the site however, Arabanoo scooped a grave in the sand with his hands, lined the hole completely with grass, and put the little girl's body into it. He finally made a small raised mound with the earth which had been removed.

The young boy and, the older man, who was assumed to be his father, were taken to the hospital, where they were quarantined. Arabanoo insisted on staying with them and treated them with kindness. The man hoarsely whispered *'Bado, bado' (water)*, and Arabanoo tried to bring relief to him by trickling water gently down his swollen throat as he murmured gentle reassurance. We can imagine the comfort that familiar words spoken in his own language and black hands gently lifting water to his lips would bring to a man dying in the territory of an alien white population. Watkin Tench saw that too:

> *By the encouragement of Arabanoo, who assured them of protection, and the soothing behaviour of our medical gentlemen, they became at once reconciled to us, and looked happy and grateful at the change of their situation. Sickness and hunger had, however, so much exhausted the old man, that little hope was entertained of his recovery.*

The man lived only a few hours; fading away without sound or protest. The young boy, Nanberry, handled the moment of the older man's death with quiet acceptance. Looking across the room, he simply said: *'Boee'* (dead). Tench wrote that *'the tenderness and anxiety of the old man about the boy had been very moving.'* Although barely able to raise his head, while he still had strength in him, he kept looking toward the child, patting him gently *'and, with dying eyes, seemed to recommend him to our humanity and protection'*.

Nanberry, who was aged about nine, fully recovered and was adopted by John White, the doctor who had tended him and his dying father. A close bond was cemented between the doctor and the boy that continued as long as the doctor lived in the colony. But the smallpox epidemic had not yet run its course. It continued to produce victims among the black population around Sydney Cove and beyond. David Collins, the governor's secretary, gives his account of events when he and Arabanoo went to look for more survivors:

...on our taking him down to the harbour to look for his former companions, those who witnessed his expression and agony can never forget either. He looked anxiously around him in the different coves we visited; not a vestige on the sand was to be found of human foot; the excavations in the rocks were filled with the putrid bodies of those who had fallen victims to the disorder; not a living person was anywhere to be met with... He lifted up his hands and eyes in silent agony for some time; at last he exclaimed, 'All dead! All dead!' and then hung his head in mournful silence, which he preserved during the remainder of our excursion.

Two more sick natives, a young man and his fourteen-year-old sister, were found and brought in on the governor's boat. Arabanoo attended them with sympathy and affection but the young man died within three days. When his sister, whose name was Boorong, realised he was dying, she crept to his side and lay quietly beside him; there were no elaborate signs of grief from her when he too silently faded away. When Boorong recovered she was taken into the household of Reverend Johnson and his wife, Mary, who saw it as a wonderful opportunity to teach the young native girl about Christianity and the advantages of a British lifestyle. When the clergyman wrote to a friend in England, he mentioned that a native girl was living with them:

I have taken pains to instruct (her) in reading, and have no reason to complain of her improvement - she can likewise begin to speak a little English, and is useful in several things about our little hut. I have taught her the Lord's Prayer and as she comes better to understand, may endeavour to instruct her respecting a supreme Being.

Boorong (also called Abaroo by some settlers due to a 'mistake of pronunciation') became known as a cheerful, light-hearted girl whose *'love of play in a great measure'* exasperated attempts at any in-depth religious discussion. However, it would quickly have become apparent to her that she was living in the home of a man of significance among the white people, similar to the *koradji (an eminent man, one of special power)* of her own people. As a happy-go-lucky girl in her early teens she must have experienced significant culture shock, going from a lifestyle in the campsite of her family on the fertile banks of the river flats at the head of the harbour, to the home of the Johnsons with their strict religious traditions.

The Johnsons however were a well-meaning couple and showed genuine interest in Boorong's culture. A few months after she went to live in their home, Mary Johnson gave birth to a baby girl who was given the native name, Milbah. Although Boorong stayed with the Johnsons for an extended period, she unsurprisingly succumbed to the pull of her own culture at times. But in the early days of the smallpox epidemic, she had no idea who of her family, among the Burramatta people, had survived. Unlike Arabanoo, she had not seen the hundreds of dead bodies around the harbour; but she must have seen the devastation in Arabanoo's eyes. As far as their white protectors were concerned, both Nanberry and Boorong were orphans.

There was a tragic ending to the episode of Arabanoo's capture and interval at Sydney Cove; he caught smallpox himself and died a little more than five months after his arrival. However, in the short time he lived among the white community, he'd formed close and genuine attachments to the people he had met. After he began tending the sick natives, his physical restraints were removed, so he could have left the white settlement at any time, but chose to stay. Arabanoo demonstrated that in different circumstances, intercultural acceptance was possible between those who were willing. We can sense the sadness Arabanoo's death generated in the white community by reading Tench's tribute to him:

> *I feel assured that I have no reader who will not join in regretting the premature loss of Arabanoo, who died of the smallpox...After languishing six days the disease burst forth with irresistible fury.*
>
> *During his sickness he had entire confidence in us. Although a stranger to our medicine, and nauseating the taste of it, he swallowed with patient submission innumerable drugs, which the hope of relief induced us to administer to him. The*

governor, who particularly regarded him, caused him to be buried in his own garden.

Nothing which medical skill and constant attention could achieve had been left untried to lessen Arabanoo's suffering and save his life.

On a practical level, the death of Arabanoo meant there was no way of conveying the intended message of *'the friendly disposition of the governor and his people'* to the native population. With the unaccountable arrival of the fatal smallpox disease, they were more guarded than ever of the white settlement. Adding to the mystery of the smallpox epidemic was the fact that none of the white population had been affected. Watkin Tench, referring to the loss of Arabanoo, lamented:

> *By his death, the scheme which had invited his capture was utterly defeated. The same suspicious dread of our approach and the same scenes of vengeance...continued to prevail.*

The little boy, Nanberry, and the young girl Boorong in her early teens, were now the only natives living in the British settlement. The governor realised that once they learnt sufficient English, they could act as interpreters, but their young age meant they held no status as mediators. He needed to re-think his strategy for building a workable relationship with the natives.

The Aboriginal people also had to consider ways of adapting to their new circumstances after the appalling toll the smallpox epidemic had taken on their numbers. New alliances would have to be formed between diminished family groups in order to survive. Governor Phillip was to learn later that at least half of their population had died from the 'fatal disorder.'

★

27

Further into the vast unknown, 1789

With the formation of a settlement at Rose Hill, the governor believed the inland would become more accessible and several journeys were attempted to learn more about the obscure wilderness further west. The countryside, however, was misleading and the alluring blue mountains continued to be elusive.

When they had first arrived in Botany Bay, the governor had gazed westward and referred to the distant range as 'hills'. From the coast they didn't look particularly challenging and he'd imagined they would be exploring and crossing them within a few months of settling. But they were to discover that the landscape of their new territory was vastly different to the countryside of England.

During their second year in the colony, excursions were made inland in the hope of discovering an easy route westward and over the mountains. In the winter of 1789, the governor, accompanied by his officer comrades John Hunter, David Collins, George Johnston and others headed north, then westward, to follow the meandering course of a wide river later named the 'Hawkesbury'. On its banks they found signs of people living there, but actually saw few natives. John Hunter recorded frequently seeing evidence of yams and other roots having been dug from along the river bank, but the food gatherers themselves were no-where in sight.

On one occasion they came across a young female who had apparently been unable to run with her companions when they'd bolted on observing the white explorers' approach. John Hunter's account describes the trepidation of the young girl on realising her hiding place had been discovered by a group of alien white men:

> *In the course of this afternoon, a native woman was discovered, concealing herself from our sight in the long grass…She had, before the arrival of our boats at this beach, been with some of her friends, employed in fishing for their daily food, but were upon our approach alarmed, and they had all made their escape, except this miserable girl, who had just recovered from the small-pox, and was very weak, and unable, from a swelling in one of her knees, to get off to any distance. She had therefore crept off, and concealed herself in the best manner she could among the grass, not twenty yards from the spot on which we had placed our tents. She was discovered by some person who having fired at and shot a hawk from a tree right over her, terrified her so much that she cried out…*

> *Information was immediately brought to the governor, and we all went to see this unhappy girl… She appeared to be about 17 or 18 years of age, and had covered her debilitated and naked body with the wet grass, having no other means of hiding herself. She was very much frightened on our approaching her, and shed many tears, with piteous lamentations: we understood none of her expressions but felt much concern at the distress she seemed to suffer.*

At this point, the men tried their language skills on the terrified girl:

> *We endeavoured all in our power to make her easy, and with the assistance of a few expressions which had been collected from poor Ara-ba-noo while he was alive, we soothed her distress a little, and the sailors were immediately ordered to bring up some fire, which we placed before her. We pulled some grass, dried it by the fire, and spread round her to keep her warm; then we shot some birds, such as hawks, crows, and gulls, skinned them, and laid them on the fire to broil, together with some fish, which she ate. We then gave her*

water, of which she seemed to be much in want, for when the word 'Baa-do' was mentioned, which was their expression for water, she put her tongue out to show how very dry her mouth was...

Next morning we visited her again; she had now got pretty much the better of her fears, and frequently called to her friends who, we knew, could be at no great distance from her. She repeated their names in a very loud and shrill voice, and with much apparent anxiety and concern for the little notice they took of her entreaties to return: for we imagined, in all she said when calling them, she was informing them, that the strangers were not enemies, but friends.

However, all her endeavours to bring them back were ineffectual, while we remained with her; but we were no sooner gone from the beach, than we saw some of them come out of the wood.

Later Governor Phillip and his friend John Hunter ventured along branches of the same watercourse hoping to solve the mystery of the mountain barrier but they found that their route wasn't possible in the boats they had; the stream became too narrow, rocky and shallow. Hunter wrote:

Both this and the last branch we examined, probably extend many miles farther than we, with our boats, could trace them; they did not appear to be navigable for any vessel but the canoes of the natives.

However, his summary of the countryside added to the stock of information that was gathering about the nature of the terrain:

The banks of this branch were the same as the last, high, steep, and rocky mountains, with many trees growing down their sides, from between the rocks where no-one would believe there could be any soil to nourish them.

The ruggedness of the mountain country however, made the challenge all the more inspiring for adventurous young officers like Watkin Tench when they heard the reports. Tench had been disappointed to miss out on the governor's river trip because he'd been *'unluckily invested with the command of the outpost at Rose Hill'* which he complained prevented him *'from being in the list of discoverers of the Hawkesbury.'*

However, enthused by a desire to know more about the country and spurred on by his robust sense of adventure, Tench set off in the same month with a small group of officers and convict servants to reach unexplored territory. They left Rose Hill at daybreak aiming for a small hill in a westerly direction and then to see what lay beyond. He tells us what he saw from the peak:

> *Here we paused, surveying 'the wild abyss; pondering our voyage'. Before us lay the trackless immeasurable desert, in awful silence...We continued to march all day through a country untrodden before by a European foot. Save that a melancholy crow now and then flew croaking overhead, or a kangaroo was seen to bound at a distance, the picture of solitude was complete and undisturbed.*

They decided to set up camp for the night and in the morning, after walking for about an hour, they found themselves on the banks of a wide river.

> *Vast flocks of wild ducks were swimming in the stream; but after being once fired at, they grew so shy that we could not get near them a second time. Nothing is more certain than that the sound of a gun had never before been heard within many miles of this spot.*

They stayed in the area for three days, following the banks of the river *'by a slow pace, through reeds, thickets, and a thousand other obstacles'*. Throughout their journey *'traces of the natives appeared at every step'*; they saw huts, bird and animal traps and canoes, but they saw no people. They returned the way they came and with pleasure reported all they'd found to the governor: forty miles from the coast there was more land that could be cultivated once the trees were removed, and a wide flowing river, which the governor decided to name the 'Nepean River'.

They told the governor about the natives' dwellings and knowing they must have been observed, they added somewhat frustrated, that they had been unable to make contact with any of them.

★

All through the journey, the natives had remained at a safe distance. They had heard the white men's shouts of delight as they'd come across the river and the huge flock of ducks. They had looked at each other with creased brows as they'd seen one of the strangers point his 'firestick' at the ducks and send them all flying away in fright.

Wasn't it obvious that such a noise would send the birds away?
Didn't they know there were much simpler ways to ensnare a waterbird?

They had observed the strangers setting up camp and watched with curious attention as so many things were unpacked from their cumbersome loads. They saw them eat meagrely from the supplies they had carried with them.

Didn't they know about the tasty yams easily found nearby?

They'd watched the white men inspecting and discussing the notches cut into tree trunks; the footholds that enabled the natives to climb to the higher branches to collect honey, bird eggs, and pounce on unsuspecting sleeping possums. They'd seen them examining their purpose-built bird traps of crisscrossed branches and reeds, strategically placed along the river bank. And although they hadn't understood the white men's words, they had seen the admiration in their gestures and expressions. They'd seen the men look into their empty bark dwellings and then scan the surrounding area in puzzlement.

Once again, in the wilderness, it had not been difficult for the black people to observe the white men while staying undetected themselves. As an officer, on a later excursion, admitted of the natives: *'They could see me although I could see nothing of them…'*

★

Toward the end of the same year, 1789, at the request of the governor, Lieutenant William Dawes and George Johnston crossed the Nepean River and made the first attempt to actually 'penetrate the mountains'. They set off on foot in early summer carrying all their food and provisions on their backs, and with high hopes of achieving their goal. It took stamina and nerve to venture into wild, unexplored territory; to tread where no white man had ever been before. There was no way of calling for backup if something went wrong in one of the deep canyons of the vast mountainous region. When Johnston left the settlement in mid-December, it was only weeks before the expected birth of his first child with Esther Abrahams, so she would understandably be apprehensive about his journey.

Who knew what danger lurked in those mysterious mountains waiting to ensnare even the most intrepid explorer?

The men however found the country *'so rugged, and the difficulty of walking so excessive'*, they were forced to abandon their outward journey after only a few days trekking. Dawes reported that making their way across a line of steep rocky precipices required as much *'caution in descending, as labour in ascending'*. It must have been a struggle; clamouring in and out of sandstone gorges, some as deep as two hundred metres, in the heat of summer. They were disappointed about turning back, but finding an alternative course required more time than their provisions allowed. They returned to Sydney tired and frustrated only about a week after they had left.

Esther would undoubtedly have been relieved to see George arrive home safely. On January 12th, 1790 the first of their children, a baby son whom they named George, came into the world. George Johnston proved himself to be a proud and attentive father. He had reason to be satisfied with his time so far in the colony; during the first weeks of the settlement he had been made aide-de-camp to the governor, making him one of the governor's senior right hand men. A year later, in February 1789, he had been promoted to Captain-Lieutenant by Major Ross. Now he was making his name as an explorer.

When reporting to the governor on the first journey into the rugged blue mountains, the explorers could claim that, despite the obstacles, they had made headway. On their return, Dawes had announced that, at the point at which they turned back, (a place they named Mount Twiss) they *'had reached further inland than any other persons ever were before or since'*.

In making their assertion, they had failed to acknowledge the families who had travelled through there for centuries and who throughout the explorer's trek, had been aware of their movements.

The most productive outcome of Dawes' journey was the detailed map he made showing topographic features and accompanied by comprehensive notes, including his supposition that *'a considerable river'* lay beyond the highest ridges which he suggested may *'fall into the sea considerably southward of Botany Bay'*. He had correctly predicted that the 'Great Divide', the watershed from where rivers ran either to the coast or ran inland, was still a considerable distance westward from the endpoint of their journey.

☆

Dawes and Johnston had demonstrated that although the mountains made for gruelling travel, the territory wasn't hostile; they had met no aggression from the natives (in fact they'd met no-one) and had encountered no ferocious wild beasts. They had however, seen the footprints of an unidentified animal; one unlike anything they'd seen before. When Johnston recounted his journey to his colleagues at the barracks and to Esther privately, there must have been speculation about the intriguing and mysterious sighting.[5] Dawes' expertise in surveying and mapping had provided a broader picture of the surrounding area but as their knowledge grew, they must have become acutely aware just how isolated and vulnerable they really were: no more than a tiny dot on the edge of an immense wilderness that sat on the brink of a vast and lonely ocean.

☆

---

[5] The description of the footprint given by the explorers does not fit any known native Australian animal. See notes for this chapter.

28

'A most unpleasant service'

Some months had passed after the death of Arabanoo before the governor decided on a repeat kidnap attempt, and by the end of 1789 he was eager to re-implement his cross-cultural scheme. William Bradley, the young lieutenant who was ordered to do the job, did it reluctantly. He admitted later that the task had been extremely disagreeable to him. He was sensitive to the fact that the natives, who he had been ordered to kidnap, would presumably have families that would grieve for them. He later told his friends, *'It was by far the most unpleasant service I was ever ordered to execute.'*

But orders were orders; a British officer would not dare disobey a command from his superior. In his diary, he wrote a nail-biting account of what happened on the day of the kidnapping:

November 1789

> *As we went down the harbour, we got some fish...We saw a great number of natives on both sides and several landed on the beach ...hauling their canoes up after them.*

> *As we got near the upper part of the cove, we held two large fish up to them and had the good luck to draw two of them away from a very large party by this bait; these people came around the rocks where they left their spears and met us on the beach near the boat and at a distance from their companions sufficient to promise success without losing any lives; they eagerly took the fish. Four of the boat crew were*

kept in the boat which was winded and backed close to the beach where the two natives were...

They were dancing together when the signal was given by me and the two poor devils were seized and handed into the boat in an instant.

The natives who were very numerous all round us, on seeing us seize those two, immediately advanced with their spears and clubs, but we were too quick for them, being out of reach before they got to that part of the beach where the boat lay, they were entering on the beach just as everybody was in the boat and as she did not take the ground we pulled immediately out without having occasion to fire a musket.

The noise of the men, crying and screaming of the women and children together with the situation of the two miserable wretches in our possession was really a most distressing scene; they were much terrified, one of them particularly so, the other frequently called out to those on shore apparently very much enraged with them, they followed the boat on both sides as far as the points of the cove and then returned to the beach...

Witnessing the black men's desperate fight for freedom, Lieutenant Bradley clearly saw the panic in their eyes as strange white hands wrestled them into the boat, and they realised their struggle had been futile. They'd become captives to devious, unpredictable white aliens. Seeing them cringe in fear when restrained in the boat and their evident distress at being torn from their own people had, no doubt, affected Bradley so intensely because he had been separated from his own family for so long. He had been married only a year when the fleet sailed from England and, like everyone in the colony, he'd received no reply to his letters sent by homebound ships. He'd had no news from his family and in particular his wife, for more than two long years.

★

When Bradley and his crew landed at Sydney Cove with their detainees, the scene was reminiscent of the arrival of Arabanoo; crowds of curious onlookers could not stop staring.

On coming ashore they were met by Nanberry, the native boy who was living in the settlement with Surgeon White, and he showed great excitement on seeing his kinfolk and called them by name, Colbee and Bennelong. Nanberry had often, since recovering from smallpox, spoken about his uncle Colbee, describing him as *'a great warrior and leading man'* among his people. He had not known how many, if any, of his kinfolk had survived the terrible disease that had swept through his family; now he knew one at least was alive.

Lieutenant Bradley escorted the detainees from the wharf to the governor's house where they were greeted by Boorong, the native girl. She also called the captive men by name and was 'quite frantic with joy' to see them. But the young native men were in no mood for a reunion; they were encumbered with leg irons and tied with ropes.

Bennelong was said to be about twenty-six years old, of good stature, and with a bold fearless expression. Colbee was shorter, approximately thirty and, it was soon learnt, Nanberry's uncle. Both men had smallpox scars, as well as initiation and battle scars. The native children were used as interpreters to explain their situation, as best they could, to the men. The governor had given orders for them to be treated liberally, but guarded closely in a small hut beside the governor's residence. Lieutenant Bradley carries on with the account:

> *They were assured by these children that they would be well treated and thereafter allowed to return to their friends, but all that could be said or done was not sufficient to remove the pang which they naturally felt at being torn away from their friends; or to reconcile them to their situation.*
>
> *It gave me great satisfaction to find by the children that neither of them had wife or family who would feel their loss, or to be distressed by their being taken away...*

These people were shaved, washed and clothed; an iron shackle was put on one leg with a rope made fast to it; a convict charged with each of them. They were very sullen and sulky, and continued so several days, yet it did not by any means affect their appetite if we may judge from the quantity they now eat, which is beyond everything incredible (12lb of fish does but little towards satisfying them for one meal).

Despite the iron shackles, the rope and the guards, the men tried more than once to escape.

They made several attempts to get away by gnawing the rope in the night, but being unacquainted with the securities on doors and windows they as well might have remained fast. When their keepers woke they found them groping about the room to find an opening by which they might escape.

The compassionate young Lieutenant Bradley must have wondered how the young black men were coping, unaccustomed as they were to being locked away behind four walls. Yet despite the apparent odds, Colbee was determined to have his freedom. He was not giving up so easily. Bradley continues the next phase of the story:

Colbee this evening got away by the very same means which had before been detected, the man who had charge of him was severely punished for his neglect, and the man who had charge of Bennelong was now chained by the wrist, the other end being fastened to the shackle on Bennelong's leg instead of a rope which was before used. Bennelong was nearly loose when the other was missed and in a minute more would have been after him. He was much alarmed, no doubt expecting punishment or to be put to death; but in the course of two or three days he became quite composed, and seemed better reconciled to his situation than before. He came on board the Sirius without the smallest apprehensions for his safety; he looked with attention at every part of the ship and expressed much astonishment.

Bennelong, now the sole captive, appeared to settle into his new role, as representative of his people, with comparative ease and in a relatively short period of time. Unlike Arabanoo, he took the officers' offer of wine with *'eager remarks of enjoyment'* and imitated the officers' raising of the glass and toast to 'The King'. Bennelong loved talking, loved humour and loved boasting about his conquests and of course, the officers encouraged him with questions:

'But the wound on the back of your hand, Bennelong, how did you get that?'

In recounting his combats, Bennelong would *'poise his lance, and show how fields were won'*, demonstrating with *'the most violent exclamations of rage and vengeance against his competitors'*. Bennelong loved being the centre of attention, much to the enjoyment of his spectators. Watkin Tench gives his assessment of their protégé:

> He acquired knowledge, both of our manners and language, faster than his predecessor had done. He willingly communicated information; sang, danced, and capered, told us all the customs of his country, and all the details of his family economy.

He was certainly a fast and co-operative learner and quickly noticed and adopted the etiquette of English gentlemen when it suited him. He understood the use of clothes to mark status by the white men and while he was in the settlement he was happy to conform by wearing a formal gentlemen's outfit, particularly the red jacket which had been given to him.

☆

Also living in the governor's household as a domestic servant, and taking in all the fascinating drama in the governor's parlour with the native Bennelong, was thirty-year-old Jane Dundas. The snippets of enthralling, though limited conversation between the governor, his officers and the native man were an endless source of curiosity for the household staff, including Jane. The native man Bennelong was a cheerful, funny fellow and had them in stiches, so accurately mimicking in word and action the mannerisms of all the white people he had met.

Jane had been convicted and transported for seven years for stealing a linen tablecloth and napkins from her employer, a judge, in whose house she had worked as a laundry maid. She had confessed at her trial that she had stolen and pawned the goods for a chance at a better life.

'It was for the lottery', she admitted in court.

In the squalor aboard ship during the voyage, she had berated herself for her stupid, futile crime believing any chance of a decent life was over, despairing at the thought of what horrors and humiliation her future held. But on being told, that because of her good conduct, she had been chosen as one of Governor Phillip's housemaids, she believed her life had indeed taken an unbelievable turn.

In the governor's household, Jane took pride in serving the leading members of the colony, where from close quarters, she could observe first-hand all the predicaments and dilemmas faced by the colony's decision maker. In the hectic household kitchen she busied herself helping to prepare meals for the governor and his visitors, including the amiable and voracious Bennelong.

29

Teachers and students

Bennelong was, according to his captors, impressed with everything he saw in the settlement and was soon seen accompanying the governor and his senior officers around the settlement and across the harbour by boat. He was also keen to show the governor places of significance to him and pointed out his own special island that, he announced proudly, his father had passed down to him. David Collins, the governor's secretary, noted:

> He often assured me that the island Me-mel (called by us Goat Island) close by Sydney Cove was his own property; that it was his father's. To this little spot he appeared much attached...He told us of other people who possessed this kind of hereditary property...

David Collins was also curious about the black men's survival skills. For example, he wanted to know how they started their fires and Bennelong took delight in explaining the procedure. Collins wrote:

> It is attended with infinite labour, and is performed by fixing the pointed end of a cylindrical piece of wood into a hollow made in a plane: the operator twirling the round piece swiftly between both his hands, sliding them up and down until fatigued, at which time he is relieved by another of his companions, who are all seated for this purpose in a circle, and each one takes his turn until fire is procured.

The governor also listened and watched with interest as Bennelong demonstrated bush skills previously unknown to the white men. Over time, a friendship of sorts developed between the men, bridging the huge cultural divide between them. As a mark of affection and respect to the governor, Bennelong bestowed on Governor Phillip his own tribal name and began calling him *'Be-anna' (father)*.

Watkin Tench considered Bennelong to be a flexible fellow, who had adjusted well to his new situation:

> *In a word...his relish of our society seemed so great, that hardly any one judged he would attempt to quit us... Nevertheless it was thought proper to continue a watch over him.*

Pains were taken to hide from Bennelong the fact that the colony was becoming very short of food and other supplies. He had an insatiable appetite and his diet was supplemented with fish whenever possible. They didn't want Bennelong to know about their alarming state of affairs in case he should pass on the information to his countrymen, who in turn, they imagined, could take advantage of their weakened state. Also, he had been brought into the settlement to demonstrate the benefits of its civilised existence; they did not want him to see any cracks in the illusion.

While the officers of the government had been pre-occupied with Bennelong's education, and he was busy teaching them, two recently married convicts, Isabella Rawson and William Richardson, decided that the children of the settlement needed an education. They were among the small number of literate convicts and as such, recognised the importance of schooling.

Isabella had been through tough times; her baby daughter had died during the voyage on the *Lady Penrhyn* and more recently she had suffered the death of her dear little boy who had lived only nine months. Now approaching her mid-thirties, she contemplated and accepted her dwindling chances of raising a family of her own in the future. Yet she loved children and wanted to do something useful, to give the isolated youngsters of the settlement the best possible chance of bettering their lives. So together, the young couple began giving reading and writing lessons to small groups of youngsters with the Reverend Johnson's backing.

Around forty children had landed with the First Fleet. Some were the sons or daughters of marines who, for the period of their employment, had opted to bring their families to the colony, but most, like little Henry Kable and Esther Abraham's daughter Roseanna, were the children of convicts.

Two years after the fleet's arrival, the number of children in the colony had increased significantly. Isabella was in her element, patiently coaching the little ones in their letters and numbers. Though still serving her sentence, she had been encouraged by Reverend Johnson to put her teaching skills to good use. Her husband's sentence had already expired and the couple had plans, down the track, to set up a proper school. It was not the policy of the British government to take responsibility for education so any initiative would have to be a private concern but the Reverend had promised to write to the 'Society for the Propagation of the Gospel' for their financial support. Johnson had been pleased to supply spelling books, bibles and prayer books brought from England to the young pupils and he would later write to the Society requesting that more be sent for *'those who appeared to be most deserving.'* Education, he believed, was paramount in such an alien and ungodly place and *'reformation... must begin with the rising generation.'*

★

30

Impatient for news

As time passed and they heard nothing from their homeland, the settlers at Sydney Cove and Rose Hill became increasingly impatient for news from England. Everyone, even the most optimistic individual, was becoming weary and dejected. Since they'd arrived and set up their remote and rudimentary settlements, they hadn't heard a word from their families, their friends, or their government. In all that time - two long years - there hadn't been a single follow-up ship with supplies from Britain. Yet every day they still hoped and expected one may arrive. At the sound of distant thunder, or the echo of a hunter's gunshot, people would pause and listen expectantly.

What was that? Could it have been a ship's gun as a signal?

And they would go racing to the headland to scour the ocean, hoping and praying there would be a sail. But it was nothing...again, and they would turn and walk slowly down the hill.

The original provisions brought with them from England had become dangerously low so when, after a prolonged interval, a supplementary food supply hadn't arrived, the governor had sent John Hunter in the ship *Sirius* to Africa to buy provisions. The stores brought back by Captain Hunter in May 1789 had alleviated the problem for a while but since that time their food crisis had worsened again.

Letters describing their plight had been forwarded on the returning First Fleet ships *to* England, but they were desperate to hear something back. When acquaintances met in the street, when convicts carted bricks or dragged logs together, when officers met on the parade ground, they talked about little else but contact from home.

Their most pressing need was for food, but they also urgently needed blankets, clothing and the necessary items of everyday life such as writing paper, thread for patching and repairing clothes, candles and soap.

'God help us. If some ships don't arrive, I don't know what will,' moaned Lieutenant Clark.

Even David Collins, the governor's secretary, usually a level headed man, wrote a letter to his father in which he couldn't conceal his despondency:

> *I find that I am spending the prime of my life at the farthest part of the world, without credit, without... profit; secluded from my family...my connections, from the world, under constant apprehension of being starved...All these considerations induce me...to embrace the first opportunity that offers of escaping from a country that is nothing better than a place of banishment for the outcasts of society.*

Like the rest of the settlers, he was obviously experiencing serious doubts about the continued survival of the colony. Chief surgeon, John White, venting his frustration in a letter to a friend, put into words what many must have been thinking:

> *In the name of heaven, what has the ministry been about? Surely they have quite forgotten or neglected us...Lord have mercy on us!*

What was going on out there? Had they been abandoned? How much longer could they endure?

With their food stock running out fast, the governor again ordered the *HMS Sirius* on a voyage to purchase urgently needed food stocks. This time they would head north to China, detouring via Norfolk Island on the way. A return journey to China would take months, but in the meantime hopefully ships would arrive from England with provisions.

Otherwise...

★

31

Survival tactics

As a precaution against the threat of starvation, it was determined by the governor that *Sirius*, accompanied by the smaller ship *Supply*, would take more convicts to Norfolk Island in the hope that by dividing the population over the two settlements, their chance of survival would be increased.

The governor decided to send Major Ross, his second-in-command, to Norfolk Island to take over the administration of the island settlement temporarily from Lieutenant King. He needed a reliable man like King to return to England to report on the dire state of the colony and to lobby the home government for the support necessary to ensure their survival as a British outpost. For Arthur Phillip, it would also be an added bonus to be rid of the belligerent and troublesome Robert Ross - the man who had repeatedly challenged his authority from the early days of the Sydney settlement. With two hundred and eighty people, comprising convicts and marines, Major Ross would set sail in March 1790.

Among the two hundred convicts sent to Norfolk Island was young teenager and former chimney sweep, John Hudson. As the governor stood watching the convicts board the ship, he was pleased that young Hudson, one of the youngest prisoners in his charge, was leaving the bad influence of some of the older men. It was common knowledge that the boy had been an orphan for much of his life but no-one knew how he'd survived his nine years prior to coming before a judge for alleged theft. The court proceedings of the boy's trial in 1783 had been brief, but spoke volumes:

Court to Prisoner: *How old are you?*
Going on nine.
What business was you bred up in?
None, sometimes a chimney sweeper.
Have you any father or mother?
Dead.
How long ago?
I do not know.

But young John *had known* what it was like to wedge himself halfway up a filthy blackened chimney stack, his eyes streaming and lungs wheezing in the narrow smoke-filled shaft. He'd known the difficulty of keeping a foothold when the sides were caked with fat and soot, and when only the thought of a beating had kept his thin legs lodged in place until the sides were scraped of muck... That life, his 'old' life, was far behind him now. As the ship sailed out of the harbour and into the vast Pacific Ocean, young John really had no idea where he and the other convicts were heading... another island, somewhere, was all he knew.

But what did it matter?

He had experienced enough in his young life to not expect too much. On the other hand, he'd already seen enough at Sydney Cove to suspect that life in the colony would be better than it had ever been for him on the streets and rooftops of London. On Norfolk Island there'd be air, light and space, even if there wasn't to be freedom.

What had he ever known of freedom anyway?

Also sailing to Norfolk Island for a short-term posting was Lieutenant George Johnston. With him went Esther Abrahams and her daughter Roseanna, as well as their newborn baby, George. It must have been a relief for Esther to be leaving the Sydney settlement during its dire food shortage. On Norfolk Island, she'd heard, there were better agricultural conditions and fewer mouths to feed. She wondered how her female companions from the *Lady Penrhyn* had fared since being sent to the island two years earlier under the command of Lieutenant King.

What had happened to those six women during that time? Had Ann Inett, the young mother forced to leave her two children behind in England, regretted her decision to be one of the women chosen as part of the island's first settlement? Esther would soon find out.

Imagine Esther's surprise on her arrival, to find Ann Inett housekeeping for Lieutenant King in the best house on the island, living as his mistress and the mother of his son, whom they had named 'Norfolk' after his birthplace. Ann was also obviously well advanced in the pregnancy of their second child.

There was only a brief time for the young women to share their stories as Ann Inett would be leaving Norfolk Island with Lieutenant King and their child as soon as *HMS Supply* was ready for its return journey to Sydney; but the young mothers saw the similarity of their situation. Both women were now under the protection of prominent men who had each openly acknowledged their illegitimate sons. Both women, prior to leaving England, had experienced the stigma and hardship of raising a child alone so they were thankful of the ongoing support of their influential partners for their colonial offspring. What a turn of events had taken place for them both since they'd been banished from England as lonely, unwanted felons.

★

32

Crucial decisions

Meanwhile back in Sydney, everyone, from the governor to the humblest convict was feeling tense and uneasy. As they had watched the *Sirius* and *Supply* sail from Sydney Cove they felt totally marooned; cut off from everywhere and everything in the known world. Those ships had been their only means of contact with civilisation, and now they were gone. Despite the daily plying back and forth of native canoes, the harbour seemed desolate.

They'd had no communication or supplies from their government; no word from family and friends at home since they'd set sail in May 1787. They felt deserted and they were hungry. Yet soon after the departure of the *Sirius* and *Supply*, the governor announced another unavoidable cut in rations:

> *...to every person in the settlement without distinction: four pounds of flour, two and a half pounds of salt pork, one and a half pound of rice,...per week.*

The governor made it known that the same rations applied to him as to everyone else in the colony, but that didn't stop the hunger pains. In today's terms, their ration amounted to little more than half a cup of flour or a small bread roll, a handful of dried meat and barely more than half a cup of rice each day. Given that the food was very stale and crawling with weevils, it was far from adequate. Again Watkin Tench gives the details:

> *The pork and rice were brought with us from England. The pork had been salted between three and four years, and*

every grain of rice was a moving body, from the inhabitants lodged within it.

We soon left off boiling the pork, as it had become so old and dry, that it shrunk one half in its dimensions...Our usual method of cooking it was to cut off the daily morsel, and toast it on a fork before the fire, catching the drops which fell on a slice of bread, or in a saucer of rice.

It was enough to keep them alive, but only just and only for so long. Things had become so grim that the hours of labour had to be reduced; nobody - convict builder, farmer or soldier - had the strength to work more than a few hours. All everyone could focus on was 'food'.

Winter would soon be on them, which meant less fish in the harbour and they would have to go further afield in search of wild greens. Some food production was being attempted but it was nowhere near enough to keep up with demand. Most of the convicts had been city dwellers in Britain and were still not adept at farming; and unlike the natives, were generally not skilled hunters. Most were fixated on simply surviving until the doling out of their next ration.

For one elderly man, even that became impossible. Just after he had received his meager food quota, he staggered outside, collapsed in front of the storehouse and was taken to the hospital where he died. During a post-mortem examination, *'his stomach was found to be quite empty'*. After investigation it came to light that, having no cooking utensils of his own, the man had been forced to eat his ration of salt pork, rice and flour raw, or give up part of his portion to a fellow convict in return for getting it cooked. The surgeon's report was *'death by starvation'*. For want of a cooking pot, a man had died.

Added to this sobering situation was the fact that most of the settlers' clothes were in shreds and their blankets were threadbare. Even the guards paraded and patrolled the settlement with holes in their clothes and without shoes. The lines of distinction between the classes of society were no longer distinct; officer, marine and convict were all in the same boat.

All the hopes of the colony and its survival were pinned on the *Sirius* returning with the needed supplies before the remaining stores ran out entirely. Had they known at that time of the catastrophe that had befallen that ship, they may have just given up completely, then and there. But they were fortunately ignorant of events outside their range of vision, and continued to hang on to a glimmer of hope.

A few days after the reduction of rations, something happened to extinguish that last ray of hope. A sail had been seen on the horizon... but something wasn't quite right.

Why hadn't news arrived from an overjoyed sentry on the headland to announce the new arrival?

Watkin Tench rushed to the observatory, hoping to confer with his friend Dawes and use the telescope to confirm or deny the rumours:

> To satisfy myself that the flag was really flying, I went to the observatory, and looked for it through the large astronomical telescope, when I plainly saw it. But I was immediately convinced that it was not to announce the arrival of ships from England; for I could see nobody near the flagstaff except one solitary being, who kept strolling around, unmoved by what he saw.

What is going on? The sail on the horizon could not belong to an English ship – the sentry posted at the headland would be acting very differently had he believed it was from home.

Tench hurried back to find the governor about to be rowed down the harbour to investigate.

'May I accompany you sir?' he pleaded.

Halfway to the headland, they saw that a row boat belonging to *Supply*, (the little ship that had accompanied *Sirius* as far as Norfolk Island) was approaching. As it came nearer, Tench saw one of the seamen aboard her make a gesture which told them plainly that something disastrous had happened.

Tench turned to the governor, *'Sir, prepare yourself for bad news.'*

It was an unnecessary statement but Tench could not help verbalising his premonition of a catastrophic report. They soon learnt that the *Sirius* had been shipwrecked off Norfolk Island. No supplies would be coming from China anytime soon. It was an unbelievable disaster, but at least everyone on board had managed to get safely ashore on the island before weather conditions changed and the vessel had been smashed against the rocks.

In the Sydney settlement, the governor had no alternative but to re-evaluate their food crisis once again. Collins, his secretary, expounded the personal lengths Phillip went to in the hope of minimising the hunger being felt in the mainland settlements.

> *The governor, from a motive that did him immortal honour, in this season of general distress, gave up three hundred weight of flour which was his private property, declaring that he did not wish to see anything more at his table than the ration which was received in common from the public store, without any distinction of persons; and to this resolution he rigidly adhered, wishing that if a convict complained, he might see that want was not unfelt even at Government house.*

The governor also called an extraordinary emergency meeting with all his officers. He must take drastic measures and he needed their support. Gravely he spelt out their predicament:

> *We have sufficient salt meat to serve us to 2nd July, flour to last until the 20th August, rice or peas until the beginning of October.*

This announcement was made in April 1790, so they had a three to six month supply of food; that was all. They would somehow have to make it last and pray that a ship would arrive soon. The Reverend Johnson, in a letter written to his friend in England in hope that it would one day be read, gives us a glimpse of how it must have been:

Dear friend,

It is now a long, long time since I have been able to write to or hear from you. I am happy to inform you we are still alive...but have had many ups & downs...Tis now about two years and three months since we first arrived in this distant country. All this while, we have been as it were buried alive, never having an opportunity of hearing from our friends... Our stock of provisions brought from England, is nearly exhausted...We have been anxiously looking out for a fleet for a long time, but hitherto none has appeared, and it is now generally conjectured that the fleet expected is either lost or taken by some enemy. Our hopes now are almost vanished, and every one begins to think our situation not a little alarming...

Richard Johnson, April 9th, 1790.

The settlement was falling into a state of lethargy; there seemed less and less incentive to plan for the future. During this dismal time however several tiny lives were added to the settlement. William Bryant, the convict fisherman, and his wife Mary, who had been among the first couples to marry at Sydney Cove, became parents to a second child; in April 1790, Mary Bryant gave birth to their son, Emanuel. For them, the event must have been met with some uneasiness and may have been the catalyst which accelerated their secret plan of escape. During the same period, the Reverend's gentle spouse Mary also gave birth to her baby girl Milbah. The young couple, despite their religious faith and the advantage of their carefully nurtured though frequently robbed vegetable garden, must have had mixed emotions about bringing a fragile new life into such a precarious world.

For the young marines who had volunteered for a 'tour of duty' to the great southern land with visions of promotion or adventure, it had become the tour to hell. With a hint of bitterness, one soldier compared his predicament with his equals in England, whose only employment he imagined, *'was to powder their hair, polish their shoes and go through the routine of a field day'.* His own situation was very different. Snippets of his letter, describing the plight of the marines gives insight into the anguish and despondency that must have pervaded the soldiers' quarters:

> *As to parade duties and show, we have long laid them aside, except for the mounting of a small guard by day and a picket at night. Our soldiers have not a shoe, and mount the guard barefoot...By the time this reaches you, the fate of this settlement, and all it contains, will be decided...the dread of perishing by famine stares us in the face...*

As well as their physical suffering, these young soldiers had the distress of having received no news from home for years. As one dejected marine put it they were in complete ignorance: *'We are no more assured of the welfare of our friends, than of what passes on the moon.'*

Nevertheless they all had little choice but to battle on as best they could. For one young marine private, the struggle of survival in the colony did become too much and he attempted to end his life by cutting his own throat. Fortunately, his quick-thinking companion, Corporal James Bagley intervened in time to prevent the tragedy. McManus survived, and later opted to stay in the colony, but his deep scar was a permanent reminder of the darkest time in the young marine's life.

★

Lieutenant King, on his return to the mainland from Norfolk Island, was shocked to see how desperate the food situation had become in Sydney Cove. With him was Ann Inett, nursing their little boy, Norfolk and well advanced in the pregnancy of their second child.

On their return to the Sydney settlement, they both knew their time together as lovers was at an end. They knew their relationship could not continue as it had on Norfolk Island, given the fact that the governor was sending the trustworthy young Lieutenant King to England to report on the distressed state of the colony, and Ann would remain in the colony to serve out her sentence. She also knew that King was an ambitious man with a clear career path in mind; he wanted to be Governor of the New South Wales colony one day.

Shortly after their arrival in Sydney, Lieutenant King was to leave again on the *Supply*; he was to sail as far as the Dutch settlement in Batavia (modern-day Jakarta) and then transfer to another ship to take him on to England. The plan was also for *Supply* to procure urgently needed food from Batavia and return to Sydney before the inevitable scarcity of the oncoming winter.

As the settlers watched *Supply,* their last hope, sail away down the harbour, some were wishing they were aboard her, escaping the confines of their hunger driven existence, but they knew that the ship could carry only fifty people at the most. Others were wondering if the aging, leaky little vessel would actually survive another trip, through the treacherous, reef strewn oceans to the north.

☆

Ann Inett stood amidst the crowd with a heavy heart watching the father of her children sail away on his mission to inform the British government of the colony's plight. She believed King's relationship with her had been more than a passing affair and she had at times, allowed herself to imagine it may continue despite their very different stations in life. They had been through a lot together during those two formative years on Norfolk Island. A consolation for Ann however was the knowledge that King had not and would not turn his back on his children by her; he had indicated as much and for that she must be grateful.

Now, as he left New South Wales, she knew he was also leaving their liaison behind; it was over. His return to the colony was anticipated as soon as he could manage it, but she knew it would be very different between them then. She knew he would visit her, address his eldest son affectionately and see his second child for the first time, but she knew it would never be the same between her and Lieutenant King again.

☆

33

The escape

Throughout the colony's prolonged period of hunger and disquiet, the governor, his officers and everyone involved in the Bennelong project, had continued their facade of sufficiency, going to considerable lengths to conceal from the captive native the fact that the colony was on the edge of starvation. Besides, they had become fond of him and didn't want to risk losing him. Watkin Tench tells us that every practical tactic was *'used to keep him ignorant'* of their dilemma:

> *Our friend Bennelong, during this season of scarcity, was as well taken care of as our desperate circumstances would allow. We knew not how to keep him and yet were unwilling to part with him.*

But Bennelong was an intelligent man and he wasn't blind, so no matter how the officers tried to deceive and distract him, he could not have missed the state of the colony. Tench relates:

> *There is reason to believe that he had long meditated his escape... About two o'clock in the morning, he pretended illness, and awaking the servant who lay in the room with him, begged to go down stairs. The other attended him without suspicion of his design; and Bennelong no sooner found himself in a backyard, than he nimbly leaped over a slight paling, and bade us adieu.*

And so after all the risk and effort involved in his capture, all the confidence placed in the scheme and all the rations forfeited on his behalf, Bennelong quietly and quickly leapt over the governor's fence and took off into the darkness; taking all the governor's hope of improved intercultural understanding with him.

That was May, 1790. By then, the concern of the governor and his senior officers was centred more on the depleting food stocks, than on the escape of Bennelong. Daily, they watched the level of meat, flour and rice reduce. They were counting down the days left before none would be left.

Most of the inhabitants of Sydney Cove were also too preoccupied with their own hunger and misery to care that the native man, whose arrival had caused so much excitement, had escaped.

★

34

Thoughts of freedom

John Wilson, a convict with his sights on life in the wilderness, was hungry too. But he told himself it was training for times when lack of food would be inevitable. He'd seen the natives tie a ligature, a cord spun from possum fur, tightly around their waists to alleviate the sensation of hunger in times of scarcity, so he would see the current food shortage in the settlement as preparation for his future life in the forest.

He didn't blame Bennelong for escaping the settlement. He couldn't wait to be free from the confines and restrictions of the white man's world either. He felt enticed by the contradictions of this strange land; the deafening buzz of the cicadas and the lulling coo of the gully birds. He was drawn to its ruggedness and the softness of its tranquility. He hankered for the freedom of just being.

But it wasn't only the bush that attracted him; it was the bush people and their ways. He'd seen how the natives lived out there and as far as he was concerned, their way of life was preferable to his. The priorities, the focus of the two cultures, the white settlers and the black natives, couldn't be more different and he knew which one appealed to him more.

He and his fellow convicts were always hungry, always working, always kowtowing to their overseers and in dread of a lashing. The native family groups fished, hunted and gathered food but then they sat around their campfire chatting, joking and playing with their children. They met together to form larger tribal groups which were occasions for music, song and dance. They had ritualised fighting sessions between young males of the various groups but, once the fighting was over, and the winners' and losers' wounds were attended to, no long-held grudges seemed to continue; the matter was settled.

Out there in the forest they were unconcerned about 'possessions'. In fact, they scratched their heads at the methods employed at the settlement; keeping stale food in boxes until they were writhing with worms seemed nonsensical. The native families gathered what they needed, fished in their simple canoes till they had enough food for the needs of their group, then enjoyed the rest of the day relaxing, swimming or making and repairing their implements. What food they'd gathered or hunted, they shared.

Wilson could see the benefits – oh yes. He was already making plans, already making connections with the young men of the forest tribe, showing them white man skills: how to utilize white man's tools, how to tie complex knots, how to make a simple three legged stool. He would make himself valuable to the tribes by supplying them with information.

He'd toe the line in the settlement as long as he could bear it. But he wasn't hanging around any longer than he had to. He wouldn't miss the salted pork that was more than two years old, or the weevil infested flour. Some of the natives' food would take time to acquire a taste for, but at least it would be fresh! Only one more year and his sentence would be over, then he'd be gone, out into the vast wilderness...and freedom.

☆

35

Letters and questions

One wintery day in June 1790 Watkin Tench was sitting in his hut pondering the fate of the colony and waning in a cloud of negativity when an unusual flurry of activity outside snapped him out of the doldrums. He could hear the sound of a woman, or rather women, shrieking.

What on earth's going on out there?

The shouting and screaming continued and it quickly registered that they weren't cries of alarm but calls of excitement. Obviously the women were beside themselves with delight about something. He flung his door open and stood gaping at the scene:

> *Women with children in their arms running to and fro with distracted looks, congratulating each other and kissing their infants with the most extravagant marks of fondness.*

'The flag's up...the flag's up!' someone was calling.

Tench, hardly able to contain himself, grabbed his pocket-glass and began running as fast as his legs would carry him to a hill.

A tiny sail spotted on the horizon on that cold, windy June day at last heralded the arrival of a ship. Could this really be a ship from England bringing supplies, carrying letters from home? Surely it must be! It would be the first news they'd had in three years.

Watkin Tench was overcome with emotion, as was the crowd around him. Looking out to sea, he couldn't stop the tears rolling down his cheeks. He turned to a fellow officer, but neither could utter a word, they were too choked:

> *My next door neighbour, a brother-officer, was with me, but we could not speak. We wrung each other by the hand, with eyes and hearts overflowing.*

He bolted back down the hill knowing that the governor, as was the custom when a ship arrived, would be putting out in a boat to meet the ship as it entered the harbour. He prayed silently that this would not be a repeat of their trip when learning of the plight of the shipwrecked *Sirius*. On reaching the wharf he was short of breath but called *'Please sir, can I join you?'*

The governor gestured his consent. Tench realised, he too, was overcome with emotion.

The weather was atrocious that day and rain lashed in the faces of the crew but the men rowed with all their strength. Every man was on the same wavelength - they all wanted to be out of their misery; they all wanted to know for certain if this ship *really* was from good old England.

'Pull away, me lads'; the crew urged each other on.

As they neared the entrance to the harbour, they saw a large ship in the distance and soon they made out the word *'London'* on the stern.

'She is from Old England! Come on, a few strokes more, and we shall be aboard! Hurrah for a bellyful, and news from our friends!' Such were the cheers and calls yelled by the boat's crew.

News from home at long last!

A few minutes later the men boarded the *Lady Juliana*, carrying two hundred and twenty-two female convicts; this was the first of several ships of the 'Second Fleet'. To everyone's surprise the ship had taken almost eleven months to make the passage from England to New South Wales; three months longer than the First Fleet. But it had arrived...with food, provisions and letters. The colonists were desperate for news from home and the questions tumbled out, everyone talking at once.

'Letters, letters!' was the cry all around.

As the bundles of mail were distributed to recipients and torn open with trembling hands, some would have had the added frustration of having to get a literate friend to read theirs aloud. There was so much news from home to catch up on, and even though they were aware that the 'news' they'd received was almost a year old by the time it reached them, their correspondence was read and re-read with speechless excitement.

Watkin Tench wrote: *'We were overwhelmed with it: public, private, general, and particular.'*

The governor learnt that a ship, *Guardian*, had left England with provisions for the colony a year before but had hit an iceberg in the southern ocean, east of South Africa. If that tragedy had not occurred, supplies would have reached New South Wales in time to avert the extreme food shortage they had suffered. The colonists also learnt to their astonishment, of the French Revolution of 1789 and that the King of England had been seriously ill but had since recovered. There was so much news to take in that Tench said it took days to absorb it all.

★

36

The Second Fleet - 1790

Shortly following the arrival of the *'Lady Juliana'*, another ship entered the harbour. It was *'Justinian'* which had been loaded entirely with provisions for the colony. At last, the settlers could return to full rations.

By the end of June, three more ships, *'Neptune'*, *'Surprise'* and *'Scarborough'* arrived with more convicts, as part of the second fleet of convict ships from England. The state of the prisoners, however, showed terrible neglect and cruelty on the part of the ship's masters, particularly Donald Trail of the *'Neptune'*. Many convicts had died on the voyage from starvation and mistreatment and as the ships entered the harbour, bodies of the recently dead were thrown overboard before reaching Sydney Cove. The natives, seeing the putrid, shrunken bodies washed ashore on the secluded beaches away from Sydney must have been appalled at the display of inhumanity. Once the ships had anchored, hundreds of dying men and women had to be carried ashore and taken directly to temporary hospital tents, where many soon took their last breath. David Collins, a witness to the horror, wrote:

> *Several of these miserable people died in the boats as they were being rowed onshore, or on the wharf as they were being lifted out of the boats; both the living and the dead exhibiting more horrid spectacles than had ever been witnessed in this country. All this was to be attributed to confinement in a small space and in irons, not put on singly, but many of them chained together...It was said, that on board the Neptune several died in irons; and what added to the horror of such a circumstance was, that their deaths*

were concealed, for the purpose of sharing their allowance
of provisions, until by chance, and the offensiveness of a
corpse, directed the surgeon...to the spot where it lay.

And though the convicts had been deprived of food and suffered crowded conditions with barely room to move, the ship's master had found room on his decks to load piles of goods to sell in the colony, knowing that the settlers would be desperately short of provisions and wouldn't be able to resist his goods, however overpriced they were.

Captain William Hill, a compassionate young member of the incoming New South Wales Corps, was appalled by the conditions he witnessed on the *Surprise* and put in a complaint:

> *The irons used upon these unhappy wretches were*
> *barbarous...so that they could not extend either leg from*
> *the other more than an inch or two; thus fettered, it was*
> *impossible for them to move, but at the risk of both their*
> *legs being broken. The slave trade is merciful compared with*
> *what I have seen in this fleet.*

Nanberry and Boorong were among the crowd that witnessed the 'horrid spectacle' of filthy, wasted bodies being brought ashore for John White as chief surgeon of the colony, to try to bring back to some semblance of humanity. Nanberry knew his foster father would give the task every ounce of energy he possessed, as he had done in saving his own young life, and many other black and white lives, on numerous occasions during the past two and a half years.

In all about five hundred dying or seriously ill convicts were landed from the Second Fleet ships and the undertaking tested John White and his assistants to their medical and emotional limits. However, despite the lack of proper accommodation and medical equipment, they managed to save nearly half of them.

★

In addition to the hundreds of convicts arriving in Sydney Cove in 1790, there were several aspiring individuals, travelling on the upper decks of the ships, who would have a huge impact on the colony's future. One was a young Irishman, D'Arcy Wentworth, with an interesting past. He was a 'voluntary passenger' in one sense and a convict in another. As a young man he had studied medicine and was certified as an assistant surgeon. But later, while living in London, he put himself on the wrong side of the law and was arrested several times for robbing people as a masked highwayman.

Fortunately for young D'Arcy he had a wealthy, influential relative and each time he appeared in court, the charges were dismissed as his victims seemed reluctant to identify him. Eventually, however, the patience of the law enforcers and his relative ran out and he was given an ultimatum: be prosecuted or take voluntary exile in the New South Wales colony. For the young rascal, a role as a surgeon in the new colony seemed a good option. Soon rumours circulated in London society that Mr D'Arcy Wentworth had *'taken passage to go in the fleet to New South Wales; and had obtained an appointment there, as an assistant surgeon'*.

On the voyage, D'Arcy Wentworth wasn't confined below deck with the convicts but would have been a lonely figure during the early part of the voyage, not being included in the officer's circle or invited to use his medical skills. He evidently spent *some* time with the convicts though, because he met and fell in love with a young Irish girl, seventeen year old Catherine Crowley, who had been sentenced for stealing clothes. Catherine's baby to him was almost due by the time they reached Sydney Cove. Within a short time of his arrival in the colony, D'Arcy Wentworth was sent to Norfolk Island, as an assistant surgeon, though without pay. Catherine accompanied him and shortly after their son William was born.

The officials on Norfolk Island found D'Arcy Wentworth's medical expertise invaluable and relied on him as a doctor to themselves, as well as the prisoners, and as a superintendent of convict work. He was liked by both officers and convicts for his fair-minded manner. Through his own experience he'd learnt that the line between being a criminal and a 'respectable' member of society could be incredibly thin and fragile. His young de-facto wife Catherine raised their son in the island community until the family returned to Sydney six years later.

During her first year on the island Catherine had the company of George Johnston's convict partner Esther Abrahams, whose situation was similar to her own; they were both serving a seven year sentence for theft but enjoyed relative security through their connection with influential men. Their sons were of a similar age and the young women would undoubtedly have supported each other through the shared experience of motherhood.

Their sons, William Wentworth and George Johnston Jnr, remained friends throughout their lives and were both to have important roles in the colony's future. But during the struggles faced by the early settlement, such predictions would not have entered the heads of the two young convict mothers.

★

The Second Fleet on which D'Arcy Wentworth sailed into Sydney, also brought two companies of a specially formed New South Wales Corps. These soldiers were part of a new unit specifically tailored for service in the colony; their responsibilities would include guarding the convicts and protecting the colony. They had been sent to replace the marines who would soon return to England. One member of the newly arrived Corps was Lieutenant John Macarthur with his young wife, Elizabeth and their baby son, Edward. Twenty-two-year-old Elizabeth had kept herself occupied during the early part of the voyage by writing a comprehensive journal in which she described how the ocean 'ran mountains high'.

The voyage had quickly developed into an ordeal for them as they had to endure a tiny airless cabin, with only a thin partition dividing them from the sick and dying convicts. John Macarthur had also become dangerously ill with a 'violent and alarming' fever and little Edward had been so sick that Elizabeth thought she was going to lose him. Added to this, a month into the voyage she'd become aware that she was pregnant with her second child. Conditions had subsequently become so bad for her that after weeks of anxiety, struggle and sleep deprivation, her pregnancy ended. She lost a baby daughter who, after living only one hour, was wrapped in a small canvas blanket and dropped into the sea as her grieving parents watched helplessly. Elizabeth wrote of this time:

...no language can express, no imagination conceive the misery I experienced...my spirits failing, my health forsaking me...

Tough as the voyage had been for them, they were fortunate to have transferred, while the fleet had berthed at Cape Town, from the 'death ship' *Neptune* on which 150 convicts died before the voyage was over, to the *Scarborough* where conditions were somewhat better.

The day they finally sailed into Sydney Cove was cold, grey and gloomy but they were grateful to have arrived safely after months of grueling travel.

When John Macarthur stepped onto the wooden pier, he was still recovering from his insidious illness. Elizabeth was extremely concerned about him and her little son, who was just over a year old. But she put on a brave face as she was led along the muddy track, across ditches bridged with cut logs, to her two roomed mud and thatched hut on the edge of the wilderness; her new home.

She was the first white woman of distinction to arrive in the early settlement and her appearance at the waterfront caused a stir. As she picked her way up between the crude dwellings, dodging puddles as she went, she was aware of the stares of the convicts and the gazes of the officers. She realised that, however crumpled her bonnet and skirts may be or however mud-stained her boots were, she was well-dressed compared with the faded, tattered and patched clothes of everyone around her.

She had traversed the vast oceans of the world, leaving her family and friends behind, to be with her husband as he embarked on his career in New South Wales. She had adapted to appalling conditions on the voyage, so she wouldn't let the primitive circumstances of the fledgling settlement faze or frighten her. She had assumed from the outset that her time in the colony would be temporary, believing that one day, when her husband's tour of duty was over, she would return to England, to her mother, her younger sister and her dear grandfather, but in that she was mistaken. During her first months in the settlement however, her focus was on the fragile health of her husband and little son. She must make the best of her situation in the small primitive hut with its earthen floor, leaky roof, and glassless 'windows'. With what few possessions she had brought from home, she began to establish a routine and with optimism she may not have felt, she wrote to her childhood friend in England:

> *Everything is new to me...every bird, insect, flower...All was novelty around and was noticed by me with eager curiosity.*

She soon heard the horror stories of near starvation before she'd arrived and the problems encountered with the native people; the thefts, killings and reprisals. She also saw the gallows where young bodies of white men had swung for stealing food. She learnt that so far the colony had two main settlements, Sydney and Rose Hill, and that the country had only been explored in a crescent of about fifty miles.

Despite her optimistic nature, Elizabeth soon became dejected by the lack of female company in Sydney. Although there were a few marines' wives, there was only one other woman of any note in the whole colony. According to Elizabeth, however, they had little in common. In a letter to her friend in England, Elizabeth hinted that Mary Johnson, the Reverend's conservative wife was not someone she could or would confide in. In her letter, she complained:

> *I wanted something to fill up a certain vacancy in my time... having no married female friend to whom I could unbend my mind, not even a single woman with whom I could converse with satisfaction...the clergyman's wife being a person in whose society I could reap neither profit or pleasure.*

However, within a short time her loneliness was lessened as she developed strong friendships with some of the officers like William Dawes who sparked her interest in the plants and flowers of the Sydney area and taught her about astronomy at his observatory. George Worgan gave her piano lessons, teaching her to play 'God Save the King' and other tunes on the keyboard he'd brought from England, and Watkin Tench took delight in showing her around the settlement and relating incidents prior to her arrival. Her husband, still ill from the voyage, had a relapse which caused her great concern and kept him too weak to have any impact or influence on the settlement. Once recovered though, John Macarthur would become a force to be reckoned with and a man who would steer the direction of the colony in coming years...but no-one had an inkling of that in the early months after their arrival.

★

Only weeks after Elizabeth's arrival, there was the frightening incident of 'the monster' in the harbour, which must have added to her apprehension of her new surroundings. A young sailor and three marines were in a small boat in the bay when a huge whale raised itself out of the water, close enough to make them extremely concerned. They rowed furiously to get away from the enormous mammal but it seemed intent on hunting them down. Watkin Tench takes up the story told to him by the only survivor of the attack:

> *Sensible of their danger, they used every effort to avoid the cause of it, by rowing in a contrary direction from that which the fish seemed to take, but the monster suddenly arose close to them, and nearly filled the boat with water. By exerting themselves, they baled her out, and again steered from it.*
>
> *For some time it was not seen, and they conceived themselves safe, when, rising immediately under the boat, it lifted her to the height of many yards on its back, whence slipping off, she dropped as from a precipice, and immediately filled and sunk. The midshipman and one of the marines were sucked into the vortex which the whale had made, and disappeared at once. The two other marines swam for the nearest shore, but one only reached it, to recount the fate of his companions.*

It was a shocking incident and made many of the colonists, including Elizabeth and other recently arrived convicts, wary about going on the harbour. They were reassured however that it was not a typical occurrence. In any event, as we shall see, the whale was soon to come to *'a sticky end'* itself, putting a close to a dramatic story; an *'unhappy catastrophe'* as Tench put it.

★

The arrival of the Second Fleet had been dramatic on many levels for the residents of Sydney. But the next major incident, occurring only months later and connected with the demise of the offending whale, would send shock waves through the colony, triggering a sequence of events that could have changed the course of Australian history...

★

37

Mayhem at Manly Cove

September, 1790

The influx of hundreds of additional convicts on the Second Fleet, the landing of much needed provisions, and the arrival of soldiers of the New South Wales Corps had been a necessary distraction for Governor Phillip. But as soon as circumstances allowed, he wanted to resume the important mission of reconciliation with the native people. In particular, he wanted to make contact with Bennelong. He was about to get his wish, but with consequences he could not have imagined.

Watkin Tench began his journal entry for September, 1790 with reference to the earlier whale incident:

> *The tremendous monster that had occasioned the unhappy catastrophe just recorded was fated to be the cause of further mischief to us.*

One spring day, in the first week of September, the colony's chief doctor, John White, his young companion Nanberry and a group of white men headed across the harbour to begin an overland expedition. As they approached the bay known as Manly Cove, they saw a group of about two hundred natives feasting around the whale that had beached itself and died. They were cooking thick slabs of whale meat on several fires when the white men approached by boat.

As this was the first contact between the two groups since the kidnap and escape of Bennelong and Colbee, both parties were wary. The natives on seeing the boat approach became agitated and picked up spears but Nanberry was instructed to call out in their language, saying the white men had friendly intentions. Eventually Bennelong and Colbee came forward and a conversation ensued. Colbee pointed to his leg to show that he had removed the iron fetter that had been attached when he'd escaped from the governor's house. From the white men's perspective, the escapees, Bennelong and Colbee, appeared cautious but willing to forgive their kidnappers. Bennelong asked for some clothes and when they were produced, proceeded to put them on for the amusement of his countrymen who continued to keep their distance.

As the white men were about to leave, Bennelong expressed a wish to make contact with the governor and asked the boat-crew returning to Sydney to take some whale meat to him; it seemed like a peace offering. However, given the perplexing incident that eventuated later that day, a different strategy may have been formulating.

★

As soon as the governor heard there was an opportunity to meet the natives on friendly terms and in particular, to speak with Bennelong, he made immediate plans to go to the meeting place. After collecting food and clothes as gifts, and fire-arms as back-up, he directed his boat crew to the beach where the natives had been feasting. David Collins his secretary, and an aspiring nineteen-year-old junior officer, Henry Waterhouse accompanied him. On the way to the beach they tested their muskets to find that only one was working. Besides Phillip's hand pistol they had no other weapons but, as they weren't anticipating trouble, it wasn't a serious concern. An account of the day's events indicates that as the white men approached Manly Cove, the gathered throng became guarded:

> *Several natives appeared on the beach as the governor's boat rowed into the bay, but on its nearer approach they retired amongst the trees.*

Phillip, believing a display of confidence was the best way to re-open communication, landed on the beach accompanied only by a seaman who carried some bread, meat and a few other articles as gifts. He had told David Collins and Lieutenant Waterhouse to wait in the boat.

Bennelong didn't immediately come forward and when he did, he had apparently changed so considerably in the five months since his escape (he'd lost weight, had battle scars and a long beard) that initially Governor Phillip didn't recognise him:

> *After calling repeatedly on his old acquaintance...he was answered by a native who appeared with several others at a distance, and as he increased his distance from the boat, the native approached nearer, and took a number of little presents, on their being laid down at the distance of a few paces; but he would not come near the governor, although in answer to the question, 'Where was Bennelong?', he repeatedly said **he** was the man. This, however, could not be believed, as he was so much altered.*

Lieutenant Waterhouse gives us his first-hand account of the same scene, when they arrived at the beach where the crowd was feasting on whale meat. The governor and his men, in the first instance, were still in the boat:

> *The Governor after desiring Captain Collins and myself to remain by the boat...told us to have the muskets ready. He stepped out and advanced up the beach with his hands and arms spread open; they did not seem much inclined to come down, however he persevered and followed them into the woods till out of our sight.*

The governor, in an effort to confirm Bennelong's identity and to re-establish camaraderie between them, produced a recognisable object:

> *At length a bottle was held up, and on his being asked what it was in his own language, he answered, 'The King'; for as he had always heard his Majesty's health drank in the first glass after dinner at the governor's table, and had been made to repeat the word before he drank his own glass of wine.*

This convinced the governor that it could be no other than Bennelong, and every method was tried to entice him to come near, but he always retired on their approaching him nearer than he wished, so that they were presently out of sight of the boat, though at no great distance from it; but on eight or ten of the natives placing themselves in a situation to prevent Bennelong being carried off, had it been attempted, he came up, together with Colbee and held out his hand.

At last, after months of wondering what would happen when they met again, the two men shook hands; Bennelong knew this was the white men's way of greeting.

After a while the governor, well pleased with himself, returned to the boat to collect more gifts and asked David Collins to walk back up to the beach with him. As a precaution he told Henry Waterhouse to stay with the boat's crew and to *'keep the boat afloat on her oars'*, as he sensed the natives were *'under some apprehensions'*. As the governor and Collins retreated from sight, Waterhouse believed their movements were being closely observed and relayed between strategically placed natives. When a messenger returned to the boat to invite Waterhouse to join the group on the beach, he sensed their tension. His account of the day, reads:

On my getting on the bank I perceived a number of natives on each side and 8 or 10 in front, all with their spears in their hands except two with whom the governor and Captain Collins seemed in earnest conversation.

At the reunion on the beach, however, the atmosphere seemed more relaxed. According to Phillip:

Bennelong appeared glad to see his old acquaintances; he was very cheerful, and repeatedly shook hands with them...

Knives, hats, and various other articles were given to him and Colbee, laughing, showed them that he had got the iron from his leg by which he had been secured when at the settlement. He also seemed glad to see his former acquaintances, and made himself very merry at the manner of his friend Bennelong's getting away from Sydney, by laying his head on his hand, shutting his eyes, and saying, 'Governor nangorar' (asleep) and imitating the manner in which his companion had run off.

Then another native, who had been standing at a distance, approached the governor and showed him, with signs and gestures, several spear wounds on his back. Bennelong also began pointing out all the wounds that he had received in the past months, since leaving the settlement. One had gone completely through his left arm and another, still looking bad, above his left eye. He indicated that his wounds had been received in a conflict with a rival at Botany Bay.

As they were speaking, the governor spotted an unusual spear and thinking it particularly interesting, asked Bennelong if he could have it. But, according to Lieutenant Waterhouse, Bennelong, '*either would not, or could not, understand him and took it and laid it down in the grass*' near a native the governor had never met. The ongoing account of proceedings reads:

In the course of this interview, they had stopped near a spear which was lying on the grass, and which Bennelong took up; it was longer than common, and appeared to be a very curious one, being barbed and pointed with hard wood. This excited Governor Phillip's curiosity, he asked Bennelong for it, but instead of complying with this request he took it where the stranger was standing, threw it down, and taking a common short spear from a native...he presented that and a club to the governor.

Taking up his firsthand story again, Waterhouse explains that earlier on the beach Colbee had shaken his hand enthusiastically, and Bennelong, he says '*took me round the neck and kissed me*'. There had been friendly conversation, Bennelong and Colbee had donned coats and hats, and everything seemed to be going well. But when the governor mentioned the spear, things seemed to change. Waterhouse tells us:

The natives now seemed to be closing round us which the Governor took notice of and said he thought we had better retreat as they had formed a crescent with us in the centre; there were then nineteen armed men near us and more in great numbers that we could not see.

The mood had altered and the governor decided it was time to get back to the boat. He assured Bennelong that he would return in two days with more hatchets and the clothes that Bennelong had been so fond of wearing when he lived at the governor's house. But Bennelong seemed to be stalling. He pointed to the stranger that was standing near the unusual spear, as if he wanted the governor to notice this particular man. Waterhouse describes the incident:

Just as we were going, Bennelong pointed out and named several natives that were near, one in particular to whom the Governor presented his hand and advanced towards him...

And that's when it all happened...As the native stepped back with one foot and took aim, the realisation of danger registered with Phillip and he called out in the native's language:

'*Weeree, Weeree', (Bad; you are doing wrong).*

But the words were barely out of the governor's mouth, when the spear entered his body with incredible force just above the collar-bone, penetrating deeply between his spine and shoulder blade. The attacker had kept his eye fixed on the weapon until it struck its target; then he'd dashed into the forest and wasn't seen again.

It all happened so abruptly and unexpectedly, there was immediate confusion. Bennelong and Colbee disappeared; several spears flew through the air, though without hitting anyone. Young Waterhouse was in complete panic:

I immediately concluded the governor was killed as it appeared to me much lower than it really was, and supposed there was not a chance for anyone of us to escape, and turned round to run for the beach, as I perceived Captain

Collins running that way and calling to the boats crew to bring the muskets up.

The governor also attempted to run holding the spear with both hands to keep the end off the ground...I suppose it could not be less than twelve feet long.

The governor was in intense physical pain and distress. The three metre long shaft of the spear was sticking out in front of him, so that as he tried to run down the beach to the boat, the butt of the shaft kept striking the ground, tearing the gash of his wound even further open.

'For God's sake, haul the spear out!' the governor pleaded, as Lieutenant Waterhouse began heading down the beach toward the boat. Waterhouse immediately turned and began tugging at the spear, but realised that by pulling the barb back through the governor's chest he was causing more damage. Instead, he tried in vain to break off the shaft without adding to the governor's agony. He describes how a surge of fear helped accomplish the task:

...just in that instant, another spear came and grazed the skin off between the thumb and forefinger of my right hand. I must own it frightened me a good deal and I believe added to my exertions, for in the next sudden jerk I gave it, it broke off.

As the men struggled down the beach toward the boat, one of the crew appeared and fired a shot toward the trees with the only musket that was working. They eventually made it to the boat with the struggling governor leaning heavily against Waterhouse:

With the help of a seaman I lifted the Governor into the boat as he was very faint. Captain Collins immediately followed with the boats crew and we put off.

I supported the Governor in my arms all the way - during which time he was conscious that a few hours must fix the period of his existence supposing the spear had gone through much lower than it really did...We got up within two hours to Sydney when the surgeons were immediately sent for...

On the way back to Sydney, Arthur Phillip was convinced he was going to die. Even when the boat arrived at the settlement and the doctor examined his wound, the governor asked how many hours he had left:

> *When the governor got home, the wound was examined. It had bled a good deal in the boat, and it was doubtful whether the subclavian artery might not be severed. On moving the spear, it was found, however, that it might be safely extracted, which was accordingly performed.*

And so the account ends on a positive note: the doctor assured the governor that there would be no *'fatal consequences from the wound'* and that within six weeks he would be able to go about his business again. But as the governor was healing, he had a lot of time to think over the events.

Why had it happened? What had triggered it?
If he'd handled it differently...maybe it could have been avoided?
Maybe the natives thought the white men intended to kidnap Bennelong again?

Over and over, he went through each step of the incident. He thought about the man who had speared him; the fact that the spearing had taken place *when* it did, at the end of the visit, in full view of the natives surrounding him. He would like to meet that man, not to punish him but to ask why?

If it had been the warrior's intention to throw the spear all along, why hadn't he done it when Phillip was alone on the beach, before Waterhouse and Collins joined him?

He wanted to believe it was an accident...

*But why hadn't Bennelong tried to stop it? Why hadn't **he** called out, 'Weeree, Weeree'?*

Governor Phillip was still trying to make sense of it when he wrote his account of events in his journal much later. As we read it, we can almost hear him thinking aloud:

It is most likely that the action proceeded from a momentary impulse of fear. But the behaviour of Bennelong on this occasion is not so easily to be accounted for. He never attempted to interfere when the man took the spear up, or said a single word to prevent him from throwing it...

Then, Phillip started to think about the strategic placement of the native men on the beach:

A few minutes before this affair happened, nineteen of the natives had been counted round our party, and the position they took showed their judgment.

Again he went over and over where everyone had stood, what had been said and what the natives may have been thinking. The spear had a smooth wooden head; it was not a weapon of execution, its plunge was not intended to be fatal. The governor then thought about the way the natives had shown him their wounds just prior to the attack.

Why had they done that?
Had they shown their wounds to him to demonstrate that it was the way they dealt with serious violation of law? Was the event a staged incident? Was it an example of their 'ritual punishment'?

But in the end the governor didn't know what to think. He concluded 'officially' that there had been no premeditated aggression; that it had been '*the business of a moment*'. Some of his officers, particularly when he had first been injured, had urged him to take punitive action but he had given strict directives that the natives were not to be attacked. He had to look to the future and didn't want this episode to interfere with his plans for a peaceful resolution with the natives. They would all get over this; he would make sure they did.

★

38

Making amends

The day following the spearing, some of the governor's men while patrolling the harbour, came across a group of natives who enquired after the governor's condition. They didn't seem afraid and they didn't appear to expect retaliation. The white men didn't know what to think.

A week later, Lieutenant Dawes and Reverend Johnson, accompanied by young Boorong, were on the harbour when they were approached by two native men in a canoe. They asked, with Boorong's help, how the governor was faring and *'seemed pleased to hear that he was likely to recover'*. One of the men was Maugoran, a representative of the Burramatta people who had lived at the head of the river before the settlers moved there. While he had the white men's attention, he told them he was from the area the British called 'Rose Hill' and that his people were displeased that so many settlers had moved there. The new settlement had disrupted their lives very much and they wanted the governor to know of their objection. The governor got the message, and pondered the situation. He commented later:

> *Indeed, if this man's information could be depended upon, the natives were very angry at so many people being sent to Rose Hill.*

But wasn't it obvious to them that he was intent on peaceful relations? Had he not tried to involve them?

One thing seemed evident to Arthur Phillip: misunderstanding on the part of the black residents was as glaring as ever. He had written his 'grand vision' for the natives of the new colony even before arriving in New South Wales: *'I mean to furnish them with everything that can tend to civilise them, and to give them a high opinion of the new guests'*. But his good intentions were apparently not getting through to them.

He would have to reinforce his peaceful objectives; make them understand his goodwill toward them. In the meantime, in consequence of Maugoran's assertion, he felt a precaution was necessary. The current detachment of soldiers at Rose Hill would likely not be sufficient to prevent trouble. He would have to reinforce the military presence as soon as possible.

★

Looking back through the mists of time, we can only imagine the internal conflict felt by Maugoran, as he paddled back up the harbour to his relocated family along the river and when the following day, he witnessed more soldiers being sent by boat to 'Rose Hill'.

Around the same time he had discovered that his daughter, Boorong, who had been assumed dead from the *'galgalla' (as the natives called smallpox)*, had been nursed to health by the white people and was content enough to stay living with them. On the one hand the white people had taken his land, yet on the other, they had saved his daughter's life.

★

Over subsequent days, around the harbour, the white men came across other natives who enquired about the governor's recovery and gave the impression they hadn't supported the attack on him. Watkin Tench made a curious comment about this; he suggested their censure of the incident was contrived:

> *Like the others, they had pretended highly to disapprove the conduct of the man who had thrown the spear.*

Tench, it seems, suspected they *did* support the actions of the man who hurled the weapon. But did he also suspect that the incident was seen by the natives as a necessary deed, an essential step to put affairs right, before things could move forward?

Had they feigned disapproval of the spearing because they suspected the white men would never understand the rules of appropriate conduct or the fundamentals of exacting justice?

Whatever anyone thought about the case, it heralded a surprising turnabout in the relationship between the black and white residents of the harbour. A week after the spearing incident, several of the officers went across the harbour, accompanied by the two native children, Nanberry and Boorong, after seeing a fire which the officers understood to be *'a signal for us to visit them'.* On landing, they met a group of natives, including Bennelong.

To break the ice, the British men had purposely taken food and other gifts which were offered among the group. Bennelong, in his typical manner, assumed the key role and when a bottle of wine, bread and beef were produced, Bennelong distributed the fare to his friends. Watkin Tench tells us, *'two of whom tasted the beef, but none of them would touch the bread.'*

Some black children were standing at a distance watching the merriment; they seemed timid and unsure of the white men but were eventually persuaded to come forward for little gifts.

Barangaroo, a woman Bennelong had often spoken of while captive in Sydney as 'his favourite', was also standing at a distance and Bennelong boasted that she was now his wife. The white men signalled for her to come closer but she was hesitant so the young girl, Boorong, was sent to coax her to join the group. Boorong, who had been carefully coached in the home of the Reverend Johnson and his wife about the importance of modesty, took a 'petticoat' for Barangaroo to put on before coming among the white men. We don't know how Boorong approached the subject of the petticoat but we can imagine the conversation between the black women: one a teenage girl who had spent over a year living with white settlers, and the other, a self-confident married woman who was completely at ease with her nakedness.

Why do the white people cover their bodies?
They say it is shameful to do otherwise.
Where does this shame come from?
I don't understand their reasons but body coverings are important to them.

When later Barangaroo eventually joined the group, she made the concession of wearing the petticoat. However, she wasn't as eager as Bennelong to try the white man's other offering; that vile tasting, blood coloured drink:

> *Wine she would not taste, but turned from it with disgust,*
> *though heartily invited to drink by the example and*
> *persuasion of Bennelong.*

She also made it clearly understood that she had no inclination to visit the white men's camp. She wasn't in any way impressed with the *Berewalgal* (*the people from far away*) as the British were being called; they had strange ways. They had kidnapped her Bennelong, they had brought disease and death to her people and they had, even recently, stolen their precious hunting and fishing equipment.

The officers could see the influence that Barangaroo had on her husband, so they instructed Boorong to take her for a walk and tell her about all the advantages of life in Sydney:

> *Supposing, that by a private conversation, she might be*
> *induced to visit Sydney, which would be the means of drawing*
> *her husband and others there, Boorong was instructed to take*
> *her aside, and try if she could persuade her...*

But clever Barangaroo turned the tables on the *Berewalgal* and spent the time talking to Boorong about the benefits of life with her own people:

> *They wandered away together accordingly, but it was soon*
> *seen, that Barangaroo's arguments to induce Boorong to re-*
> *join their society, were more powerful...*

Barangaroo must have been convincing because it was with reluctance, and after repeated coaxing, that Boorong got back into the boat that day to return to Sydney with her white guardians and when she did, she sat in the boat, *'in sullen silence, evidently occupied by reflection on the scene she had left behind.'*

Another subject had been raised just before the British men left to return across the harbour, possibly at the instigation of Barangaroo:

> *Before we parted, Bennelong informed us that his countrymen had lately been plundered of fish-gigs, spears, a sword, and many other articles, by some of our people, and expressed a wish that they should be restored.*

The British officers returned to Sydney, not doubting that the accusations of theft were true, and made a search of the settlement for stolen goods.

The following day, they returned across the harbour as promised with a large quantity of native property that had been recovered from the white camp:

> *All the stolen property being brought on shore, an old man came up and claimed one of the fish-gigs, singling it from the bundle, taking only his own; and this honesty, within the circle of their society, seemed to characterise them all...*

> *Among other things, was a net full of fishing lines and other tackle, which Barangaroo said was her property and, immediately on receiving it, she slung it around her neck.*

The white men, feeling that stability was being restored, invited Bennelong to visit the recovering governor in Sydney but Bennelong was insistent that the governor must visit him first:

> *At parting, we pressed him to appoint a day on which he should come to Sydney, assuring him, that he would be well received, and kindly treated. Doubtful, however, of being permitted to return, he evaded our request, and declared that the governor must first come and see him, which we promised should be done.*

The governor seeing this ultimatum as progress, rose from his couch only ten days after his operation, gingerly climbed into a boat and crossed the harbour to meet with Bennelong. Phillip used the opportunity to assure Bennelong that if he returned to the Sydney settlement in future he would not be restrained in any way. He would *'be his own master, and go and come when he pleased'*. Not immediately, but within weeks of the governor's spearing, Bennelong (without Barangaroo) and a group of his friends paddled across the harbour to visit the settlement, and in particular, Governor Phillip.

On hearing of their arrival, an inquisitive crowd quickly gathered at the wharf but the black men, undaunted by the large assembly, filed with self-assurance directly to the governor's house. Bennelong and the governor greeted each other warmly and some bread and beef was offered and eagerly accepted. Bennelong then decided to give his kinfolk a tour of the governor's house:

> *Bennelong seemed to consider himself quite at home, running from room to room with his companions, and introducing them to his old friends, the domestics, in the most familiar manner. Among these last, he particularly distinguished the governor's orderly sergeant, whom he kissed with great affection, and a woman who attended in the kitchen…the tenderness which he had always manifested to children he still retained; as appeared by his behaviour to those who were presented to him.*

The only person, in the whole settlement, that Bennelong and the other native men deliberately avoided was the governor's gamekeeper, a convict by the name of John McEntire for whom, as Tench put it, they showed *'dread and hatred'*.

☆

In the months following Bennelong's courtesy visit, friendly relations continued to develop between many of the natives and the Sydney settlers. Even Barangaroo's resistance to the British soon softened. Deciding it was time to learn more about the strange white people her husband was so absorbed with, she compromised and visited the British settlement; but she never again wore the peculiar body coverings they called 'clothes' to conform to their strange ideas. Even when, on regular occasions, she dined at the governor's house, she wore nothing but painted decorations on her body and at times adorned her pierced nose with a small piece of tapered bone.

Elizabeth Macarthur, with apparent pleasure, described the visits of native people after Bennelong's resolution with the governor. In a letter to her friend in England, she wrote:

> Since that period the natives visit us every day, more or less; men, women and children come with great confidence without spears or any other weapon. A great many take up their abode entirely among us and Bennelong and Colbee with their wives come in frequently. Mrs Colbee, whose name is Daringa, brought in a new born female infant of hers for me to see...It was wrapped up in the soft bark of a tree.

John Hunter provides more detail on native women's use of paperbark blankets, one of which he had seen Barangaroo carrying 'nicely folded up', and which she intended to use for her unborn infant:

> The bark of the tea-tree is thick in proportion to the size of the tree, and is composed of a great number of layers of very thin bark...but it is so very soft, that nothing could be better for the purpose for which it was intended.

Hunter also recorded the kind of collaboration taking place between the two cultures and the confidence that was growing among them. He described one occasion at which Daringa, Colbee's gentle wife, and her companions were keen for the English doctor to become involved in one of their regular procedures:

> Colbee's wife had a young female child in her arms, about three or four months old (who) had a ligature round the little finger...in order to separate the two lower joints, which in the course of three weeks or a month it effected: I saw it just

as the finger was about dropping off, but as it hung by a bit of skin, they begged Mr White, the surgeon, to take it off, which he did, with a pair of scissors, and which the child did not seem to feel.

What Hunter described (the removal of the top part of a little girl's finger), was termed *'malgun'* by the natives and was understood to be customary in enabling native women to use their fishing lines more adeptly. It was gratifying for the governor to witness the trust and cordiality that was developing. This was the turn-around he had hoped for.

☆

William Dawes, the young astronomer, was also delighted to have native callers at his small dwelling near the observatory on Sydney Cove's western point. The new acquaintances would sit for hours on the flat sandstone elevation in front of his hut, teaching and learning words and phrases. As his tutors patiently modelled and repeated expressions for him, Dawes meticulously recorded them in his notebook.

From his notebooks we get glimpses of lighthearted days, full of fun and laughter between the men, women and children interacting with Dawes. We also get an indication of how comfortably the two cultural groups were beginning to communicate. In one instance, a little native girl was trying to put on a petticoat belonging to a young black woman, named Pattye.

'It's too long', Dawes had said playfully to the black child.
'I will hold it up', the little one had responded confidently and impishly.

On another occasion, while Dawes was shaving Bennelong amid the chatter and camaraderie of the group, Barangaroo teased that Dawes might cut her husband. Boorong and Nanberry were also often part of the gathering outside the Lieutenant's hut and one day Dawes, being a spiritual young man, tried to turn the conversation to religion and get an understanding of their beliefs but, he later told his friend Tench, their *'love of play in a great measure defeated his efforts'*. It was their nature to be fun-loving and carefree, however, Tench later wrote in his journal:

When they attended church with us (which was common practice) they always preserved profound silence and decency, as if conscious that some religious ceremony on our side was performing.

The caring, conscientious and deeply religious Mr Dawes must have been pleased with that.

★

As the number of black families visiting Sydney increased, language barriers were overcome with signs, gestures and good humour on both sides. There were certain pronunciation issues though, as Tench recorded:

The 's' is a letter they cannot pronounce, having no sound in their language similar to it. When trying to pronounce sun, they always say tun; salt, talt, and so on...

As an aside to this, Tench noted a comical scene when Bennelong was showing off his superior knowledge to his companions in the governor's house. The pronunciation issue was irrelevant to Bennelong's companions but was amusing to the English onlookers:

He undertook to explain the use and nature of those things which were new to them. Some of his explanations were whimsical enough. Seeing, for instance, a pair of snuffers, he told them that they were 'nuffer for candle', which the others not comprehending, he opened the snuffer and holding up the fore-finger of his left hand, to represent a candle, made the motion of snuffing it.

Seeing that his friends had no idea what he was talking about *'he threw down the snuffer in a rage and reproach at their stupidity'* and stamped out of the room.

Just as the British saw the native's language issues and cultural interpretations as entertaining, the black locals were equally amused

178

that the British could not produce some of their sounds. Tench referred to several which were *'difficult for English mouths to pronounce'*: one was the sound he described as *'dy'*.

Despite the inevitable hitches, great headway was being made in race relations around the Sydney settlement. When anyone, black or white, couldn't work something out, or had a cultural query, it was Bennelong they consulted, although he was evidently still adjusting to the role himself:

> *...he had lately become a man of so much dignity and consequence, that it was not always easy to obtain his company. Clothes had been given to him at various times, but he did not always condescend to wear them. One day he would appear in them, and the next day he was to be seen carrying them in a net slung around his neck. Further to please him, a brick house of twelve feet square was built for his use, and for such of his countrymen as might choose to reside in it, on a point of land fixed upon by himself.*

> *Elated by these marks of favour, and sensible that his importance with his countrymen arose in proportion to our patronage of him, he warmly attached himself to our society.*

Bennelong had achieved reconciliation with the white leader and made an informed decision to enjoy the benefits of the white men's camp. He had negotiated for his people unrestricted access to the settlement and had been promised an ongoing supply of 'white men's' provisions: bread, meat, liquor, iron hatchets, blankets and clothes. He believed he had claimed a stake for his clan in the white men's political structure while still retaining their treasured independence. The brick house, built for Bennelong at his request on the eastern point of Sydney Cove became his 'headquarters'; a place where the native people of the cove met around their communal fire by day and where they sang and danced together at night. The location of his house is still known as Bennelong Point, and is now the site of the world-famous Sydney Opera House.

Bennelong and his comrades had chosen peaceful co-existence with the British assuming they had entered a mutually binding obligation of respect. The commitment was never put in writing and not all the Eora, as the black people referred to themselves, agreed with their choice.

One of the people who didn't share Bennelong's confidence in the white people was Pemulwuy, a native whose name meant 'man of the earth'. He was a tall, muscular warrior of the clan known as the *Bediagal*, and whom the white men later referred to as *'a leader of the tribe that resides about Botany-Bay'*. He would become a force to be reckoned with; by the end of 1790, Pemulwuy would make his entrance into the scene of the colony with major consequences.

★

39

Pemulwuy

The year 1790 had been turbulent for everyone in the settlement, but particularly for Governor Phillip. There had been thefts, hangings, injuries and attacks by blacks and whites on each other's property and a predictable cycle of retaliation. The population had endured a terrible food crisis and scarcity of all the basics deemed necessary to a civilised existence. Then, with the arrival of the Second Fleet, they'd been inundated with more sick and decrepit dependents which, in some ways, had outweighed the relief felt by the lessening of their food crisis.

Shortly after the advent of the Second Fleet, a recently arrived convict, John Turwood masterminded the theft of a single-masted boat and disappeared with four other convicts into the Pacific Ocean. They had presumably perished in the treacherous ocean storms prevailing at the time and the governor hoped their apparent failure at freedom had quelled ideas of copycat schemes. Nevertheless, it was a blow to the government to lose one of the colony's few reliable vessels.

There had also been the devastating shipwreck of *HMS Sirius* on the hazardous approach to Norfolk Island, and last but not least, the spearing attack on the governor himself. If the white leader was hoping that the year would end without further drama, he was to be disappointed. He was away at Rose Hill when a disturbing event, which led to serious repercussions, occurred in bushland south of Sydney.

It centred on John McEntire, a convict who had found favour with the governor as a skilled game-hunter, while attracting hatred from the Aboriginal people, including the brooding warrior, Pemulwuy, a native man who had thus far remained low-key on the scene of British settlement. McEntire had apparently been involved in some incident away from Sydney to draw such a strong negative reaction from the black population in general, and Pemulwuy in particular. The time had arrived for a response from the young warrior.

At the beginning of December, McEntire and two other convicts under the supervision of a sergeant, set out on an overnight hunting trip to the Botany Bay area. Their plan was to rest in the late afternoon, until sunset, then hunt kangaroos during the evening which was their main grazing time. The group had settled down for an afternoon nap in a makeshift hut, when rustling sounds were heard in the undergrowth. One of the men peered out between the cracks and spotted a number of natives creeping toward the hut.

'Don't be afraid, I know them', McEntire told his anxious, now wide-eyed companions.

He cautioned the other convicts and the sergeant to stay put, assuring them he would fix things. He left the shelter unarmed and walked toward the natives, speaking to them in their language. One of the eyewitnesses later reported that, at first the natives appeared to back away from McEntire, then one of them *'without the least warning of his intention'*, launched his spear at him, embedding it in his left side. From the view inside the hut, the violence appeared to be unwarranted. McEntire doubled over, immediately sensing his fate was sealed:

'I am a dead man', he cried. *'Get me back home; I don't want to die out here'.*

His anxious companions immediately began an excruciatingly slow return to Sydney with him. McEntire was bleeding profusely and it wasn't until the early hours of the morning that they staggered back into the settlement where one of the surgeons examined his wound. But it was too late for medical help and McEntire knew it. The spear, still protruding from his side, was no ordinary hunting weapon. He'd seen this type of spear before and knew how it worked. If an attempt was made to extract it, the numerous, small stone barbs attached to the tip of the timber shaft and already penetrating his lung, would tear off and lodge inside him. He was a goner!

According to Tench, the wounded convict began to *'utter the most dreadful exclamations, and to accuse himself of crimes of the deepest dye... too terrible to repeat'.*

'Oh God have mercy on me', he wailed.

The following day, Colbee, already aware of the incident, was questioned about the identity of the man who'd thrown the spear and gave the attacker's name as Pemulwuy, 'a man of distinction' from the Botany Bay district. When taken to see McEntire, by then extremely weak, Colbee confirmed the surgeon's suspicion: if an attempt was made to extract the wooden shaft, death would be immediate. If it was left alone, he would linger but not recover.

McEntire did linger for a further ten days. Although soon after the attack, he had allegedly spluttered confessions about his treatment of natives on previous hunting trips, as his death approached, he had retracted his admission of guilt, saying he'd only ever shot at natives in self-defence. Tench suggested however because of McEntire's *'general character and other circumstances ...most people doubted the truth of this'.*

After questioning eyewitnesses of the spearing, the governor however was not convinced of its justification. Phillip's reaction to the incident was unpredictable, uncharacteristic and dramatic.

40

Retaliation

Governor Phillip, absent from Sydney at the time of the attack on McEntire, only heard of it on his return from Rose Hill. According to those at the scene of the assault, McEntire had not merited the violence; the hunting party had been resting inside the hut when their aggressors approached. The governor valued the gamekeeper's hunting abilities and saw him through rose coloured glasses. He felt justified in having a decisive response issued:

> *The governor, in order to deter the natives from such practices in future, has ordered out a party to search for the man who wounded the convict McEntire in so dangerous a manner on Friday last, though no offence was offered on his part...*

> *A party, consisting of two captains, two subalterns, and forty privates, with a proper number of non-commissioned officers from the garrison, with three days provisions, are to be ready to march tomorrow morning at day-light, in order to bring in six of those natives who reside near the head of Botany Bay; or, if that should be found impracticable, to put that number to death.*

Events were about to take a significant and irreversible turn.

☆

The McEntire incident was apparently the last straw in what had been a trying year for the governor, and marked a very different attitude in his dealings with the natives. He paced the room waiting for Watkin Tench to attend a private meeting in his office. When the officer arrived, the governor informed him he was to lead the punitive expedition. Tench recorded the mind-boggling orders in his journal:

> *We were to proceed to the peninsula at the head of Botany Bay...we were, if practicable, to bring away two natives as prisoners; and to put to death ten; that we were to destroy all weapons of war but nothing else; that no hut was to be burned; that all women and children were to remain uninjured...*

> *That we were to cut off and bring in the heads of the slain; for which purpose hatchets and bags would be furnished. And finally, that no signal of amity or invitation should be used in order to allure them to us...for such conduct would be not only present treachery, but give them reason to distrust every future mark of peace and friendship on our part.*

As the young lieutenant stood before the governor hearing his instructions, he tried to keep his expression blank but his heart was pounding. Had he heard correctly? The words echoed in his head:

... 'to put to death ten...cut off and bring in the heads of the slain ... hatchets and bags...'

He stood mute, wanting to question such drastic action but it wasn't his place. The governor however answered his unspoken query: he believed *'the principal aggressors'* of various killings and injuries on settlers were men of the Botany Bay tribes. He needed to send a message to the antagonists. He told Tench he was *'determined to strike a decisive blow'* in order to impart a widespread fear which, he hoped *'might operate to prevent further mischief'*.

But why such extreme measures this time? Watkin wanted to ask.

The governor, as if reading his officer's mind explained that he had delayed use of violent methods for so long because he believed that in every former instance of hostility, the natives had acted either in reaction to injury done to them, or from misunderstandings. He continued:

> *To the latter of these causes, I attribute my own wound, but in this business of McEntire, I am fully persuaded that they were unprovoked...I have separately examined the Sergeant, of whose reliability I have the highest opinion and the two convicts; and their story is short, simple, and alike. I have in vain tried to stimulate Bennelong, Colbee, and the other natives who live among us, to bring in the aggressor...So we have our efforts only to depend upon...*

The governor explained his rationale: he planned to punish the offence publicly, hoping the natives would see it as a *'most exemplary'* penalty and deterrent:

> *I am resolved to execute the prisoners who may be brought in, in the most public and exemplary manner, in the presence of as many of their countrymen as can be collected, after having explained the cause of such a punishment; and my fixed determination to repeat it whenever any future breach of good conduct on their side renders it necessary.*

Here the governor paused and heaved a sigh. His earnest hope had always been to keep peace with the natives. He had continually directed that none of their blood would be deliberately shed... but now a check on the attack on an unarmed man seemed absolutely necessary. He was at his wit's end; the responsibility he carried on his shoulders was immense. He looked at the young officer, Lieutenant Watkin Tench, and said purposefully:

> *If you could propose any alteration to these orders under which you are to act, I am prepared to listen to you.*

Encouraged by the prospect of lessening the appalling impact of his mission, Tench put forward a more lenient approach:

Sir, instead of destroying ten persons, would not the capture of six better answer all the purposes for which the expedition is to be undertaken...?

The governor agreed immediately to adopt his officer's suggestion, but then added:

If six cannot be taken, let this number be shot. Should you, however, find it practicable to take so many, I will hang two and send the rest to Norfolk Island for a certain period, which will cause their countrymen to believe that we have dispatched them secretly.

As the young officer left the room, the governor felt the weight of his command. *Had he been hasty?*

Did the spearing incident necessitate such a show of British strength? What would he do if the murderer and the murdered had both been white? What would the Eora, the black men, do if the murderer and the murdered had both been black?

He was in an unenviable position; there could be no win-win outcome.

✭

41

Conflict and bungles

Watkin Tench walked away from the governor's headquarters and went to see his friend William Dawes at the observatory, as they were both to be involved in the operation. They had individually developed close friendships among the Eora; only weeks before Tench had written in his journal:

> *During the intervals of duty, our greatest source of entertainment now lay in cultivating the acquaintance of our new friends, the natives.*

...but Tench knew that Dawes' connection with some of them was particularly strong. A deep bond of mutual respect had developed between Dawes and his black friends and Tench anticipated an emotive reaction from his colleague. In this, he was not mistaken.

'*No!*' declared William Dawes, '*I will not do it...I will not go!*'

Tench tried to reason with his agitated friend, but Dawes was adamant that he could not conscientiously take part in such an expedition. With shaking hands he began writing a letter of refusal to the senior officer of his detachment, Captain Campbell. On receiving the letter, the shocked officer did his utmost to persuade the young lieutenant of his military obligation; even pointing out that his refusal to participate could result in his arrest. But Dawes was unwavering in his resolve; he would not go. That is, until finally in the early hours of the morning the Reverend Johnson was woken and brought to speak to Dawes. After a long and intense discussion with his spiritual advisor, the young man agreed reluctantly to submit to the governor's instructions. He had been reminded of his duty; he must follow orders, without question.

The expedition set off at four o'clock in the morning. The detachment, besides Lieutenants Tench and Dawes, included several other officers, two surgeons and forty soldiers: in all, fifty men. They were provided with three day's rations, rope to bind the prisoners, and hatchets and bags to cut off and contain the heads of the slain; natives were to be brought in dead or alive. It was mid-December, the hottest part of the year, but in the time honoured tradition of the British military, they wore tight-fitting, long-sleeved, red woollen jackets and leg-hugging trousers. By mid-morning, their small rimmed black hats would not have given much protection from the blazing sun. Tench records the first uneventful, yet noteworthy day of the mission:

> By nine o'clock this terrific procession reached the peninsula at the head of Botany Bay, but after having walked in various directions until four o'clock in the afternoon without seeing a native, we halted for the night. At daylight on the following morning our search recommenced.

Incredibly, though not surprisingly, after twelve hours marching, they had not seen one single native. By the end of the second morning, due to *'a mistake of the guides'* the band of soldiers became lost. After reaching dead ends created by gorges and marshes and wasting hours in retracing their tracks, they saw five natives on a distant beach. The soldiers, according to the official report, attempted to surround them but by the time the ambushers reached the spot, the natives had gone.

Accounts of the expedition reveal a series of further mishaps, which had it not been for such a grim purpose, must have seemed farcical, in hindsight, to Watkin Tench. Imagine over fifty British soldiers in the stifling heat of summer, lugging their heavy provisions, clad in their body-hugging, bright red jackets trying to sneak up on experienced native bushmen. It is likely the natives heard or smelt them even before they saw them.

Tench's account reveals they then marched to another area where they knew a small native campsite was situated. They had hoped to surprise them, but again, as they approached:

> ...*three canoes, filled with natives, were seen paddling over in the utmost hurry and trepidation, to the opposite shore... All we could now do was to search the huts for weapons of war: but we found nothing except fishing equipment which we left untouched.*

Next, as they returned the way they had come, they saw a lone fisherman in the shallows and although they were on a mission to shoot natives or seize hostages, Tench decided it was not practical 'in such a situation' to do either. He records:

> *I therefore determined to pass without noticing him, as he seemed... quite unintimidated at our appearance. At length he called to several of us by name, and in spite of our formidable array, drew nearer with unbounded confidence. Surprised at his behaviour I ordered a halt.*

Soon, to Tench's further surprise, the man approached them with *'familiarity and unconcern'* and they recognised him as Colbee. They quickly realised that he was completely aware of the purpose for their mission, as he told them that Pemulwuy was miles away; so far in fact that there was no way the party could follow him without a fresh supply of provisions. Colbee then attached himself to the party, nonchalantly invited himself back to their camp depot for a meal and when he was ready, left to go about his own business.

It had been a tense, exhausting day in the mid-summer heat; they were dusty, sweaty, edgy and very weary. That evening the group camped near a freshwater swamp but the following morning the men struggled out of their blankets complaining of a sleepless night due to swarms of mosquitoes and sand flies that bit and stung all night.

They headed homeward exasperated and grumpy, and after wading chest-high through two inlets of the sea too extensive to go around, they arrived back in Sydney late afternoon where Tench reported to the governor that their expedition had failed to complete its mission.

The governor suspected the natives had been tipped off, so to Tench's dismay, he was sent in charge of a second assignment with exactly the same objective two weeks later. This time, in order to mislead the natives and prevent them from repeating their previous forewarning tactic, the detachment pretended their preparations were directed northward rather than to the south. It was also decided, that being a full moon, the operation should be performed at night, both for the sake of secrecy, and to avoid the extreme heat of the day.

After leaving the camp, they veered southward toward Botany Bay where they planned, as a shortcut, to wade across a tidal stretch of water when the current was low. They waited till the early hours of the morning before the water had receded enough and carrying their provisions, firearms and ammunition on their heads, they waded across, carefully dodging holes and obstacles. They crossed other watercourses in the same way and eventually came to a wide creek which didn't look too deep, as again the tide was out. After indecision about whether to attempt a crossing or take the much longer route around the area, Tench decided to send some men the long way with the bulk of their equipment, while most of the men waded across. However, the first men to step into the water had not even reached half way when disaster struck:

> We were immersed, nearly to the waist in mud, so thick and tenacious, that it was not without the most vigorous exertion of every muscle of the body, that the legs could be disengaged. When we had reached the middle, our distress became not only more pressing, but serious, and each succeeding step, buried us deeper. At length a sergeant of grenadiers was stuck fast and declared himself incapable of moving either forward or backward; and just after, Ensign Prentice and I felt ourselves in a similar predicament, close together.

'I'm sinking, 'I can't move!' was echoed on every side. It was a terrifying situation, every moment becoming more urgent as they could feel themselves gradually being sucked further into the thick, gluggy mire.

Fortunately, some of the men had not yet stepped off the bank when the cries of their companions alerted them to danger and one man, quickly assessing the situation, had the forethought to cut branches from trees and use them as lifelines for the stranded soldiers. It was a near disaster and Tench praised the diligence of the soldier:

> ...a lucky thought, which certainly saved many of us from perishing miserably; and even with this assistance, had we been burdened by our knapsacks, we could not have emerged; for it employed us near half an hour to disentangle some of our number. The sergeant of grenadiers in particular, was sunk to his breast-bone, and so firmly fixed in that the efforts of many men were required to extricate him.

They managed to pull the traumatised soldier out of the mud with one of the ropes that had been destined to bind their captives, by fastening it under his arms and dragging him to safety. It had been a lucky escape but they were all drenched, shaken and covered in thick mud which oozed from their boots and weighed them down. A rest would have been most welcome but it was almost morning so there was no time to waste. They had to push forward, obey their orders and accomplish their objective. They headed to the small native campsite that they'd found deserted on their last visit. Watkin Tench tells us his plan to surround and surprise the camp:

> Here I formed the detachment into three divisions, and having enjoined the most perfect silence, in order, if possible, to deceive native vigilance, each division was directed to take a different route, so as to meet at the village at the same moment.

> We rushed rapidly on, and nothing could succeed more exactly than the arrival of the several detachments. To our astonishment, however, we found not a single native at the huts; nor was a canoe to be seen on any part of the bay...On closer examination it appeared that many days had elapsed since a native had been on the spot, as no mark of fresh fires, or fish bones, was to be found.

By now the men were almost dropping with fatigue; they had marched all night, waded through several rivers and nearly drowned, only to have made an unsuccessful and embarrassing ambush. They were covered in mud, aching and frustrated. All they wanted to do was rest but that wasn't possible:

> *On consultation it was found that unless we reached the rivers, we had so lately passed, in an hour it would be impossible, on account of the tide, to cross to our baggage; in which case we should be without food until evening. We therefore pushed back, and by alternately running and walking, arrived at the fords, time enough to pass with ease and safety.*

> *So excessive, however, had been our efforts, and so laborious our progress, that several of the soldiers, in the course of the last two miles, gave up, and confessed themselves unable to proceed farther. All that I could do for these poor fellows was to order their comrades to carry their muskets, and to leave with them a small party of those men who were least exhausted, to assist them and hurry them on. In three quarters of an hour after we had crossed the water, they arrived at it, just time enough to affect a passage.*

After crossing the stretch of water they rested, as it was the hottest part of the day, and recommenced their mission after four o'clock in the afternoon:

> *Our march ended at sunset, without our seeing a single native. Our final effort was made at half past one o'clock next morning; and after four hours toil, ended as those preceding it had done, in disappointment and vexation.*

They returned to Sydney, to report another unsuccessful expedition. Whether or not Governor Phillip lamented his decision, after that brief but highly charged period, cannot be fully known. However, Collins his secretary later wrote that the governor had 'resorted with reluctance' to the action but that it had been deemed 'absolutely necessary'. Collins also suggested after the event, that there had been 'little probability' of the troops actually finding the people they had been sent to punish. But it was hoped that the mere 'threat' the expedition had posed may have been enough to put the fear of the British into the 'accused' band of natives. His actual words were:

> *The very circumstance of a party being armed and detached purposely to punish the man and his companions who wounded McEntire, was likely to have a good effect, as it was well known to several natives in the town of Sydney, that this was the intention with which they were sent out.*

Had they really hoped the rumour mill would resolve the issue without the use of hatchets and bags?

✬

Lieutenant Dawes, who had struggled with his conscience throughout the excursion, made a bold announcement on his return to Sydney. He had been appalled by what he had been persuaded to do and made it formally known that he would never again obey such an order. The governor, of course, could not allow such insubordination. He labelled Dawes' reaction as 'unofficerlike' and demanded an unconditional apology, which the young officer was not prepared to give. Under different circumstances, the situation would have led to a court martial but in their isolated state, the governor later claimed it was necessary at times *'to pass over improprieties which could not otherwise have passed unnoticed'*. Dawes, with his engineering and surveying skills, was a talented and very useful young man. However, when he applied to stay in the colony for a further three years, he was informed that his only option was to transfer to the New South Wales Corps which would involve taking a demotion. Although other officers and marines were given incentives to stay as settlers, it was unfeasible for Dawes to remain in the colony.

✬

In the meantime, individuals and groups among the black community were pondering their response to the white leader's military operation.

Bennelong and others could see opportunities and advantages in maintaining a relationship with the white settlers and therefore persevered in trying to understand the strange workings of the white camp.

Pemulwuy, the man the governor had set out to punish, had a considerably different viewpoint. He had eluded the white men by fading back into the wilderness but he was not finished with the British yet...He would bide his time, but he would never back down.

★

42

Growth and adjustment

Sydney - 1791

The new year heralded in a short period of positivity for the British colony. Collins tells us that on the first day, *'the convicts were excused from all kind of labour'* to welcome the forthcoming year. The colony seemed to take on a new tempo and exude fresh confidence prompting wishes for happiness and prosperity to be exchanged between the settlers. The place had a more established feel due to its increased population; the arrival of convicts from diverse backgrounds and the influx of many black residents had introduced a multicultural component. By then too, the colonists were finally seeing some results for their initial hard work in agriculture. At last there were tangible rewards for all their perseverance and planning. Watkin Tench wrote of an incident which he labelled 'trivial' but by its very inclusion in his journal, he clearly found deeply satisfying:

> *On the 24th of January, two bunches of grapes were cut in the governor's garden, from cuttings of vines brought three years before from the Cape of Good Hope. The bunches were handsome, the fruit of a moderate size, well filled out and the flavour high and delicious.*

The governor was feeling optimistic about the colony's prospects, writing that *'its future independency as to the necessities of life'* was not in doubt. He also marked January 26th, *'in commemoration of the day on which formal possession was taken of this cove three years before'* by hoisting the British flag.

However, as summer set in, the settlers began experiencing their hottest summer yet. One day at Parramatta, Tench recorded the temperature to be 109° (over 40° Celsius), saying the wind *'felt like the blast of a heated oven'*, scorching everything in the gardens and farms.

> *Our dogs, pigs and fowls, lay panting in the shade, or were rushing into the water. But even this heat was far exceeded in the latter end of February, when the north-west wind again set in, and blew with great violence for three days.*

On the coast, in Sydney, it must have been just as hot and windy as people recorded seeing bats and birds literally drop out of the trees:

> *An immense flight of bats driven before the wind, covered all the trees around the settlement, whence they every moment dropped dead or in a dying state, unable to endure the burning state of the atmosphere... In several parts of the harbour the ground was covered with different sorts of small birds, some dead, others gasping for water.*

The hot gusty conditions of the summer of 1791 were accompanied by drought which seriously affected Sydney's water supply. As the streams around the cove began to dry up, and fresh water became ever scarcer, Elizabeth Macarthur, experiencing the effects of her first southern summer, realised she had never before really understood or appreciated the importance of rain. In a letter to England, she described the hot winds and heat of the summer of 1791 as 'oppressive'. Trying to explain the weather conditions to her English friend, on the opposite side of the world where cool weather and gentle showers were the norm, she wrote of how they dealt with the scorching hot winds:

> *...we have no other resource but to shut ourselves in our houses and to endeavour to the utmost of our power to exclude every breath of air.*

In the same letter, she described her faintheartedness during ensuing summer storms.

These winds are generally succeeded by a thunderstorm so severe and awful that it is impossible for one who has not been a witness to such a violent concussion of the elements to form any notion of it; it is so different from the thunder we have in England. I cannot help being a little cowardly...

Though she found the force of her first Sydney storms frightening beyond her imagination, she soon began to welcome the rumble of distant thunder and the anticipation of a pounding deluge. Water was then caught in buckets, bowls and whatever else would hold it during those downpours because, except for brief storms, there was little other rain.

As the freshwater stream that ran through the Sydney settlement began dwindling, the governor, always thinking ahead, began plans for the stonemasonry gangs to cut large 'tanks', as reservoirs, out of the rock beside the stream in the hope of reserving enough water *'to supply the settlement for some time'.* The innovation took months to complete and ever after the watercourse was referred to as the 'Tank Stream'.

In the meantime, the blistering heat must have been unbearable for those compelled to work outside under the blazing sun; the struggle to grow vegetables under those conditions must have been disheartening. Tench describes some unfortunate effects of that extreme summer:

Gardens were plundered, provisions pilfered, and the Indian corn stolen from the fields where it grew for public use... The governor ordered convict offenders either to be chained together or to wear singly a large iron collar with two spikes projecting from it, which effectually hindered the party from concealing it under his shirt; and thus shackled, they were compelled to perform their quota of work.

In addition, the natives in and around the settlement complained that they were still being robbed of their spears and fishing tackle. Tench recorded the punishment of a male convict after he was found to have stolen fishing equipment from Daringa, wife of Colbee:

198

The governor ordered that he should be severely flogged in the presence of as many natives as could be assembled, to whom the cause of punishment should be explained. Many of them, of both sexes, accordingly attended.

But the spectacle had not received the reaction the governor had anticipated from the natives:

There was not one of them that did not testify strong abhorrence of the punishment and equal sympathy with the sufferer. The women were particularly affected; Daringa shed tears, and Barangaroo, kindling into anger, snatched a stick and menaced the executioner.

Evidently, the Aboriginal men and women were still not accustomed to British forms of justice; and Barangaroo, being an assertive, compassionate and somewhat impulsive woman had been unable to stand by and watch a fellow human being viciously flogged while suffering the indignity of being tied up. As she took matters into her own hands and single-handedly confronted the attacker, the British saw further evidence that Bennelong's wife had a mind of her own.

★

43

Life and death

During 1791, Bennelong and Barangaroo, whose immediate family thus far had included several orphaned black children, welcomed their own baby into the world; a little girl they named Dilboong, meaning 'bell bird'. Bennelong had wanted his baby's birth to take place at Government House, as a way of forging stronger bonds with the powerful white leader, but the governor had suggested the hospital as a better option. In being born within the perimeter of the white settlement Bennelong's child would forever have a connection to that place, thereby cementing ties to the white man's camp. When the time came however, Barangaroo gave birth in a secluded place of her own choosing a short distance from the settlement. There, she placed her newborn daughter on a soft, specially-prepared paperbark blanket while she sterilised a splinter of bone over fire before cutting the baby's umbilical cord. To Barangaroo, childbirth was women's business.

Sadly, Barangaroo didn't live long after the birth of her baby girl. The cause of her death wasn't recorded, but as she was estimated to be in her forties by that time, her age could have been a factor.

A contributing cause may also have been a fight between her and her husband close to the time of Dilboong's birth: Barangaroo and Bennelong had been known to have a passionately volatile partnership. Their relationship had vacillated between heated arguments resulting in Barangaroo's treatment by Surgeon John White for blows to her head; at other times, they had showed tenderness and devotion to each other.

Tench remembered an argument between the couple soon after his introduction to Barangaroo which demonstrated what could happen when she was unhappy with her husband. The disagreement had arisen because she had not wanted him to visit Sydney:

> *When she found persuasion vain, she had recourse to tears, scolding, and threats, stamping the ground and tearing her hair. But Bennelong continuing determined, she snatched up in her rage one of his fish-gigs, and dashed it with such fury on the rocks, that it broke...*

Bennelong, however, proved he could be equally explosive:

> *Bennelong, eyeing the broken fish-gig, cast at her a look of savage fury and began to interrogate her, and it seemed more than probable that the remaining part would be demolished about her head had we not intervened to pacify him.*

Yet, in the end, Barangaroo had won. Bennelong, it appeared, was easily charmed by his wife:

> *The conduct of Barangaroo succeeded in subduing Bennelong who, when we parted, seemed anxious only to please her.*

Barangaroo, by her beauty, as well as her temperament, had made an impression from the day she had first agreed to visit Sydney with her husband. John Hunter had commented at the time:

> *...she is very straight and exceeding well made; her features are good, and though she goes entirely naked, yet there is such an air of innocence about her that clothing scarcely appears necessary.*

Barangaroo's dynamic personality had been impossible to ignore and her sudden demise would leave a void. When she died, her grieving Bennelong asked his friend, Governor Phillip, to be his daughter's foster father and to find a white woman to nurse his baby. During his earliest phase in the settlement, Bennelong had given the governor the privileged title *'Be-anna'* (father). Now the governor, who was childless, was to learn this also brought family ties and responsibilities. David Collins explains the native custom:

> *On inquiry we were informed, that in case a father should die, the nearest of kin, or some deputed friend, would take the care of his children; and for this reason those children called them Be-anna, though in the lifetime of their natural parent.*

> *Bennelong confirmed to us at the death of his wife...the care of his infant daughter Dil-boong (who at the time of her mother's decease was at the breast) went to his friend Governor Phillip, telling him that he was to become the Be-anna or father of his little girl.*

Barangaroo's funeral took place in the governor's garden with Judge Advocate, David Collins, Chief Surgeon John White and Governor Phillip standing alongside the grieving Bennelong and his kinfolk. After being wrapped in an English blanket, she was cremated with her basket of fishing gear placed beside her.

When little Dilboong died shortly after her mother, she was also buried in the governor's garden, where Bennelong sat vigil until the following morning. Collins recorded this incident too:

> *The ceremony of sleeping at the grave of the deceased was observed by Bennelong after the death of his little child Dilboong; he and two or three other natives passing the night in the governor's garden, not very far from the spot where it was buried.*

Collins, always interested in Aboriginal practices, related another observance associated with the death of their loved ones. Bennelong had told his British friends not to mention the name of the deceased; it was an important observance, *'a custom they rigidly attended to themselves whenever anyone died'.* Wanting to know more about his beliefs about life and death, Collins approached the subject with his black friend:

'Where do the black men (or Eora) come from?' he asked Bennelong, careful to record his question accurately in his journal:

> *His answer was, they came from the clouds (alluding perhaps to the aborigines of the country); and when they died, they returned to the clouds (Boo-row-e). He wished to make me understand that they ascended in the shape of little children, first hovering in the tops and in the branches of trees...*

Collins added that his discussion with Bennelong had *'excited a smile'* that the natives' beliefs about life were not so very different to his own.

☆

44

Forward planning

As 1791 progressed, Governor Phillip continued to plan ahead for the settlement, but he also began formulating personal plans. He was feeling weary and during the past few years had been increasingly unwell and in pain. As a result, he decided to officially apply to the authorities in England for a replacement and for permission to return to England:

> *I have never been a week free from a pain in my side, which undermines and wears me out, and though this colony is not exactly in the state in which I would have wished to have left it, another year may do much, and…if settlers are sent out, (will) answer in every respect the end proposed by government in making the settlement.*

His paternal attention to the colony had been hampered by the lack of cooperation and ongoing offences by the marines and convicts; but he remained optimistic about its future. Ideally he hoped the British government would send free settlers, but in the meantime his strategy for building the colony involved the convicts whose sentences had expired or would soon expire; many of them had served years of their conviction in English prisons before being sent to New South Wales. He wanted to encourage as many of them as possible to stay on as farmers. Watkin Tench recorded the governor's policy:

> *On the first of May, many allotments of ground were parcelled out by the governor to convicts whose periods of transportation were expired, and who voluntarily offered to become settlers in the country.*

It was an incredible opportunity for convicts, who in Britain would never have been given such a break. On the other hand, it was a complete disregard for the rights of the original custodians of the land. The governor's decision may have been well-meant, but it presumed that the land was vacant.

Before the year ended, more than a thousand white settlers would move westward to the town of Parramatta and its surrounds, in addition to the hundreds already there.

★

When Pemulwuy, the man who had speared McEntire and prompted the governor's punitive expedition, heard that many more white people were moving inland, he knew something would have to be done. He had no idea of their actual numbers, but the impact of the *Berewalgal (men from afar)* on the land of his people was sadly apparent wherever they settled. There must be a response to the displacement of his people and Pemulwuy knew he would be the one to lead it. But he would not be impulsive. He would continue to bide his time, building support among his people for a defensive strategy against the incursion into their land.

The regions now being cleared and developed were traditionally areas where yams were dug, edible ferns and other greens were gathered and animals were hunted. These food sources were particularly important when fish was scarce. The areas the white men had built on were places where material for weapons, canoes and fishing gear had customarily been collected and crafted by his people. The white men's clearing methods were not justifiable.

Pemulwuy was well aware that his people had superior knowledge and expertise in bush survival and that they could use these skills to advantage. The white men were heavily dependent on the produce they farmed, so sporadic attacks on their crops would send a message to the settlers that not all the black people would watch passively as their land was taken. He would devise a way to counter the white men's powerful weapons and make his move when the time was right. But that time was not yet.

★

45

New territory

By autumn 1791 Watkin Tench knew his days in the colony were dwindling. He would be leaving before the year's end and he wanted to make the most of the remaining time. The colony had been settled for almost four years and no-one had conquered the Blue Mountains to the west of the settled areas. He thought about the earlier expeditions that had been made and how much tougher they had been than anyone expected. Another expedition westward was being planned, across the impressive river he had found west of Rose Hill, and into the unknown wilderness beyond. He was looking forward to seeing what was out there.

Unbeknown to them at the outset, this journey would prove to be their most significant yet and would add greatly to the explorers' knowledge of the mysterious interior and the natives who lived there. The expedition this time included Governor Phillip, David Collins, Dr White the surgeon, Lieutenant Dawes and some soldiers, gamekeepers, and servants and of course our gallant correspondent Watkin Tench; over twenty men altogether. Two natives, Colbee and another well-liked young native man, Ballooderry, volunteered to accompany the expedition (into territory unfamiliar to them also) after assurances that the explorers would *not stay out many days*' and that there would be *plenty of provisions*' taken. Colbee also stipulated *with great care and consideration*' that, during his absence, his wife and child would be cared for in the Sydney settlement.

Tench outlined in his journal the preparation involved for such an arduous journey for the benefit of his British readers who, in all likelihood, were only familiar with ambling along well maintained roads in the relative tameness of the English countryside. Painting the picture, Tench explained that the explorers must be prepared *'to drag through morasses, tear through thickets, ford rivers and scale rocks'*:

> *But before we set out, let me describe our equipment, and try to convey...an account of those preparations which are required in traversing the wilderness. Every man (the governor excepted) carried his own knapsack, which contained provisions for ten days. If to this be added a gun, a blanket, and a canteen, the weight will fall nothing short of forty pounds. Slung to the knapsack are the cooking kettle and the hatchet, with which the wood to kindle the nightly fire and build the nightly hut is to be cut down.*

In addition to carrying their hefty loads of at least twenty kilos each, the men knew from previous experience that their clothes and shoes had to be sturdy enough to withstand the harsh terrain: the thick prickly brushwood, the uneven, stony surface and dangerously steep mountain-sides. They really didn't know what they would encounter this time, but tried to be mentally and physically prepared. Tench, obviously relishing the image of himself at the centre of a journey thwart with difficulties, continued to paint a picture of the hardships they would face in the untamed mountains; contrasting the experience with the relative ease of a traveller in rural Britain who could stop for rest and a meal at a farmhouse or inn:

> *The march begins at sunrise, and with occasional halts continues until about an hour and a half before sunset. It is necessary to stop early to prepare for passing the night, for... instead of the cheering blaze, the welcoming landlord and the long bill of fare, the traveller has now to collect his fuel, to erect his wigwam, to fetch water, and to broil his morsel of salt pork. Let him then lie down, and if it be summer, try whether the effect of fatigue is sufficiently powerful to overcome the bites and stings of the myriads of sand-flies and mosquitoes which buzz around him.*

Once the expedition got underway, his account tells us that not far west of Rose Hill the terrain became difficult and exhausting for the white men:

Monday, April 11, 1791.

At twenty minutes before seven o'clock, we started from the governor's house at Rose Hill...The country for the first two miles...was good, full of grass and without rock or underwood. Afterwards it grew very bad, being full of steep, barren rocks, over which we were compelled to clamber for seven miles...Our fatigue in the morning had, however, been so oppressive that one of the party collapsed; and had not a soldier, as strong as a pack-horse, undertaken to carry his knapsack in addition to his own, we must either have sent him back, or have stopped at a place for the night which did not afford water.

Tench's good friend William Dawes was assigned the job of steering by compass, counting and noting the number of paces, and tallying up the distance covered each night. Despite the governor's misgivings about Dawes since their disagreement over the punitive expedition to Botany Bay, he was well aware of the young Lieutenant's valuable skills as a navigator; they were all very mindful of the inherent danger of getting lost in the vast wilderness. Tench noted:

...by observing this precaution, we always knew exactly where we were, and how far from home; an unspeakable advantage in a new country, where one hill, and one tree, is so like another that fatal wanderings would ensue without it.

Colbee and Ballooderry, never having been so far inland before, had been uneasy about going into unknown territory so they were impressed with the white men's compass, naming it *'naamoro' (to see the way).*

On the first evening of the expedition, as the men were chatting by the fire side and preparing to settle down for the night, they heard voices in the bush a short distance away. Feeling the safety of their numbers, and assuming Colbee would act as intermediary they asked him to call out and invite whoever was out there to come closer, to assure them of good treatment and something to eat. Colbee called out the customary signal of invitation, in a loud hollow cry:

'Cooo-eee!' (Come here; I am here.)

Eventually, according to Watkin Tench's account, after some *'whooping and shouting on both sides'*, a man with a lighted stick approached the campsite. Tench and the others watched with interest, comprehending only a few words as Colbee and the stranger introduced themselves:

'I am Colbee, of the tribe of Cadigal.'

The stranger replied: *'I am Bereewan, of the Boorooberongal.'*

The visitor was invited to join them at the fireside and when the stranger hesitated, Colbee approached him, took him by the hand and led him within the circle of white men. Tench portrays the scene:

> *By the light of the moon, we were introduced to this gentleman, all our names being repeated in form by our master of ceremonies, who said that we were Englishmen... that we came from the sea coast, and that we were travelling inland.*

'Budyeeree', *(They are good men.)* Colbee assured the stranger confidently, pointing to the group of unusually pale beings standing in the firelight in their strange body coverings. After a long conversation between the two black men, and having accepted some provisions, the visitor departed 'highly satisfied'. It was a good start to their inland trek and the white men turned in for the night feeling optimistic. It was the first time they had actually encountered a black man so far inland.

During the following days the group travelled over varied landscape: trudging through swampy ground, scaling and sliding down rock faces and tumbling amidst prickly undergrowth. During the journey, Colbee and Ballooderry apparently amused themselves in making light of the difficulties encountered by the white men. Tench records:

> *They walked stoutly, appeared little fatigued, and maintained their spirits admirably, laughing to excess when any of us either tripped or stumbled...*

There was apparently banter going on from all sides. When any of the white men cursed or snapped at their native companions after being *'stung at once with nettles and ridicule, and shaken near to death by his fall'*, Colbee or Ballooderry immediately responded by calling back *'their favourite terms of reproach, 'goninpatta',* which Tench wrote, *'signifies an eater of human excrement'*. (An expression which he acknowledged had an equally descriptive English equivalent.)

At the end of the third day Tench described the white men's fatigue as excessive; but said their native companions seemed *'rather enlivened than exhausted by it'*:

> *...their principal source of merriment again derived from our tumbling amidst nettles, and sliding down precipices, which they mimicked with inimitable drollery.*

Soon however Colbee and Ballooderry began to get tired of wandering aimlessly around unfamiliar bush, living off the contents of backpacks and began asking continually and urgently when they would be heading home, making it clear they wanted to go back to the comforts of Rose Hill. Watkin Tench recorded their sentiments:

> *'At Rose Hill', said they, 'are potatoes, cabbages, pumpkins, turnips, fish and wine; here are nothing but rocks and water.'*

> *These comparisons constantly ended with the question of, 'Where's Rose Hill? Where?' on which they would throw up their hands and utter a sound to denote distance.*

The two Aboriginal men had apparently already decided that for them, life in the township of the white men was preferable to life in unfamiliar bushland. To pacify them the white men, still wanting to continue their exploration, said they would be heading home to Rose Hill 'soon', but *'avoided naming how many days'*.

☆

In due course the travellers came upon a river but were unsure which of the previously discovered 'Hawkesbury' or 'Nepean' rivers it was, and whether in fact those rivers were one and the same. Soon after, they met natives from the new territory. Tench's journal tells us:

> We had not proceeded far when we saw several canoes on the river. Our natives made us immediately lie down among the reeds, while they gave their countrymen the signal of approach. After much calling, finding that they did not come, we continued our progress until it was again interrupted by a creek, over which we threw a tree and passed upon it.
>
> While this was happening, a native from his canoe entered into conversation with us, and immediately after, paddled to us with a frankness and confidence which surprised everyone. He was a man of middle age, with an open cheerful countenance, marked with the small pox, and distinguished by a nose of uncommon magnitude and dignity...
>
> Two stone hatchets, and two spears he took from his canoe, and presented to the governor, who in return for his courteous generosity, gave him two of our hatchets and some bread, which was new to him, for he knew not its use, but kept looking at it, until Colbee showed him what to do, when he ate it without hesitation.

Though Colbee hadn't met these inland natives before, he took delight in playing host and introduced each of the white men by name to the black visitor. The explorers were keen to continue their course, and their new acquaintance pointed out the best path and walked ahead of them along the riverside. A man and small boy in a canoe appeared and stayed abreast of them, paddling gently as the white men followed the water's edge. The wives and children of the black guides were on the opposite bank and the black men frequently spoke with them as they continued down the river. Tench was surprised that the natives did not appear suspicious or uneasy of the white men's intentions. When they stopped for the night, their guide introduced the man from the canoe as Yellomundee. This man, and his children, would play a significant role in the precarious interactions between black and white in future years. For now both parties were intrigued and intent on learning about the other.

Later in the evening the natives gathered around the fire with the white strangers, shared their biscuit and pork and drank from their water bottles. The explorers recorded that they were astounded at the friendliness of their hosts; *'the ease with which these people behaved among strangers... without betraying any symptom of fear, distrust or surprise'.*

Watkin Tench wanted to know more about how the natives survived in the forests, away from the coast. He asked a lot of questions, with signs and Colbee's help, about their language, medicine and food. He noticed when Colbee and Yellomundee spoke, although each understood the other, many of the most common and necessary words were different. It became apparent that the coastal natives and the inland forest people spoke different dialects. Tench was particularly curious to know what they lived on, as the white men on their previous expeditions had never found anything edible in the woodlands:

> *What we were able to learn from them was that they depend little on fish...and that their principal support is derived from small animals which they kill, and some roots (a species of wild yam chiefly) which they dig out of the earth.*

The men continued their easy camaraderie late into the evening, where stretched out before a fire *'all sides continued to chat and entertain each other'.* The white men listened with curiosity as the older man pointed to battle scars on his body, telling them his combat stories. Colbee told Yellomundee he had the splintered remains of a spear shaft in his chest and asked the man to use his special powers to remove them. Colbee explained to his white companions that Yellomundee was a man with special healing skill, a *koradji.* Tench recorded this to mean 'renowned doctor'.

Yellomundee went through a complicated process, as the white men looked on, intrigued. Using water he sprayed Colbee's wound, then extracted the spear splinters by putting his mouth over the wound. He withdrew from the group then immediately re-joined them at the fireside. The white men weren't sure what to think, but when they observed the serious, silent attention given by the other natives, they knew they were witnessing something mystical.

At the end of the procedure, Colbee demonstrated that the wound was now healed. The white men examined the place where Colbee swore there had been a gash and it appeared undamaged. But in the end Watkin Tench was dubious:

> *The operator pretended to receive something in his mouth... With this he retired a few paces, put his hand to his lips and threw into the river a stone, which I had observed him to pick up...When he returned to the fireside, Colbee assured us that he had received benefit from the operation...We examined the part, but it was smooth and whole, so that to the force of imagination alone must be imputed to both the wound and its cure.*

It was then Yellomundee's turn to learn more about the white men:

> *Colbee informed him who we were; of our numbers at Sydney and Rose Hill, of the stores we possessed and, above all, of the good things which were to be found among us, enumerating potatoes, cabbages, turnips, pumpkins, and many other names which were perfectly unintelligible to the person who heard them, but which he nevertheless listened to with profound attention.*

The men of both cultures had shown an openness to learn about the other.

> *The native men remained with us all night, sleeping before the fire in the fullness of good faith and security. The little boy slept in his father's arms...*

In the morning the good-natured companionship continued between the newfound friends, as the whole party breakfasted together. The white men then watched a demonstration, given by one of their hosts, of their tree climbing technique. The performance made them gape in awe:

He asked for a hatchet and one of ours was offered to him, but he preferred one of their own making. With this tool he cut a small notch in the tree he intended to climb, about two feet and a half above the ground, in which he fixed the great toe of his left foot, and sprung upwards, at the same time embracing the tree with his left arm. In an instant he had cut a second notch for his right toe on the other side of the tree into which he sprung, and thus, alternately cutting on each side, he mounted to the height of twenty feet in nearly as short a space as if he had ascended by a ladder, although the bark of the tree was quite smooth and slippery and the trunk four feet in diameter and perfectly strait.

To us it was a matter of astonishment, but to him it was sport; for while employed thus he kept talking to those below and laughing...He descended with as much ease and agility as he had raised himself. Even our natives allowed that he was a capital performer...for as they subsist chiefly by fishing, they are less expert at climbing on the coast.

Later that morning the governor and his men shook hands with their hosts and they reciprocated enthusiastically. Colbee bade goodbye to his new acquaintances with *'a nod of the head, the usual salutation of the country'*. As the white men walked away from the scene, Watkin Tench thought about how much territory had been covered in a few days - not merely physical territory - he was pondering the *'unabated friendship and good humour'* that had existed between the two groups of men. This was the explorers' first encounter with the inland, 'freshwater' people of the Hawkesbury region. Governor Phillip's goal of an amicable relationship with the natives was expanding into new territory.

To the 'great joy' of Colbee and Ballooderry, the following day the governor decided to head homeward. When it was learnt that a boat was due to leave from Rose Hill for Sydney that afternoon, they rushed ahead in order to catch it. They could not wait to *'communicate to Bennelong and the rest of their countrymen the novelties they had seen.'*

☆

A month later Watkin Tench and William Dawes returned westward and *'settled the long contested point about the Hawkesbury and Nepean'*. Tench wrote with obvious satisfaction: *'We found them to be **one river.**'*

On this journey they met three different native men who were equally friendly and helpful to those met on the previous trip. On hearing the traditional native expression, *'Cooee', (Come here)* they responded in the same way:

> *When we heard a native call...we directly answered him and conversed across the river for some time. At length he launched his canoe and crossed to us without distrust or hesitation. He presented us with two spears and a throwing-stick, and in return we gave him some bread and beef.*

The native man offered to guide them along the river and paddled his canoe as the white men walked alongside, on the riverbank. Further along, the explorers indicated that they were going to try to cross over the river and the native immediately offered his canoe to them. The white men gratefully accepted and their provisions were paddled across without getting wet. Other natives willingly made three trips across and back to bring all the explorers' provisions across the water. The explorers were impressed with the honesty of the natives who could have stolen their food and guns while they were separated from their provisions by the river. Tench, after experiencing the dishonesty of the white population in Sydney, admired the natives' integrity:

> *During this long trial of their patience and courtesy, in the latter part of which I was entirely in their power... they had manifested no sign of taking advantage of the helplessness and dependence of our situation; no rude curiosity to pry into the packages with which they were entrusted; or no sordid desire to possess the contents of them; although among them were articles exposed to view, of which it afterwards appeared they knew the use, and longed for the benefit.*

Later, when Tench shot a hawk that fell and got caught in the branches of a tree, one of the black men offered to climb for it and was lent an iron hatchet to hasten the process. He was so delighted with the hatchet that he asked if he could keep it; a small token for the generous help he had provided. As Tench needed the hatchet to chop wood for their evening fire, he promised that if the man visited them the following morning, it would be given to him:

> *Not a murmur was heard; no suspicion of our insincerity; no mention of benefits conferred; no reproach of ingratitude. His good humour and cheerfulness were not clouded for a moment. Punctual to our appointment, he came to us at daylight next morning and the hatchet was given to him, the only token of gratitude and respect in our power to bestow.*

★

In mid-winter 1791 Tench and Dawes made their final excursion together into the unknown territory of the vast southern land which had so intrigued them. Tench's comments on his trip centred on the striking scenery spread before them one frosty morning, and the extreme coldness they endured while camping in sub-zero temperatures:

> *The sun arose in unclouded splendor and presented to our sight a novel and picturesque view; the country as white as if covered with snow, contrasted with the foliage of (evergreen) trees... Nothing but demonstration could have convinced me that so severe a degree of cold ever existed in this low latitude...Part of a leg of kangaroo, which we had roasted for supper, was frozen quite hard, all the juices of it being converted into ice.*

On their final journey, Tench and Dawes must have been disappointed that they hadn't made any extraordinary 'discoveries', but they had nonetheless added another valuable piece of information for future explorers about the land so disconcertingly full of contrasts and extremes.

★

46

Great escapes

The official expeditions of Watkin Tench and his adventurous companions were not the only excursions outside the known territory of the colony during 1791. There were also a number of daring escapes by convicts. The most audacious and courageous getaway happened one night in March and involved the escape of William and Mary Bryant by sea, with their two small children and seven male absconders. Their determination to flee the colony was evident by their meticulous planning.

William and Mary originally came from the same fishing district in England and had been among the first convicts to be married in the colony. William, due to his experience with commercial fishing, had been entrusted with the oversight of the colony's fishing operations and the couple had, at first, been allowed to live in their own hut beside the water. However, William had found himself in trouble for selling fish privately, allegedly for his own profit and had been publically disgraced and punished with a hundred lashes. The family had also been expelled from their little cabin by the water and moved into the main camp where William could be closely monitored. The governor however had retained him in his role as chief fisherman, as his experience and talent was too valuable not to exploit.

William was burning with resentment at this treatment and had begun plotting his escape in earnest. Mary was anxious to leave too; she wanted a better future for her children and was willing to take great risks to achieve freedom. So William began making discreet enquiries from visiting sailors and began stashing equipment for their escape. The governor had his informers though:

William Bryant, who had been continued in the fishing-boat after the discovery of his malpractices, was, at the latter end of the month, overheard consulting in his hut after dark, with five other convicts, on the practicability of carrying off the boat in which he was employed. This circumstance being reported to the governor, it was determined that all his proceedings should be narrowly watched.

The governor or his watchers could not have seriously believed that a young man and his wife, with two very small children, would be reckless enough to attempt escape into the open sea without compass, charts or provisions. But of course, they had underestimated Bryant.

By this time, the arrival of ships to the harbour was not the rarity it had been a year earlier with the advent of the Second Fleet from England. However when an East Indies trader, *Waaksamheyd* sailed into the harbour in late 1790, it had been a welcome sight. Bryant, taking advantage of the fact that the ship's Dutch captain held a grudge against the British, had managed to buy from him the necessary navigational equipment, as well as gleaning information that would assist him in his passage northward. Cunningly, he also turned a series of other circumstances to his advantage. The colony's best fishing boat, an open, six-oared cutter, used for travel across the harbour and short distances along the coast, had been in an accident and needed repairs so it had just been fitted with new sails, mast and oars. In the meantime, William and his co-conspirators had stashed stolen fishing nets, muskets, ammunition and tools. Mary had accumulated food and gathered medicinal herbs from the bush, including vine leaves commonly used to brew 'sweet tea' by the convicts (now known to be *Smilax glyciphylla*).

The Bryants were clever about their timing too by waiting until just after the *Waaksamheyd* left Sydney to make their move. Then there would be no ships left in the harbour capable of overtaking fugitives in a boat.

It must have been a nerve-racking few hours as Mary, William and their accomplices silently made trips back and forth in the dark to load the boat, push it off shore and row past the sentries on the headland without detection. March 28th was a moonless night and the wind and tide were favourable in aiding the small boat down the harbour and out through the headlands into the vast Pacific. Collins, the governor's secretary records the details:

> In the course of the night of the 28th, Bryant…eluded the watch that was kept upon him, and made his escape, together with his wife and two children (one an infant at the breast) and seven other convicts, in the fishing-boat, which, since the accident at the latter end of the last month, he had taken care to keep in excellent order. Their flight was not discovered until they had been some hours outside the heads.
>
> They were traced from Bryant's hut to the Point, and in the path were found a hand-saw, a scale, and four or five pounds of rice, scattered about in different places, which, it was evident, they had dropped in their haste.
>
> On searching Bryant's hut, cavities under the boards were found, where he had secured the compass and such other articles as required concealment: and he had contrived his escape with such address, that although he was well known to be making an attempt, yet how far he was prepared, as well as the time when he meant to go, remained a secret.

Once they had made it past the high sandstone headlands that marked the entrance to Sydney harbour, they rowed north, keeping the coast in sight whenever possible. Their plan was to head to the islands north of Australia, to the Timor Sea where there were Dutch colonial settlements. Once there, they planned to pose as shipwreck survivors. Many of those remaining in the colony sympathised with their daring actions. One marine, John Easty, wrote in his diary:

> …it's a very desperate attempt, to go in an open boat…and in particular for a woman and two small children, the oldest not above three years of age – but thoughts of liberty from such a place as this is enough to induce convicts to try all schemes to obtain it, as they are the same as slaves all the time they are in this country.

The Bryants and their companions had at first been ecstatic at their new found freedom, but soon reality set in. They had endured violent storms and been soaked by torrential rain and squally seas for days on end. With the boat leaking and in constant fear of sinking they had to continually bail out water to keep it afloat. At other times they were driven far from the coast with no sight of land for long periods; then they were sunbaked and parched for lack of drinking water. When forced to land through starvation and thirst, they experienced frightening encounters with natives along the coast. An account from convict James Martin, a survivor of their ordeal, describes the waves as *running mountains high*:

> *I will leave you to consider what distress we must be in; the woman and the two little babies were in a bad condition; everything being so wet that we couldn't light a fire. We had nothing to eat except a little raw rice.*

Of course, details of their journey and their final fate were not known in Sydney until almost two years later when a visiting ship brought news from the outside world. However, when an account of their disappearance became public in Sydney the day after their escape, it created uproar.

☆

The Bryant's daring escape and their imagined success must have inspired other convicts to try their luck. However, to prevent similar attempts, the sentry guarding all boats was strengthened and the governor directed that only small boats of limited dimensions could be built under strict supervision. So, without opportunity and the necessary equipment or skills for sailing, most of the escapees went inland.

From the founding of the colony there had been many attempts at freedom in the wild forests. The governor and his officials had not suppressed stories of death by starvation in the bush in the hope of discouraging absconders. One man, on returning to the settlement, said he had seen:

...more than fifty skeletons, which the natives assured him had been white men, who had lost their way and perished. This account was corroborated by different European articles which were scattered about, such as knives, old shoes, and other things which were known not to belong to the natives.

But despite these tales, by the end of 1791 mass escapes were becoming more common. In one instance, twenty men and one pregnant woman took to the bush with their clothes, working tools, bedding, and a week's worth of provisions which had just been issued to them. As they were sneaking into the forest from the settlement at Rose Hill, a curious convict settler wondering what was going on, asked where they were headed. A unanimous answer was whispered:

'To China.'

A detachment of troops was sent into the bush after them but after a harrowing and far-reaching search they returned without success. Within a week, however, most of the absconders had staggered back into camp or had been found half-starving by travellers in the outlying bush. When questioned about their escape, they admitted that they had been deceived into believing that China was easily reached, being separated only by a river. Watkin Tench went to the hospital where four of them were recovering from their ordeal:

I asked these men if they really supposed it possible to reach China. They answered that they were certainly made to believe that at a considerable distance northward existed a large river, which separated this country from the back part of China; and that when it was crossed...they would find themselves among a copper-coloured people, who would receive and treat them kindly.

But it had not been as easy as they had anticipated. They told Tench that on the third day of their decampment, one of the party died of fatigue; another they saw attacked by the natives who, finding them unarmed, confronted them and put them to flight. After starvation had taken hold, several of them agreed their scheme wasn't going to work and decided to return to Rose Hill. But they had great difficulty finding their way and when they eventually staggered back into the camp, they were almost dead. The horror stories and failures, however, didn't stop others trying their luck a few months later, as reported by Collins:

> ...*forty-four men and nine women were absent and unaccounted for; among which number were included those who were wandering in the woods, seeking for a new settlement, or endeavouring to get into the path to China!*
>
> *Of these people many, after lingering a long time, and existing merely on roots and wild berries, perished miserably. Others found their way in, after being absent several weeks, and reported the fate of their wretched companions, being themselves reduced to nearly the same condition, worn down and exhausted with fatigue and want of proper sustenance.*
>
> *Yet, although the appearance of these people confirmed their account of what they had undergone, others were still found ignorant and weak enough to run into the woods impressed with the idea of either reaching China by land, or finding a new settlement where labour would not be imposed on them, and where the inhabitants were civil and peaceable.*

Those who saw the bleeding feet, sunken cheeks and battered bodies of the escapees dubbed 'Chinese travellers' recognised their quest for freedom was so strong that *'no risk was too great'*. But it was easy for the officers and marines to criticise the lengths others had taken in the pursuit of liberty. Their own escape from the colony was looming large on the horizon; they would soon be going home to Britain. They'd had word that *HMS Gorgon*, the ship that was commissioned to take them home, was on its way. They could begin formulating plans for life in their homeland.

★

47

Family matters

When Lieutenant George Johnston returned to Sydney from his one-year posting on Norfolk Island in mid-1791 he, like his fellow officers, knew his tour of duty was drawing to a close and that he must make critical decisions regarding his future.

Should he stay in the colony or go home to Britain?

By then he was openly acknowledging his partnership with Esther, writing that, '*Hetty and the two children*' had embarked with him at Norfolk Island bound for Sydney. Nevertheless, it would not have been easy for him to commit to remaining in the colony where life was still a struggle. In the months before *HMS Gorgon* arrived to take the First Fleet officers home, he had voiced sentiments similar to his colleagues:

> *I hope we shall soon see the Gorgon here to carry us to England... I hope we shall soon be in the Land of Plenty.*

However, as the year advanced and the time came for final decision making, Johnston had several important considerations in the reckoning. He was a family man now: as well as the care of Esther's daughter Roseanna, he and Esther had a toddler whom they adored and another baby on the way. He wanted Hetty, as he affectionately called Esther, to be part of his future. She was caring, discreet and industrious, but she was still serving her sentence.

Beside family considerations, there would be material advantages to staying in the colony: the probability of further promotion and encouraging economic prospects. So, although his homeland was exerting a strong pull and New South Wales still lacked the comforts of an established colony, he decided to stay and see what opportunities lay ahead.

Sydney had become a very different place to the town he and Esther had left only a year earlier. While on Norfolk Island they had heard reports of the goings-on in Sydney, but they hadn't been there to witness the dramatic events. They'd missed the spearing of the governor and the arrival of hundreds more convicts on the Second Fleet. The most noticeable change in Sydney however was the large number of black families who had come to live in the town. The governor's cultural project, in which George Johnston had played a major role in the kidnap of Arabanoo in 1788, appeared to have finally brought results. Many Aboriginal people now lived in the homes of white settlers as part of their extended families. The population of Sydney had expanded and diversified; farms were beginning to produce consistently and ships were arriving with provisions. The place was beginning to look as if it had a future; one in which he and Esther could build a life together.

★

48

Arrivals and departures

The arrival of a 'Third Fleet' of ships during the second half of 1791 brought much needed supplies and of course, more convicts. This time, many of the convicts were 'political prisoners' from Ireland adding yet another dimension to the colony. The newly arrived prisoners strongly voiced their grievances to the governor about cruelty and ill-treatment on the voyage. They complained of not receiving an adequate food allowance, and by their pale faces and frail condition it was also evident they had been crammed below deck in extremely unhygienic conditions. Judge Advocate, David Collins, was outraged that the ship's masters had withheld rations and used space that should have been allocated for convicts, to cram in as many 'saleable' items as possible. Believing he spoke for many in the colony, he wrote:

> ...what crime could be more offensive to humanity, than cutting a ration...to derive an advantage from the miseries of our fellow-creatures!

However, as soon as these masters had unburdened the ships of their cargo of convicts, they set up temporary shops offering 'articles of comfort' to settlers at prices way above their usual value; prices which the colonists were evidently coerced into paying. David Collins, in a letter to his father, described the situation:

> ...we now purchase every little article of comfort or convenience from the shipping at the most exorbitant prices; three, four thousand per cent being charged on many articles...

The matter was reported to England for investigation in the hope of preventing similar cases in the future. In the meantime, the ships' masters, knowing the settlers had been living without basic necessities for some time, sold their goods for the highest possible profit. What they couldn't sell in Sydney, could be traded in India on their return journey.

As convicts arriving on the recent ships were adding thousands to the population of the colony, other convicts, whose terms of transportation were at an end, were in a position to leave if they had the means. The governor, following instructions to persuade as many as possible to stay in the colony, offered incentives:

> *The convicts whose terms of transportation had expired were now collected and by the authority of the governor informed that such of them as wished to become settlers in this country should receive every encouragement...Those desirous of returning to England were informed that no obstacle would be thrown in their way, they being at liberty to ship themselves on board such vessels as would give them a passage.*

But those wishing to return to their homeland were in an unenviable situation; there was no such thing as a free ride back to England for convicts. The return passage had to be paid for by work, money or by some other sort of sponsorship, and as convicts were not generally capable of meeting the payment, there were many attempted stowaways on ships returning to Britain.

One of those ships was the lately arrived *HMS Gorgon*, commissioned to take the marines and officers of the First Fleet back to England at the end of 1791. Many of them, including Watkin Tench and William Dawes, would be leaving the colony for good, as their 'tour of duty' had ended. They would be sailing across the great expanse of ocean to the opposite end of the earth once again. This time however, they were heading to the familiar sights of England, to the assured comforts of civilisation and the waiting arms of their families. They were going home.

★

As the marines were preparing to embark on the recently anchored *Gorgon*, some important dignitaries were disembarking. Captain Paterson of the NSW Corps and his young wife Elizabeth were to enjoy a short stop-over in Sydney, en route to Norfolk Island. Also returning to resume his command of Norfolk Island was Lieutenant King, and with him, to the surprise of his colleagues in Sydney, was his new wife Anna Josepha. An added element to the unexpected news of his marriage was that King's wife was almost eight months pregnant. To the delight of Elizabeth Macarthur, here at last was the longed-for female company she had been missing. She looked forward to socialising with ladies of her own standing after being so long deprived.

Governor Phillip put on a dinner party enabling the young wives to become acquainted, and tours of the harbour and elaborate picnics were also arranged for the entertainment of the new arrivals. As the dignitaries were shown around Sydney and its environs, their reactions were eagerly observed by the longer-term residents of Sydney, and they were pleased to note that Lieutenant King's young wife showed enthusiasm for everything she saw. Elizabeth Macarthur described Anna Josepha King in a letter to England as having *'a great share of good nature and frankness'*; the prospect of her company she said, was a *'pleasant consideration'*. Lieutenant Clark made a private observation in his journal that *'Mrs King appears to be a genteel woman'* but *'not very pretty'* and that *'Mrs Patterson, a good cosy Scott lass, fit for a soldiers' wife.'* The new arrivals were evidently quite a novelty and as such, the topic of the moment. Mrs Parker, the *Gorgon* captain's wife, was described by Elizabeth Macarthur as *'a very amiable, intelligent woman'*. The Captain's wife, in turn, gave a glowing description of the colony, the countryside and the governor:

> We made several excursions up the cove to the settlement at Parramatta. I was surprised to find that so great a progress had been made in this new settlement which contains above a thousand convicts besides the military.
>
> The gentle ascents, the winding valleys and the abundance of flowering shrubs render the face of the country very delightful...the fatherly attention of the good Governor on all

*occasions with the friendly politeness of the officers rendered
our sojourn perfectly happy and comfortable.*

But to the disappointment of Elizabeth, her time of socialising with young women of her own social standing was to be short-lived. Captain Parker and his wife would be returning to England on *Gorgon*, and the Patersons and the Kings, after a five week stopover in Sydney would be on their way to Norfolk Island, where Captain Paterson was to take up a posting with the NSW Corps and King would recommence his command of the island, as Lieutenant Governor.

☆

When Lieutenant King had arrived in Sydney with his pregnant young wife on his arm, Ann Inett knew he would eventually visit her. Despite his recent marriage, he had his 'other family' to consider and he had assured his convict mistress in the past that he would take responsibility for the welfare of his two illegitimate sons by her. The Lieutenant would have things to discuss with her. He would want to see his sons, Norfolk, who was by then over two years old, and little Sydney (named after his birthplace) who was by then fifteen months old. It was possibly an uncomfortable meeting but the past lovers had a shared interest in the well-being of their sons.

King told Ann that he wanted to give his boys the best chance in life; he would make sure they both had a good education and fulfilling careers. He said he had explained their relationship to his new wife, a wonderfully understanding woman who had agreed to take the little boys into her care as part of the King family. Ann had at first been dazed but decided that her sons' future must take precedence over her own needs. It was not the first time she had parted with her children; she'd had no choice but to leave her two young ones behind in England when she had been transported in the First Fleet. It was happening again, but at least this time she could be confident they would benefit from her sacrifice. It was arranged that two year old Norfolk would accompany King and his new wife when they left the mainland a month later and little Sydney would follow when he was older.

★

Accompanying the Kings to Norfolk Island, as a domestic servant would be the *'quiet and sober'* female convict, Jane Dundas. She was the young woman who had landed herself in prison in England for pawning her employer's linen in the hope of winning the lottery with the proceeds. She had subsequently, by her *'good conduct'*, secured herself a role in the household of Governor Phillip who had, with the arrival of the Kings, recommended and offered Jane's services to them. Once on Norfolk Island with the Kings, Jane's role would be the wearying task of attending to the needs of the family in relatively basic conditions, but she would again be working for the most prominent household in the community. She had not won the lottery but she had landed herself another enviable position and would become a valued companion to Mrs King.

★

With the departure of the Kings to Norfolk Island, Ann Inett was in no doubt that her relationship with the lieutenant was over and knew she must move on. She would marry Richard Robinson, a steady, reliable man who had been transported to the colony with a life sentence on the same ship as the Macarthurs, though he had travelled in the bowels of the *Scarborough* with the dying and the dead. Ann was aware that on parting with her little boys - when they had both become part of the King household - she may never see them again; in due course they would likely be sent to England to be educated. She would have to focus on the benefits for her children and not allow herself time to dwell on the past. She must busy herself, look to the future with her new husband and make plans that didn't include her little boys. It was all for the best she must tell herself.

★

49

Nanberry and Ballooderry

Meanwhile, during the second half of 1791, Nanberry was another little boy making his way in the world in the care of a foster-parent. When his small black body had been carried feverish and listless into the camp, in the aftermath of the smallpox epidemic two years earlier, he had been taken into the home of the doctor, John White. As the adopted son of the colony's Chief Surgeon, he had mixed with the leading members of white society. He had quickly learnt and copied all the manners and habits that were seemingly of great importance to his British hosts, complying with their codes of social behaviour as he could see they expected. He had enjoyed extravagant dinners at Government House and at Governor Phillip's table he had delighted in impressing the softly spoken, pretty white lady, Elizabeth Macarthur with his table etiquette. According to his hosts, young Nanberry had showed little desire to return to '*the society of his birth*' and '*stuck very close*' to his new white friends.

In reality however, Nanberry often felt the pull of his own culture and frequently returned to play in the bush around the harbour with the young black children who lived in the vicinity. At times he willingly acted as informant to members of his own race when he thought they were in danger of getting the poor end of the bargain in some retaliatory action from the governor. On one occasion of that nature, he had stripped and run naked through the bush undetected to warn his good friend Ballooderry that Governor Phillip had sent a party of soldiers to apprehend him.

The whole sad story of the trouble between Ballooderry and Governor Phillip must have affected Nanberry deeply. The unhappy episode began during a period when many natives, including Ballooderry, had taken up the practice of bartering some of their surplus catch of fish in exchange for bread and salt meat with the white residents at Parramatta. Ballooderry was a well-liked young man and had a good rapport with Governor Phillip. In fact he frequently stayed at Government House and the governor had talked about taking him to England.

He was very proud of his new trading enterprise in his recently built canoe, so imagine his distress on returning to the banks of the Parramatta River one day to find it had been smashed to pieces. David Collins tells us:

> *There were among the convicts some who were so unthinking, or so depraved, as wantonly to destroy a canoe belonging to a fine young man, who had left it at some little distance from the settlement and he hoped out of the way of observation, while he went with some fish to the huts. His rage at finding his canoe destroyed was inconceivable and he threatened to take his own revenge and in his own way...*

Ballooderry, devastated by the demolition of his treasured canoe, was assured by the governor that the guilty party would be punished. But he decided to take matters into his own hands and deal with the issue according to tribal law which held that payback could extend to other members of the offender's mob. In the days following the destruction of his canoe he speared and wounded a convict unrelated to the incident, someone who just happened to be passing by.

> *This act of Ballooderry's was followed by the governor's strictly forbidding him to appear again at any of the settlements; the other natives, his friends, being alarmed, Parramatta was seldom visited by any of them, and all commerce with them was destroyed...Those who knew Ballooderry regretted that it had been necessary to treat him with this harshness, as among his countrymen we had nowhere seen a finer young man.*

As Watkin Tench suggested at the time:

> *The truth was, some mischievous person belonging to us had wantonly destroyed his canoe, and he revenged the injury on the first of our people whom he met unarmed. He now seemed to think the matter adjusted; and probably such is the custom they observe in their own society in similar cases.*

Ballooderry however was banned from the settlements. When he was sighted near the town and a band of soldiers were sent to bring him in, it was young Nanberry who took off into the bush along a short-cut to warn his friend that the soldiers were on their way. John Hunter recorded the incident in his journal:

> *...a party of soldiers were ordered out to secure Ballooderry; but before they got sight of him, the boy Nanberry heard what was going on and left the place...true to his countrymen, on seeing the soldiers form on the parade, ran into the woods, and stripping himself, that he might not be known, joined the natives, and put them on their guard; after which he returned and seeing the governor go past with some officers, while he was hid in a bush, he afterwards showed himself to an officer's servant and asked where the governor and the soldiers were going, and being told, he laughed, and said they were too late, for the natives were all gone.*

Over the ensuing months Bennelong tried to act as arbitrator and end the disagreement between the men who had previously been on good terms, but Governor Phillip remained adamant that the young man must answer for his attack on an uninvolved, unarmed individual. That was until several months later when he learnt that Ballooderry was extremely ill and in need of medical attention. Governor Phillip immediately sent Surgeon White who found Ballooderry in a fever:

> *...the first question (Ballooderry) asked was whether the Governor was still angry, or if he would let him be brought to the hospital to be cured.*

Bennelong still acting as intermediary returned with the surgeon to Governor Phillip who said he was not angry and told him to bring Ballooderry to the settlement...

> At first, (Ballooderry) seemed under great apprehensions, but they presently subsided, on the governor taking him by the hand, and promising that when he was recovered he should reside with him again...Poor Ballooderry appeared to be very ill, and went with the surgeon to the hospital.

Although Bennelong and his companions were willing to see their friend treated at the hospital, they were eager to administer their own methods of healing too. The English doctor, after doing what he could for Ballooderry, stepped aside and made way for Bennelong to perform a procedure he hoped would bring a cure:

> Bennelong applied his mouth to those parts of his patient's body which he thought were affected, breathing strongly on them, and singing: at times he waved over him some boughs dipped in water, holding one in each hand, and seemed to treat him with much attention and friendship.

Two days later a *koradji, (man of special power)* came to the hospital to perform a healing ritual. The period of Ballooderry's illness shows how those involved from each culture tried to understand and respect the ways of the other. However, at the end of the day, all the remedies in the world (or the governor's change of heart) could not save their much-loved Ballooderry.

> He was at this time at our hospital; during the night his fever increased, and his friends, thinking he would be better with them, put him into a canoe, intending to take him to the north shore; but he died as they were carrying him over. This was immediately notified to us by a violent clamour among the women and children; and Bennelong soon after coming into the town, it was agreed upon between him and the governor that the body should be buried in the governor's garden.

233

*In the afternoon it was brought over in a canoe...the body
was wrapped up in the jacket which he usually wore, and
some pieces of blanketing tied round it...At the request of
Bennelong, a blanket was laid over the corpse, and Cole-be
his friend sat by the body all night, nor could he be prevailed
on to quit it. They remained rather silent till about one in the
morning, when the women began to cry, and continued for
some time.*

Boorong was there, mourning the death of her older brother. She had
learnt only a year or so earlier that some of her family, including her
brother Ballooderry, had survived the smallpox epidemic and he had
subsequently come to live in the settlement. But now she was saying
goodbye to him. Collins' account gives a moving insight into the cross-
cultural nature of Ballooderry's funeral:

*At daylight Bennelong brought his canoe to the place, and
cutting it to a proper length, the body was placed in it, with
a spear, a fiz-gig, a throwing-stick, and a line which Ba-loo-
derry had worn round his waist...The father stood alone and
unemployed, a silent observer of all that was doing about his
deceased son, and a perfect picture of deep and unaffected
sorrow...*

*After this they proceeded to the grave which had been
prepared in the governor's garden. Bennelong had earnestly
requested that some drums might be ordered to attend, which
was granted, and two or three marches were beat while the
grave was preparing; Bennelong highly approving, and
pointing at the time first to the deceased and then to the
skies, as if there was some connexion between them at that
moment...*

Great care was taken by Bennelong and Colbee to position Ballooderry's
body so that 'the sun might look at it as he passed'; shrubs and branches
were trimmed to make sure that the sun's rays reached the burial
site. Then, working as a team the young man's black and white friends
together filled in his grave.

As Maugoran, Ballooderry's grieving father, stood quietly watching the white men join in the burial of his son he must have felt a sense of disorientation mingled with his grief. When David Collins recounted the funeral, he described the effect that Ballooderry's death had on his father:

> *When Ba-loo-der-ry, a very fine lad who died among us, was buried, I saw the tears streaming silently down the cheek of his father Mau-go-ran; but in a little time they were dried, and the old man's countenance indicated nothing but the lapse of many years which had passed over his head.*

Twelve-year-old Nanberry, dejectedly witnessing the proceedings, must have had stirring images flashing through his young head; recent memories of times fishing and hunting with his friend and mentor: Ballooderry had taught him the native skills he'd missed out on while growing up in the white man's camp. He and Ballooderry had exchanged names to signify their bond of friendship, but now he must give up the name; now his friend was gone.

We can only imagine what Arthur Phillip, with the benefit of hind-sight, was feeling as he too stood observing the moving tribute to the young black man he had thought so highly of as to propose taking him to England.

✫

50

Maugoran's family

Ballooderry's father, Maugoran, had lived near the head of the harbour for most of his life; that is, until the white men had built a township on his ancestral land. He had been the man who had boldly represented his clan in letting the white governor know, shortly after his spearing, that the people of Burramatta were angry; the settlement the governor had initially named 'Rose Hill', and later changed to Parramatta, had been a significant disruption to their lives and livelihood.

Maugoran and his family however, with the passing of time, had found ways to adjust to their new situation. The white men had promised to provide those who lived amicably among them in the settled districts with bread, salt meat, liquor and blankets; and so far they had kept their promise. His sons, Ballooderry and Yerranibe had found niches for themselves in the British settlements where they had lived comfortably. Ballooderry had been particularly pleased with his new-found bartering role, until the regrettable incident of his demolished canoe.

In the aftermath of the *'galgalla' (smallpox epidemic)*, Maugoran had learnt that his daughter, Boorong had survived due to the medical attention of the white doctors and the on-going care received in the household of the Reverend Johnson and his wife Mary. He understood that the man distinguished as 'Reverend' by the white men was in fact akin to a *koradji,* an eminent man of his own people. The healing man, surgeon John White who had treated Boorong and adopted Nanberry, had a similar status. The natives often visited the doctors in the British camp to have their wounds dressed after an injury or skirmish with other black men; even Maugoran had sought out the surgeon to have his lacerations treated after a fight over whale meat with men of the north-shore clan.

In accepting the white man's provisions, Maugoran and his people had been conscious of not relinquishing their treasured independence and had carefully guarded their right to come and go. When Boorong told her white guardians that she wanted to marry a man of her choice, from her own people, they had not interfered. She had informed her foster-parents, Richard and Mary Johnson, of her decision to leave them soon after the spearing of Governor Phillip and after a long talk on the beach with Bennelong's wife, Barangaroo. It was on that occasion that Boorong had been urged by the white officers to convince Barangaroo of the advantages of white society, but the older woman had instead persuaded the young girl to re-join her own people.

That day, Boorong, obviously deeply affected, had returned grudgingly to the settlement with her white guardians. A few days later, when she and Nanberry had been in a boat on the harbour with some officers acting as interpreters with a group of natives, she discovered some who were of her own clan. John Hunter had recorded what had eventuated that day:

> ...the girl was very desirous of remaining with them; she was now of an age to want to form a connection with the other sex, which she had no opportunity of doing in the clergyman's family where she lived, and very innocently told him, when she asked to go away, that she wanted to be married.

Knowing that it would be difficult to prevent her, her British carers reluctantly agreed that she should go whenever she pleased; urging her to take all her clothes with her; and that whenever she chose to come and see her friends, *'whatever she wished for would be given her'*. The trigger, that finally caused her to leave, came a few days later:

> ...a canoe with Bennelong's sister and several young people coming to one of the points of the cove, the girl who had now lived seventeen months with the clergyman's wife, joined them, and was so desirous of going away that it was

consented to: the next day she was seen naked in a canoe,
but she put on a petticoat before she joined the clergyman
and some others who went to visit her; she appeared to be
pleased with having her liberty.

It seemed it was time for the white settlers to farewell the happy-go-lucky youngster who had played a pivotal role in building bridges across the cultural divide and who many in the settlement considered to be their friend. It was with regret that the Reverend and his wife said goodbye to the girl they had hoped to cultivate as their first Christian convert. As they watched her walk away with her bundle of clothes and other souvenirs of 'civilisation', they wondered if the parting would be permanent.

★

51

More goodbyes

December, 1791

Elizabeth Macarthur stood amid the crowd on the quayside, waving her friends goodbye with a heavy heart. She was about to part with more of her cherished, yet dwindling social network. *HMS Gorgon* was about to leave on its return voyage to England and her dear friends Watkin Tench and William Dawes were on board. She would miss her conversations with Mr Tench on poetry and literature, and with the thoughtful, intelligent Mr Dawes no longer living at the observatory, there would be little incentive for her to walk the track to the little peninsula that would continue to bear his name. Although several of the chief officials, George Johnston, David Collins, Doctor White and of course Governor Phillip, were remaining in the colony, it wouldn't be the same with so many of the officers now taking their leave.

Earlier in the year she had farewelled other good friends on the *Waaksamheyd*. Among them were Captain Hunter and her patient piano teacher George Worgan, the talented young doctor who, prior to his departure, announced he was leaving his keyboard with her. She still missed the musical evenings gathered around the piano, with George playing and her husband John and his colleagues, singing songs from home. At the time of their departure, she had admitted in her journal that her spirits were quite low at the loss of these friends. Now, as *Gorgon's* departure loomed, she once again felt *'a considerable branch of her society was being lopped off'*. Only a few weeks earlier she had stood on the same wharf farewelling the Kings and the Patersons as they left to take up their appointments on Norfolk Island. She pictured lonely days ahead.

Anna Josepha, Lieutenant King's young wife, had impressed her new acquaintances during her brief time in Sydney with her cheerful nature and quiet acceptance of her husband's illegitimate children. She had taken little Norfolk aboard the departing ship with loving attention while at the same time heavily pregnant with her own baby. In taking on such a responsibility, she had opened to her step-son a life of privilege and opportunity. Elizabeth Macarthur, also expecting another child, would miss sharing the experience of motherhood with the companionable Anna Josepha. Their shared excursions and dinner parties had been a wonderful diversion but it had been fleeting. Pondering the Kings' domestic situation, Elizabeth admired King for shouldering responsibility for his illegitimate sons, and Anna Josepha, a frank, good-natured woman, for taking on his mistress' children. She wondered if, in similar circumstances, she would be as willing to do the same.

There were no female confidantes with whom she could discuss such things; no-one with whom she could share a little gossip. She had nothing in common with the reserved chaplain's wife, Mary Johnson, and although she wrote to her dear friend Bridget in England, she had to wait such a long time for a reply.

Admittedly, there were a number of convict women who were by no means unrefined; some were even relatively educated. There was Esther Abrahams, the convict partner to Lieutenant George Johnston, one of her husband's closest military colleagues. She was clearly an intelligent, discreet woman, and though they would inevitably continue to cross paths, it would be socially unacceptable for them to be more than passing acquaintances. Elizabeth comforted herself with the thought that free settlers to the colony were expected any time now. Surely among them, would be women of a more suitable status.

☆

From the deck of *HMS Gorgon*, Watkin Tench looked ashore to the diverse crowd seeing them off. Among the throng were many black faces for whom he readily admitted feeling *'some share of affection'* and from whom he had learnt a great deal. In his summary of the natives in general, he had written:

240

I do not hesitate to declare that the natives of New South Wales possess a considerable...sharpness of intellect, which bespeaks genius.

On a personal level, he would carry with him fond memories of Arabanoo, Bennelong, Colbee and 'many others'. What an extraordinary four years it had been since he had landed on the shores of Botany Bay. He vividly remembered his first encounter with the natives there: the day he had cautiously walked up the beach toward them, holding the hand of a seven-year-old child. He recalled the gentleness shown by an old native man toward the little boy as he had warily come forward and laid his hand on the youngster's hat, felt his clothes and muttered in astonishment at the whiteness of the child's skin. Tench had recorded that experience, and his many early interactions and discoveries in the colony in his first journal which he'd dispatched on one of the ships returning home to England in 1789.

His first journal had been published with huge success in Britain, ahead of other 'accounts' of the colony, as a pocket-sized booklet called *'A Narrative of the Expedition to Botany Bay'*. He had been extremely pleased by its popularity with the British public and encouraged to make his follow-up account even more comprehensive and intriguing. So, in the days prior to embarking on *Gorgon*, he had visited Rose Hill and its surrounding settlements to gather material for his second book to be published as, *'A Complete Account of the Settlement at Port Jackson'*.

Aware that his readers would enjoy stories rather than statistics, Tench while including some facts and figures, kept his account conversational. Among the recently arrived convicts was one of particular interest: a celebrity-criminal, by the name of George Barrington. Tench knew British readers would be keenly interested in the legendary prisoner's fate. The convict in question had been a notorious, high-class thief who had gained widespread publicity for his pick-pocketing expertise among the rich and famous of Britain and Europe. Tench was curious to view the man *'of famous memory'*.

But before I bade adieu to Rose Hill, in all probability for the last time of my life, it struck me that there yet remained one object of consideration not to be slighted: Barrington.

Originally from Ireland, George Barrington had infiltrated fashionable London society in the early 1770s. His elegant attire and polished manners had been convincing enough to allow him to circulate among the social elite while helping himself to the contents of their purses and pockets without detection for some years. Eventually however, people began putting two and two together and stories began appearing in the printed press about the handsome young socialite's likely but mostly unproven involvement in the thefts. Thriving in his celebrity status Barrington, poised and self-confident, had even hit back with accusations of defamation.

His reputation had reached its most sensational when he'd attempted to steal a diamond studded snuff-box, estimated to be worth £30,000, from the pocket of Russian Prince Orlow as they were seated at London's Covent Garden theatre. When the prince had felt something being removed from his pocket and turned to confront Barrington, the article had quickly been slipped back into the royal gentleman's pocket. Like many of Barrington's victims, the self-conscious prince had failed to prosecute. However a full account, and even an artist's impression of the incident, had later appeared in newspapers.

The British press knew the public loved to hate a rogue and accounts of Barrington's continuing escapades regularly made the print media. When he appeared in court, his stylish outfits were described in detail and his polished speeches to judge and jury were published. In his last, widely publicised trial in 1790, Barrington made an eloquent appeal to the jury:

> *Life is the gift of God and liberty is its greatest blessing: the power of disposing of either is the greatest man can enjoy... great as that power is, it cannot be better placed than in the hands of an English jury; for they will not exercise it like tyrants, who delight in blood, but like generous and brave men, who delight to spare rather than destroy; and who, not forgetting they are men themselves, lean when they can, to the side of compassion.*

However, Barrington's flattering speech had not prevented a 'guilty' verdict, nor his imprisonment and subsequent transportation to New

South Wales. Tench knew the English public would be eager for an update on the famous pick-pocket since his arrival in the penal colony.

Prior to visiting him, Tench admitted to having a mental image of Barrington in all his finery, as the newspapers had portrayed him in his heyday, and was taken aback to see him dressed as a convict:

> *I saw him with curiosity... Of that elegance and fashion, with which my imagination had decked him (I know not why), I could distinguish no trace. Great allowance should, however, be made for depression and unavoidable deficiency of dress.*

In addition to his altered appearance, Barrington it seemed had reformed his character since his conviction and he had impressed the authorities by his amazing transformation:

> *Both on his passage from England, and since his arrival here, his conduct has been irreproachable. He is appointed high-constable of the settlement of Rose Hill, a post of some respectability, and certainly one of importance to those who live here.*

Within a few weeks of landing it seemed the celebrity-thief had found a very different niche for himself in his new home. Tench thought his knowledge of the criminal mind would serve him well in his capacity as law-enforcement officer and could not help being impressed:

> *I cannot quit him without bearing my testimony that his talents promise to be directed in future to make reparation to society for the offences he has heretofore committed against it.*

Barrington had certainly stepped across a great divide.

☆

Tench, continuing his rounds of Rose Hill, had focussed on the situations and prospects of ex-marine and convict settlers. Among them he listed Anthony Rope and his wife Elizabeth, a convict couple who had married in the early months of the colony. Still in his early twenties, Rope had learnt the trade of bricklaying since his transportation, was listed with an allotment of 70 acres and had two children. The couple had come a long way in under four years.

Some settlers, Tench believed, *'were men of great industry'*; others he wrote *'were in a state of despondency'*. He was critical of a few who, he thought, would never adapt well to life on the land.

He was particularly derisive of young Matthew Everingham who had been an attorney's clerk in London, and at the age of about fifteen had been convicted for selling stolen law books to pay his board. At the end of his seven year sentence in 1791 Everingham had opted to try his hand at farming with his wife, Elizabeth. But Tench, although confessing himself to be *'a man of so little experience of these matters'*, declared Everingham to be out of his depth in farming. Referring back to the misconduct for which the young convict had been transported, Tench wrote with uncharacteristic scorn:

> *I dare believe that he finds cultivating his own land not half so easy a task as he formerly found that of stringing together volumes of tautology to encumber, or convey away, that of his neighbour.*

Time would prove Watkin Tench to have been unfair in his judgment of Matthew Everingham. Despite many setbacks the ex-convict became a highly respected pioneer and patriarch of an extensive family who would set precedents in the crossing of social, cultural and physical divides. Everingham was one of the few literate convicts who later documented his own perceptions of life in the early colony.

In the meantime, Tench added a poetic phrase as he summed up his opinion of farming prospects in New South Wales:

> *He who looks forward to eat grapes from his own vine, and to sit under the shade of his own fig-tree, must labour in every country. Here, he must exert more than ordinary activity.*

He had documented the colony's milestones and detailed every fascinating event in his journal, but his posting in the remote settlement was over and he was happy to hand over the charge of recording future episodes to someone else. The final words of his journal were:

> *Here terminates my subject...I leave to others the task of anticipating glorious, or gloomy, consequences, from the establishment of a colony, which unquestionably demands serious investigation.*

Tench, like most of the officers, was more than ready to leave the colony, but his close colleague William Dawes had wanted to stay. He had many friends among the Aboriginal people but had developed a particularly close relationship with a young woman, Pattyegarang, or Pattye as he fondly called her. He had spent some of the happiest days of his life on the secluded peninsular at his observatory learning about her ways, her language and her people; he had even begun teaching her to read. From the early days, he had sympathised with the native people and their situation; he had deplored the governor's retaliatory actions, and for that he had been discredited and was on his way, back to England.

During their time together, he and Pattye had discussed the simmering bitterness of her people. On one occasion he broached the topic of an attack on a white man near Sydney, asking why the black men had done it:

'Gulara.' (Because they are angry, Pattye had answered.

'Minyin gulara eora?' (Why are the black men angry?) Dawes asked, already suspecting the answer.

'Inyan ngalwi - Tyerun kamarigals' (Because white men are settled here... The black men are afraid).

'Minyin tyerun kamarigals?' (Why are they afraid?)

'Gunin' (The guns), was Pattye's short but direct answer.

Dawes had seen the impact of white settlement on the lives of the black people; especially in the outlying district around Parramatta where land had been cleared indiscriminately and without consultation, where their food sources were dwindling and access to water courses was increasingly being denied them. Fear and anger - always the precursors to racial conflict - were the emotions Pattye had attributed to the black men's attack. Standing beside his friend Watkin Tench aboard the *Gorgon*, William Dawes felt helpless. He was leaving the colony forever. He would never see Pattye again.

★

52

A time of transition

With the departure of *HMS Gorgon,* Elizabeth Macarthur was not the only one in the colony feeling flat; in the closing weeks of 1791 David Collins, the governor's loyal secretary was also in a despondent frame of mind. The little ship *Supply,* which had served the colony so unfalteringly since its arrival with the First Fleet, was also returning to England, prompting him to write soon after the ships sailed:

> *The cove and the settlement are now resuming that dull uniformity of uninteresting circumstances which had generally prevailed. The Supply and the Gorgon had departed, and with them a valuable portion of our friends and associates.*

The early months of 1792 however, heralded in a series of challenges that kept the governor and his secretary busy. A reduction in rations had become necessary once again. Scores of convicts, male and female, had absconded into the wilderness in search of 'China'. And others, whose sentences had expired, decided that rather than work for the government any longer, they would simply take themselves 'off the government stores' and live 'independently'. This resulted, Collins recorded, in bold thefts *'being nightly committed on the outskirts of the town, and at the officers' farms, by some of these vagrants.'*

In February, a daring plot was uncovered in which *'a great body of convicts'* had conspired to seize weapons and *'proceed to the sea-coast, where, destroying every person who should oppose them',* they planned to build a ship and make their escape. The ringleader, when seized, soon implicated his co-conspirators and the men were chained together until the situation was deemed safe enough to return them to their usual labour.

According to Collins, the cycle of thieving, plotting and punishment was never-ending. Added to this, was the governor's continuing health concern; not a day went by that he didn't suffer pain in his side from an unknown cause.

So when the *Royal Admiral* sailed into Sydney Harbour in the spring of 1792, bringing more convicts, provisions and government dispatches, Arthur Phillip was delighted to also receive news of a personal nature. It was information he knew would create upheaval so he waited some weeks before announcing it publicly. To some, the governor's announcement would be a bombshell, to others it would be a welcome surprise, but no-one in the settlement would be unaffected. Governor Phillip had received permission to quit the colony and would be leaving within weeks of his announcement.

★

The departure of Phillip, the man who had been pivotal to the existence of all classes of society in the colony over the past five years would naturally evoke diverse reactions. Collins said the governor's announcement created *'no small degree of concern in the settlement'*, but other sentiments were probable.

To the convicts with whom he had dealt leniently, Phillip's departure would no doubt create a high degree of uncertainty. *How would future policy makers treat them?* To the emancipists, those who had already gained their freedom, a new leader could adversely affect their opportunities. But for some of the officers and marines of the newly formed New South Wales Corps, a change of governance, one more sympathetic to their situation, would be a welcome thought. Someone, like the recently arrived incoming administrator, the easy-going Major Grose, was just what they needed; someone they trusted would give preference to the military once he was in charge.

✵

As Arthur Phillip's governance came to its end, three young female residents were looking to the future with mixed, but mostly optimistic emotions.

The three English women, Elizabeth Macarthur, Esther Abrahams and Susannah Kable may not have realised it, but they had quite a lot in common, despite their different backgrounds and circumstances. Esther and Susannah were still serving their time as convicts, while Elizabeth, having arrived as the wife of one of the New South Wales Corps, enjoyed the freedom her privileged status afforded. However, regardless of the women's differing social standings, each of them had faced similar challenges since arriving in the colony, and each had reason to look forward to increasing prosperity for her colonial family.

Each woman had arrived in Sydney Cove weighed down with anxiety for the young infant she had brought with her to New South Wales under difficult conditions; to have the responsibility of a tiny life in such a precarious setting was not to be envied. Although Esther Abrahams, with baby girl Roseanna, and Susannah Kable with little Henry, had suffered the added horror of confinement in dreadful surroundings below deck during their voyage, Elizabeth Macarthur had also endured appalling conditions aboard *Scarborough*, a convict transport of the Second Fleet. She had undergone the loss of her baby girl on the voyage and had almost lost her husband to an illness that still left him weakened; her little boy Edward had also arrived at Sydney Cove in precarious health. Yet each of the women, through her private and personal experience of hardship, had built the strength of mind necessary to take on future trials.

In the initial months after their arrival, each young mother had adjusted bravely to her new circumstances, nursing her infant through illness, living in makeshift huts in an environment very different to her homeland. Although Elizabeth had the benefit of convict servants, she like the other women, had endured the horror of spiders, ants and other crawling creatures that frequently found their way into their homes and the maggots that were a constant threat to their foodstuff in summer. Elizabeth, like the other women had gradually become accustomed to the terrifying electrical storms that visited the settlement areas, the stifling heat that felt like *'the blast of an oven'*, bringing choking dust storms which, no matter how well the gaps in walls were plugged, left all their belongings covered with a thick powdery film.

Unbeknown to all three women, due to the future decisions and actions of their ambitious husbands, each would find it necessary to preserve the stability for their young growing families through various trials. At a future time each would have to take over the reins while their husbands faced serious charges. Yet, each woman would maintain fierce loyalty to her industrious spouse under testing circumstances. All three women would remain in the colony for the rest of their lives, never seeing their homeland again. Each woman would suffer the heartache of losing more than one child, yet each would become the matriarch of a large colonial family. At the time of Governor Phillip's departure, all three women, were expecting another child.

By the end of 1792, Susannah Kable, the convict woman who had captivated the British public before leaving England with the saga of her enforced separation, then reunion with her baby son and his father, had every reason to be content with her lot. Her husband Henry, continuing to enjoy Governor Phillip's approval, had been appointed as a constable on the night patrol, and as consequence of his valuable service, had received a free pardon. The couple already had two colonial born children under the age of three, as well as their English born son, Henry. Within the year she would give birth to another child in their extended, though still simple dwelling. The New South Wales colony had well and truly become home and would become an increasing source of wealth and respectability for her offspring.

Esther Abrahams, the young Londoner, convicted for stealing a roll of lace, also had reason to feel satisfied with her family situation. When she and her baby girl Roseanna, had been loaded onto the *Lady Penrhyn,* she had wondered what life held for her little daughter. But she had caught the eye of Lieutenant George Johnston and her life had taken a turn for the better. She now had the security of an influential protector, recently promoted to Commanding Officer of the New South Wales Corps, with whom, since arriving in the colony she had produced a healthy son and to whom she was about to deliver another child. George Johnston had proved to be a devoted father to their children and though she knew discretion was imperative, Esther Abrahams was enjoying the relative freedom her association with a senior officer of the Corps had brought. George had invested money in a cartel with other officers and soon, it was rumoured, a large grant of land would be confirmed.

Life, for Elizabeth Macarthur, was looking particularly rosy as 1792 drew to a close. Her husband's career prospects were extremely promising and the likelihood of a substantial land grant was more than probable. Though she missed the lush green fields of England, she loved the unspoilt beauty of her new land. In her letters home she described the harbour and its surrounds as *'agreeable and romantic'* and *'so beautifully formed that I can conceive nothing equal to it.'* She was however, still feeling homesick.

Writing to her friend Bridget in England, she confessed that though she was *'sincerely happy'* she had *'yet great hopes of seeing grandfather once more'*. When she gazed at the starry night sky above Sydney, seeing the constellation of the Southern Cross that Mr Dawes had pointed out from his observatory, she imagined her grandfather gazing up at the bright Northern Star above England. Her confidence in seeing her family again had sustained her when times had been trying, yet she could not see herself returning to her homeland in the foreseeable future; her husband's career was just taking off.

Despite her nostalgia, Elizabeth Macarthur wrote that she was *'abundantly content'*. She shared her husband's foresight and could see the possibilities her adopted country afforded as a source of great prosperity for her young family. She could see opportunities ahead for the New South Wales Corps, and expected prospects would brighten considerably after the departure of Governor Phillip. The incoming administrator, Major Grose already seemed to be much more agreeably inclined toward the military sector.

Her belief in the colony and its potential was not misguided. The promotion of her husband and consequent *'handsome addition to his income'* in the closing weeks of 1792 was just the beginning of the influence and fortune that would later benefit the Macarthur family.

★

53

Pondering the known and the unknown

Sydney Cove – December 1792

Governor Phillip read through the report he was preparing to take to England. His time in the settlement was fast drawing to a close. All in all, he was satisfied with the progress that had been made. At Rose Hill, now officially re-named 'Parramatta', farms were producing consistently and the time was in sight when many settlers would be independent of government assistance. The township boasted an established marketplace, a town hall and a recently completed hospital.

Sydney was expanding at a steady pace and more substantial buildings of brick and stone were being constructed. The white population of the colony had increased to around four thousand and there were more black faces amongst them than ever. In the harbour, shipping activity was growing, government boats were being built and whaling ships from America and Europe were visiting Sydney. A new phase was beginning for the colony.

He thought back to the beginning, when they had all first landed; they had overcome so many unforseen obstacles, endured unimagined hardships and taken great risks. The diverse reactions of the convicts to their newfound situation in an alien land had always been a source of amazement to him. Some had knuckled down, taken the good with the bad and made something of their new circumstances. Others had carried with them their same old habits of theft and vice, and they had suffered accordingly.

Well, now it was someone else's turn to take over the task of building this place into something more than a colony of convicts; more than a small settlement on the edge of a still virtually unknown wilderness. He had done all he could.

He had offered incentives to marines to remain in the colony as farmers, and more than fifty had taken the opportunity to settle. Watkin Tench had suggested that those who stayed did so because of their *'infatuated affection to female convicts'*. Maybe that was so, but they would also have seen the material benefits in settling in New South Wales.

As well as land grants, he had donated as breeding stock, a sheep or a goat to each marine and married convict settler. It was a valuable gift and he hoped that those who received such a bonus *'would see the advantage it might prove to them, and cherish it accordingly'*. Throughout the year, he had introduced incentives for families and individuals to stay in the colony, aware that many convicts would soon be coming, or had already reached, the end of their sentences. He had undertaken that each 'settler' would be fed and clothed 'from the public store' for eighteen months from the term of their becoming settlers. He had also allowed them:

> *...to be furnished with tools and implements of husbandry; grain to sow their grounds, and such stock as could be spared from the public. They were likewise to have assigned them the services of such a number of convicts as the governor should think proper, on their making it appear that they could employ, feed, and clothe them. Every man had a hut erected on his farm at public expense.*

Some convicts had been working their farms under these circumstances for about twelve months and Phillip was gratified to see that his inducements were already working. As Collins' draft report testified:

> *At the time of the governor's departure, many of them, by their own industry, and the assistance he had afforded them, were enabled to have one or two convicts off the store...In general they were not idle, and the majority were comfortably situated.*

Phillip, acutely aware that the colony needed good men at the helm, had recommended Lieutenant George Johnston for promotion and urged him to stay as a commanding officer of the incoming military administration. Fortunately for the colony, Johnston had accepted the offer and had recruited marines to stay under his command, as part of the NSW Corps for a five year term. Phillip had also sought permission from Britain to grant larger land allotments to officers; the forthcoming agreement would be conditional on their farming enterprises not detracting from their military and civil responsibilities. Johnston had shown initiative in farming from the outset and with the new incentive he would be among the colony's first 'landed gentry', with very promising economic opportunities.

Phillip thought about Major Francis Grose, Commander of the NSW Corps, who had arrived in Sydney in early 1792 to take over administration of the colony. He would manage the colony once Phillip left, as Lieutenant Governor, until the next governor arrived. Phillip could see that Francis Grose was a pleasant enough man but he had already shown himself to be easily manipulated when certain officers had attempted to influence events for their own financial advantage. The officers, with the organising skills of John Macarthur, and the apparent support of Captain George Johnston, had come up with a scheme to pool their resources and charter a ship to Cape Town to buy *'many articles of comfort which were not to be found in the public stores among the articles issued by government.'* Grose had penned the request on behalf of his men to the governor. He said he gave his support because he sympathised with their position. He wrote regarding:

> *...the situation of the soldiers under my command, who at this time have scarcely shoes on their feet and who have no other comforts than the reduced and unwholesome rations served from the stores.*

Phillip had his misgivings about the project and made them known; he couldn't see it benefiting the colony as a whole. However he gave his consent and the officers hired Captain Raven, owner of *Britannia*, to make the trip to South Africa to buy livestock and other goods for them. Captain Raven had a fishing license and had intended a whaling venture along the New South Wales coast but as the officers' proposal was potentially more lucrative for him, he postponed his whaling endeavour. Plans for the chartering contract could easily be discussed between the captain and the officers as Captain Raven, during his stay on-shore in Sydney, was very conveniently, living in paid accommodation at the residence of Esther Abrahams, well known to be Johnston's partner. When the *Britannia* left Sydney harbour in October 1792, George Johnston, John Macarthur and other officers who had contributed to the cartel, were well placed as budding importers; their elite group was going to profit immensely from the scheme.

Phillip wondered if Grose was being naïve. How would the colony fare with a monopoly on trade by the military? He wondered how Grose would manage the task ahead of him; particularly with strong characters such as John Macarthur who had already conveniently offered his services to relieve the Lieutenant Governor of any administrative worries. And Grose, it had become evident, was more than happy to delegate work. John Macarthur would have an impact on the colony, Phillip could see that...

He turned his mind to the other lives that had been, and would be, changed by Sydney: the Aboriginal families, the convicts, all those who would stay when he left in December.

What lay ahead for them?

There was the builder, James Bloodworth who had been an asset to the colony and had been appointed master bricklayer for his fine building work. He had been duly rewarded:

> *James Bloodworth received the most distinguishing mark of commendation which the governor had in his power to give him, being declared free, and at liberty to return to England whenever he should choose to quit the colony. Bloodworth had approved himself a most useful member of the settlement, in which there was not a house or building that did not owe something to him...*

Phillip was glad Bloodworth, now free to do as he wished, had agreed to stay in the colony; the place needed men like him. Other convicts had come a long way too since arriving in the hold of a transport ship. William Richardson and his wife Isabella had set up a school and were teaching the children of convicts and marines. When the Reverend Johnson had praised the young couple's initiative and recommended their appointment as teachers, Phillip had readily agreed.

Now there was a school in Sydney and one in Parramatta. The convict children were taught for free but the marines were expected to make a contribution for the education of their youngsters. Phillip allowed himself a rare smile. What strange circumstances the colony had created when ex-convicts, those who had started out in chains, could receive a fee for teaching the children of marines.

One of the Richardson's young pupils, the son of Henry and Susannah Kable, had been an infant when his convict parents came ashore at Sydney Cove. Now he was six years old, a 'promising little fellow' with a little sister and a baby brother. The Kables would certainly make something of themselves in the colony; their success was already evident. When they had been married in 1788, they'd 'signed' their names with an X, but since then they had both begun to learn to write. Kable had served his sentence and in acknowledgment of his good conduct, he'd been made a constable on the night watch. He and Susannah had made themselves relatively comfortable; particularly as a result of the court hearing which had granted them compensation of their 'lost' property. Susannah must, from time to time, ponder the time five years earlier, when her baby had been dragged from her arms and life had seemed so bad that she had threatened to kill herself. As far as Governor Phillip was aware, the family had no plans to return to England; their future was with the colony.

It was inevitable that one day Sydney would become a significant port town. Though the British East India Company still had a monopoly on commerce in Asia and the Pacific, an official blind eye was already being turned to the sea-trading activity of the colony. Trade would eventually flourish, and with it, opportunity for all kinds of commercial enterprise would follow. The children of convicts were positioned well to take advantage of the situation.

The frame for a small transport vessel had been sent from England and was sitting in the government dockyard ready to be assembled, lined and waterproofed for use in the colony. Builders, shipwrights, tradesmen of any kind, would never be short of work in a place like Sydney; anyone with an ounce of initiative would see the opportunities the colony afforded. As long as food production could keep up with the growing population, the colony had a future.

Phillip's thoughts went to James Ruse, the farmer, and his wife Elizabeth. He felt encouraged by their significant progress which had vindicated his belief in the country's potential - against the many doubters. The new society needed individuals with determination and persistence rather than people who gave in to despair when the going got tough. In the very same month that William Bryant and his group had escaped the colony by boat, Ruse had announced his ability to support his family from the produce of his farm; and he had achieved such a promising result after only fifteen months working his plot. It was gratifying for Phillip to read over the report about Ruse and his wife:

> *His Excellency thought fit to exercise the power vested in him...by granting an absolute remission of the term for which Elizabeth Perry had been sentenced. This woman came out in the 'Neptune' in 1790, and had married James Ruse a settler. The good conduct of the wife, and the industry of the husband, who had for some time supported himself, his wife, a child, and two convicts, independent of the public store, were the reasons which restored her to her rights and privileges as a free woman, for extending to her the hand of forgiveness.*

Watkin Tench had interviewed Ruse at the time regarding the success of the experiment and had taken notes on Ruse's farming techniques. Ruse had been pleased to oblige:

> *My land I prepared thus: having burnt the fallen timber off the ground, I dug in the ashes, and then hoed it up...it was not like the government farm, just scratched over, but properly done. My straw, I mean to bury in pits, and throw in with it everything which I think will rot and turn to manure.*

Ruse had met the challenge; he had shown that convicts could become self-supporting and that agriculture was viable for the colony. As a reward, the governor allowed Ruse to keep the land he had cultivated, making his farm the first land grant on the vast mainland of New South Wales. In his report, Tench had referred to Ruse as *'a humble adventurer, who is trying his fortune here'*, rather than labelling him an 'ex-convict'. People like Ruse and his wife inspired hope in the future of the colony; and they had found a niche for themselves. He and his wife now lived in a comfortable brick house and had over eleven acres of his land under cultivation.

But what would the future hold for them? Would they eventually return to England? Or would they stay on and create greater opportunities for themselves in this still largely unknown land?

What about the restless young man John Wilson who had recently served out his sentence? It was well-known that Wilson was attracted to the wilderness but would he be tempted by the offer of his own land? Would he settle down and take up farming? Or, like William Bryant, his wife Mary and the other escapees who'd taken the plunge into the immense Pacific, would he take off into the vast unknown in search of his own version of freedom? It remained to be seen.

The Bryant's story - now there was a saga. News had got back to the colony through a visiting ship's crew that all eleven escapees, including the Bryant's two small children, had actually made it over 3,000 miles (5,000 kms) to Timor in the small, fishing-boat they had stolen! Incredibly the journey had taken them just under ten weeks but they had endured violent storms, starvation and thirst, and when they had tried to land they had experienced dangerous encounters with natives along the coast. On arrival in Timor, they had posed as shipwreck survivors and, for a time, their tale of distress had been believed and they were treated kindly. But soon, a slip of the tongue had aroused suspicion and on being further interviewed, the true circumstances of their escape had become known. They were then imprisoned by the Dutch governor of Timor until they could be handed over to the next visiting English ship bound for Britain.

Phillip hoped that as the story of the escapees' detention circulated, their ultimate failure at freedom would overshadow the fact that they had managed to reach Timor in an open boat. He trusted a further deterrent against imitators, would be that the Dutch would not readily accommodate suspicious arrivals a second time.

The governor however, could not miss the irony of the Bryant's fate. After all their meticulous planning and incredible suffering on their death-defying journey, the fugitives would ultimately be escorted back to England to be thrown into prison once again. He wondered what the final outcome would be for them.

Phillip was well aware that there were more than a few, who were still as intent on returning to their birthplace as the day they'd been forced to leave Britain on the First Fleet. The tough old biddy Dorothy Handland, who had been listed in the ships records as eighty-two when the fleet sailed (though most now suspected she just looked that old), had only a few months of her seven year sentence remaining. Having the distinction of being the oldest female transportee on the fleet, many had doubted she would survive the rigors of life in the colony, but she had managed to serve her time to date without incident, and was still bent on sailing back to the 'old country'.

There were many convicts, Phillip was aware, whose life was far from easy. Work for an unskilled labourer at the brickfields would be backbreaking. The convict gangs were constantly at work producing thousands of bricks and clay roof tiles required to complete a substantial building, such as a military barrack. As there still weren't bullocks available to pull the brick-carts, there was no alternative but to use men like work-horses. Work was just as unremitting for the carpenters, sawyers, blacksmiths and stonemasons, without whose forced labour the developing colony could not be built.

Phillip looked out across the harbour, where on the opposite shore he could see the smoke of native fires drifting upward like fingers of mist. He imagined the families gathered around their campsites; some repairing their hunting spears, some preparing food as their children played nearby. He had often watched the black children playing their favourite game; lined up, each with a stick in hand trying to be the first to strike a ball as it was rolled from one end of a row of children to the other. He thought about the native people and their varied reactions to the white settlement.

How would they face the unprecedented transition they were now facing?

He thought of Bennelong, his good-humoured, open-minded friend, who could also be infuriating. Phillip knew Bennelong wanted the best for his people and had made compromises to improve the relationship between his culture and the settlers, whose lifestyle was so different to his. In the end after several standoffs, it appeared he had decided that the advantages of the British camp outweighed the disadvantages. Phillip admired his tenacity; Bennelong was a true diplomat.

Then there were those of Pemulwuy's persuasion who were making it plain they saw no advantages in the white man's culture. These men simmered with resentment and aversion to the changes that had been wrought on their people and their land. Over the preceding months, settlers at Parramatta had complained of attacks on their crops, and Phillip suspected Pemulwuy was behind the activity. David Collins, the Judge Advocate had summarised what he imagined were the feelings of men like Pemulwuy, and their situation:

> *While they entertained the idea of our having dispossessed them of their residences, they must always consider us as enemies; and upon this principle, they made a point of attacking the white people whenever opportunity and safety concurred.*

How would men like Pemulwuy fare in their struggle against dispossession and the rights of their people? What would become of Pemulwuy?

There were also people like Colbee and his wife Daringa, who had kept a foot in both camps; trying to make the best of both worlds while keeping the strongest ties with their own culture. Daringa had visited the home of Elizabeth Macarthur, where the young women talked about their babies and Daringa shared her know-how of bush skills and remedies, but their conversations were restricted by the little they had in common.

Boorong and Nanberry, the young small-pox survivors, had continued to live in the settlement with white families; for most of the time anyway. Boorong had abandoned white society briefly after living a year and a half with Reverend Johnson and his wife Mary, to marry and be with her own people. But she had returned a short time afterward and had subsequently seemed content to live across both cultures. Phillip read over the account from the end of 1790:

> *Boorong, the native girl who had lived with the clergyman, returned to him again, after a week's absence: some officers had been down the harbour, and she was very happy to embrace that opportunity of getting away from the party (of natives) she had been with.*

> *By her own account, she had joined the young man she wished to marry, and had lived with him three days; but he had another wife, who the girl said was jealous, and had beaten her; indeed, evident marks of this appeared about her head, which was so bruised as to require the surgeon's attention...*

When Boorong had first been brought into the settlement as a thirteen year old, it was assumed she was an orphan, but over time she had learnt that some of her immediate family had survived the smallpox epidemic. Her father Maugoran, displaced by the settlement at Parramatta, had relocated to the northern banks of the Parramatta River with his second wife, and eventually her brothers Ballooderry and Yerranibe had come to live in Sydney. Boorong knew that many of her people were not happy with the impact the white population had had on their lives. But she had seen the good and the bad aspects of life in the colony and, like Bennelong, she had adapted her life to take advantage of both cultures. She was regularly seen naked in a canoe, fishing with Bennelong's sister, but she always donned a petticoat when in the company of the Reverend Johnson and his wife, Mary.

Young Nanberry was still part of Surgeon White's household and when in the settlement, wore a shirt and trousers and complied with the norms of his step-father's society. Though seemingly content to live in the town, he had at regular intervals, stripped off his clothes, rolled them into a ball and left them under a tree to go running on the beach, to feel the sun on his skin and to go swimming naked in the sheltered inlets of the bay.

Phillip remembered the time when the little boy, having spent the day in the company of black friends and seeing the campfires of native families, had felt the appeal of their lifestyle, and wanted to remain with them:

> *...the boy, Nanberry, now wished to stay with the natives all night; he was left behind, but the next morning he returned to the surgeon, with whom he lived, and having fared but badly, did not seem inclined to go to them again.*

Phillip knew that soon Nanberry would reach an age when his culture required that he go through an initiation ceremony, symbolised by the removal of a front tooth. Phillip knew Nanberry looked to Bennelong and Colbee as role models; they were warriors among his people. Phillip also knew Nanberry was quite attached to John White, the man who had raised him from a boy of nine; but Surgeon White was not expected to stay in the colony for much longer. The diligent, hard-working doctor was worn out and wanted to return to England.

What choices would Nanberry make in the future?
How would he react to the departure of his white guardian?

In the end, could Boorong and Nanberry keep their own heritage strong while successfully living as part of the colonial world? What would be the result for them and their children?

At times, Phillip had been at pains to prove the advantages of the British culture and superiority of its justice system to the natives who were increasingly moving into the white settlements. He knew he had played a pivotal role in the massive changes that had been brought to their lives but he must believe and be confident that they would reap the benefits with time. He was leaving the colony but his role in demonstrating the advantages of English society was not over yet. That was where Bennelong came in.

Bennelong was going to the land of the 'Berewalgal' - the land of the people from far away.

☆

Governor Phillip stood on board *Atlantic*, the ship that was taking him home to England and looked across at Bennelong. He felt fondness for this young man who had given him so many headaches! How would he cope in England? Phillip realised Bennelong, and the other young adventurer Yemmerrawanne, who had also volunteered for the sojourn at the last minute, had no idea how far they were going. Though he had tried to make them understand the distance, they had no idea how long they would be away from their homeland. The changes they would have to face would be immense: the weather, the language, the people, the landscape. The sights they would see would be mind-boggling.

If Bennelong had been impressed with the faded red jackets of the officers, what would he think when he saw the gentlemen in their silk waistcoats and top hats, and the ladies in their wide crinoline dresses?

What would he think of the shops in Oxford Street, London, stocked with every kind of gaudy toy imaginable? If he had been impressed with the little brick house built for him on the eastern point of the cove, what would he think when he saw the King's palace? He had thought the wheelbarrows used in the settlement amazing, so what would he think when he rode in an ornately decorated carriage pulled by six white horses?

☆

Bennelong was trembling. It had been a harrowing farewell with his kinfolk, especially with the loud show of distress by his second wife. He knew, had his beloved Barangaroo still been alive, she wouldn't have liked him going to the land of the British either. But it was something he wanted to do and his excitement was difficult to contain. He stood on deck with Governor Phillip waving to the receding crowd on shore until they became dots against the landscape. He was going at last; far, far away across the sea where none of his race had ever been before.

As *Atlantic* sailed from the little cove, towards the sandstone citadels that formed the entrance to the harbour, Phillip had mixed feelings too. There was so much unfinished business. Those elusive blue mountains to the west had not been conquered. They were still a mystery. What lay on the other side? Was there a great inland sea? Were there strange animals yet to be discovered? Was there another civilisation? Or was there just a great stretch of impenetrable nothingness as some had predicted?

As they sailed into the vast expanse of the Pacific Ocean, the first governor of the colony of New South Wales and his protégé exchanged a nervous nod. So many unspoken questions were yet to be answered.

'The End'

In the following painting, the eastern point of Sydney Cove is viewed from outside surgeon John White's cottage, near the hospital on the cove's western shore. Government House can be seen on the hillside above the government wharf on the opposite (eastern) shore. A ship in full sail is passing a small brick house on the cove's headland, known by all those living in the Sydney settlement as Bennelong's Point. The ship is heading eastwards towards the harbour entrance which opens into the Pacific Ocean.

The painting is attributed to convict, Thomas Watling, also known as the 'Port Jackson painter' and gives a view of Sydney Cove as it was around the time of Governor Phillip's departure to England accompanied by Bennelong.

'A partial view of Sydney Cove taken from the sea side before the Surgeon General's House'

The world famous Sydney Opera House now stands on Bennelong Point.

Image and details courtesy of the trustees of the Natural History Museum (London).
The museum's stamp is visible on the top right corner of the painting.

265

The following paintings are also attributed to the 'Port Jackson painter'. *A View of Sydney Cove - Port Jackson March 7th 1792'* gives an impression of the cove as it appeared before Governor Phillip and Bennelong departed for England later the same year.

It provides a view of Sydney Cove, looking towards the wooded area around the Tank Stream, which flowed into the head of the cove and is positioned close to the centre of the painting. Wharves can be seen on both sides of the cove: the jetty on the right bank later became known as the public wharf. Above the left bank, a wide track leads up the hillside from the government wharf towards the governor's house and gardens. To the right of Government House, a row of houses extends down to the Tank Stream.

On the western side of the cove, a number of buildings and smaller houses are dotted along the hillside, with the hospital and its gardens by the shoreline at the extreme right of the painting. The cultivated ground and gardens are enclosed and separated from the wooded areas beyond by paling fences.

An Aboriginal family is depicted paddling a canoe in the centre foreground. Behind them two small boats are moored near the wharf.

'A View of Sydney Cove - Port Jackson March 7th 1792'

The painting below: 'A View of Governor Philips House Sydney Cove, Port Jackson taken from NNW', gives a view of Government House with its outbuildings and gardens as it would have appeared around the time of Phillip's departure. The government buildings and gardens were contained within low wooden fences, with smaller houses to the right, including a small gabled construction with panels and a single door with a small window above. It is thought to be the pre-fabricated house brought from England to accommodate Governor Phillip until an official residence could be built.

Government House itself is shown as a symmetrical building of two levels, with an arched door-frame, nine windows and a lightning conductor rising from the centre of the roof. It was constructed of pale buff-coloured stone quarried from nearby, with a blue-grey roof. In front of it there is a walled courtyard patrolled by two soldiers carrying bayonets and protected by two cannons, with piles of cannon balls on either side of a gate. The gate leads to the surrounding pathways, gardens and grassed areas. To the right of the main building there is a well and outbuildings.

The construction of Governor Phillip's residence was supervised by convict, James Bloodworth, as were most of the other buildings in Sydney at that time.

'A View of Governor Philips House Sydney Cove, Port Jackson taken from NNW'

Image and details courtesy of the trustees of the Natural History Museum (London).

These and other painting relating to the First Fleet can be viewed interactively at:

http://www.nhm.ac.uk/nature-online/art-nature-imaging/collections/first-fleet/art-collection/
collections.dsml?disp=list&stype=colls&notes=true&desc=true

People associated with the colony, 1788 - 1792 and what became of them:

Governor Arthur Phillip, though intending to return to the colony one day, never did. However, he remained interested in its progress till his death in 1814.

David Collins, Secretary & Judge Advocate, left for England in 1796. He returned in 1803 to found a settlement in Van Diemen's Land.

Captain John Hunter later became the second Governor of the colony.

Lieutenant-Colonel Philip Gidley King later became third Governor of the colony.

Reverend Richard Johnson left Sydney in 1800, returning to England with his wife and two colonial born children.

George Johnston established himself permanently in the colony with Esther Abrahams and their seven children.

Watkin Tench never returned to Sydney though he stayed in touch with many colonists, including the Macarthurs.

Bennelong, shown in British clothes. After sailing to England with Phillip, he gladly returned to his homeland in 1795.

Elizabeth Macarthur became matriarch to a large colonial family, but never realised her dream of returning to England.

John Macarthur became a wealthy landowner but was embroiled in many disputes with ensuing governors.

Lieutenant William Paterson became Lieut. Governor of the colony briefly in 1795.

Frenchman, La Pérouse sailed from Botany Bay in March 1788 but vanished in the north Pacific Ocean

Notes & sources

See Bibliography for full publication details

Abbreviations:

ADB	Australian Dictionary of Biography
HRA	Historical Records of Australia
HRNSW	Historical Records of News South Wales
ML	Mitchell Library, State Library of New South Wales, Sydney

Introduction – setting the scene

See Watkin Tench's introduction to his journal: *'A Narrative of the Expedition to Botany Bay'*, in Flannery, ed. 1996, p.15, 16. For reference to convict letters, see ibid. p. 18.

Speculation on cannibalism in New South Wales: see newspaper article in *General Evening Post*, November 9, 1786, Issue 8262: *'Botany bay scheme...a settlement in those regions of the South, the habitation of cannibals':* (This prediction was found to be unsubstantiated). See also John Hunter's journal, *'An Historical Journal of the Transactions at Port Jackson and Norfolk Island'*,(1793), Ch. 3, Jan 1788 to August 1788, p. 44.

See David Collins' journal for his comments about entering 'a state unknown' in, *'An Account of the English Colony in New South Wales'*, Volume 1: Introduction: A Voyage to New South Wales, Section II, p. 53, (2008, Echo Library, facsimile edition).

The fleet's arrival at Botany Bay, see John White's *'Journal of a Voyage to New South Wales'*, diary entry January 20th, p. 43. (Gutenberg Project e-book edition).

1. The end and the beginning

The scenario depicted in this chapter is based in part on a painting by colonial artist, Joseph Lycett with the title, 'Aborigines spearing fish, others diving for crayfish, a party seated beside a fire cooking fish', (J. Lycett, 1817).

Reference to the landings at Botany Bay & Aborigines' reactions, given in evidence by Mahroot (last surviving man of the Botany Bay tribe) in NSW Legislative Council Proceedings, Sydney 1845, *'Minutes of Evidence taken before the Select Committee on the Aborigines'* See, 8 Sept 1845: information by Mahroot alias the Boatswain to question 190 of 209.

See also Willey, K, *'When the Sky Fell Down'*, (1979), pp. 50-53, for more accounts of Aboriginal beliefs about the appearance of the white strangers, and for Mahroot's account of British settlement and its aftermath for Aborigines in the Botany Bay area, pp. 217 – 220.

Evidence of Aboriginal storytelling through song and dance, see Tench's, *A Complete Account of the Settlement at Port Jackson*, (ed. Flannery) p. 262. Tench refers to the natives' songs as *'speaking pantomimes'...'At their dances I have often been present... Like their songs, they are conceived to represent the progress of the passions and the occupations of life...These dances consist of short parts, or acts...'*

See also Smith, *'Bennelong'* (2001, Kangaroo Press), p. 99, *'a corroboree was, and is, the ritual acting out of stories and myths through a fusion of song, music and dance.'* Smith suggests the Gweagal clan at Botany Bay devised a 'contact corroboree' to depict their changed circumstances since the arrival of whites in 1788. See Hunter's journal, op. cit. p. 230.

See examples in Reynolds (2006) *The Other Side of the Frontier*, p. 3-5, 13-14 of oral histories of north Australians in which stories of 'seeing white men' for the first time were passed down.

Expressions used by Aborigines from the shoreline, see Collins, Vol. 1, p.58, '*all greeted them in the same words, shouting everywhere, 'Warra, warra, warra*'', (signifying 'Go away') Note there are various spellings of recorded expressions, depending on the incident and whose journal is quoted. Collins, ibid. p. 504, lists '*Woroo woroo'* to mean '*Go away.'*

Newton Fowell gives an account of the natives with spears shouting 'Worra worra Wea' in Letter 16 (part 2) of 'The *Sirius Letters – the complete letters of Newton Fowell: 1786-1790'* (edited by Nance Irvine, The Fairfax Library, 1988) p. 67.

2. First encounters – Botany Bay, January 1788

For what the officers saw from the ships & the governor's encounter with the natives, see George Worgan's journal of 1788, '*Sydney Cove Journal'* Part One pp. 18-31 (Reproduced by the Banks Society with Introduction & notes by J. Currey, 2010).

Natives' reaction to white men coming ashore & another account of the above, see: '*The Journal of Philip Gidley King: Lieutenant, RN. 1787 -1790'*; notes for January 18th p. 32.

For the native's encounter with the party of white men and the seven year old boy, and the exchange of objects and questions, see Tench's account, op. cit. pp. 41, 42.

Natives' doubt about the gender of the white men and their query, '*What kind of creatures are these?'* see Worgan, op cit. p.29 ; the account the natives' curiosity, their decorative scaring, nose piercing and missing front tooth of the men, ibid. pp. 18-29.

Tench's interpretation of '*Whurra* ', to mean 'be gone', & British objective: Tench, op. cit. p. 42.

Aboriginal people thinking the white visitors may be reincarnated ancestors: see Collins, op. cit. p. 366; convict escapees later related that the natives believed they '*were undoubtedly the ancestors of some of them who had fallen in battle, and had returned from the sea to visit them again'.* Also see similar account by William Buckley, an escaped convict who spent decades living with an Aboriginal group. His story is told in Ward (1987) p. 62: '*They think all white men previous to death were belonging to their own tribes, thus turned to life in a different colour.'*

Fowell gives an account of natives with spears in his Letter 16 (Part 2) op. cit. p. 67.

The 'fishing incident' & demonstration of weapons: see White's '*Journal of a Voyage to New South Wales'*, entry for Jan 23rd.
For reference to 'gooroobeera' to mean 'stick of fire', see Tench, op. cit. p. 266.

William Bradley's summation of the natives' reaction to the white men's departure from Botany Bay, see: '*Voyage to New South Wales Dec 1787 - 1792',* available online the State Library of NSW website: www.si.nsw.gov.au An entry for January, '1788 reads: '*The Natives were well pleas'd with our people until they began clearing the ground at which they were displeased & wanted them to be gone; At sun set when the boats left the shore, several of the natives came down to the water side & then went to their huts.'* Transcript a138059 [page 59].

3. A line in the sand

For Phillip's exploration of Port Jackson, see Collins, op. cit. p. 57-60. For Phillip's official dispatch regarding the 'Manly encounter' and naming of Sydney Cove, see Historical Records of Australia, Series 1, Vol. 1 pp. 18, 25. Also see, *'The Voyage Of Governor Phillip to Botany Bay and Norfolk Island'*, (Project Gutenberg e-book version), entry for 22nd Jan,1788, p. 38, for the naming of Sydney; the 'line in the sand' incident, see Jan 23rd, ibid. p. 39. Also see Tench, op. cit. p. 45.

'Warran' for Sydney Cove, see *William Dawes' Notebooks on the Aboriginal Language of Sydney, 1790-1791*, published by Hans Rausing Endangered Language Project & School of Oriental and African Studies, London, 2009. See Notebook C, pp. 52-53.

4. Strange comings and goings

The unexpected arrival of French ships in Botany Bay: see Collins, op cit. p. 59. Also Tench's account, op. cit. pp. 38,39; see also Lt. Ralph Clark's *'The Journal & Letters of Lt. Ralph Clark, 1787 – 1792'*, p.264, *'the day that we left Botany Bay there came in two strange ships which not a little surprised everybody, for we as soon expected to see Saint Paul coming in the bay as two strange ships.'*

La Pérouse's voyage & time at Botany Bay, see Turbet, (2011) *The First Frontier*, pp. 21-25

Interaction & marriage between the people of Botany Bay (Kameygal, Bediagal and Gweagal) & the Cadigal people (whose territory extended south of Port Jackson) & the Wangal (whose territory surrounded Sydney Cove and westward on the southern side of the Parramatta River) was shown by recurrent communication between the clans. For example, Bennelong, a member of the Wangal, Colbee (or Colbee) a member of the Cadigal, and 'Botany Bay Kolbi' were friends. Colbee's wife, Daringa, was from the Botany Bay district and returned there to visit family and give birth: see Hunter's Journal op. cit. p. 232. See, Smith (2001) pp. 88, 129. Also, Collins', op. cit. p. 375, reported, Bennelong's sister, *'came in haste from Botany Bay'* to visit Bennelong'. Bennelong's second wife, Go-roo-bar-roo-bool-lo (or Kurubarabulu), was from the Botany Bay district.

Tench, op. cit. p. 257: *'I saw a woman…carry her new-born infant from Botany Bay to Port Jackson, a distance of six miles.'*

See map of names for clans around Botany Bay
http://www.cityofsydney.nsw.gov.au/barani/themes/popups/group_locations.htm

See also, Turbet, *'The Aborigines of the Sydney District before 1788'* (2001) pp. 20-27 for a map and explanation of territories, language groups and clans. See a map in Kohen (2009) *'The Aborigines of Western Sydney'*, p. 2; Also *'Aboriginal Clans of the Sydney Region'* in Kohen (1993) *'The Darug and their neighbours'*, pp. 20-21; For 'Kamay' as the Aboriginal name for 'Botany Bay', see Dawes. Notebooks, op. cit. Notebook C, p. 54.

See Collin's mention of Gweagal on the southern shore of Botany Bay, op. cit. p. 454. Also see Willey, (1979) p. 8, for a map; p. 15, for explanation.

Officers' positive opinion of encounters with natives at Botany Bay: see Collins, op. cit. p. 58.

5. Sydney Cove 1788

Reference to Sydney Cove's previous name 'Warran' or 'Warrane', see *Dawes' Notebooks,* op. cit. Notebook C, p. 52-53. Also see a map reproduced in Smith (2001,) op. cit. p. ix

Collins described a site adjoining Sydney Cove on which natives performed a special initiation ceremony known as *'Yoo-lahng erah-ba-diahng',* (involving the extraction of the upper front tooth of young males). It was performed in a specially prepared sacred space known as 'Yoo-lahng'. Collins described the ceremony as taking place at the head of the little cove known to the natives as Wogganmagule (see reference to the map in Smith, 2001). The place was named 'Farm Cove' by the British & is now the site of the Sydney Botanical Gardens. See Collins op. cit. pp. 351-364 (The ceremony also took place in other locations.)

For evidence of natives watching boats enter Port Jackson then retreating into the shadows, see *'The journal of Arthur Bowes Smyth: Surgeon, Lady Penrhyn, 1787 – 1789',* p. 64: 'Upon entering the Harbour mouth, we saw many natives on the top of the high rocks; none of them have appeared since we anchored.'

George Johnston's coming ashore at Sydney Cove on the back of James Ruse: see *Sydney Gazette,* 20th June 1827: *'Colonel Johnston claimed the honour of being the first who landed, but it appears he was carried ashore on the back of Ruse'.* Whether or not Johnston or Ruse were the first ashore is not debated in this book; it is only claimed that Ruse carried Johnston ashore, as he asserted. We know that on 25th Jan 1788, while the fleet was still at Botany Bay, Lt. Johnston was among officers ordered to transfer to *Supply* to go ahead of the main fleet with a group of male convicts to Sydney Cove. He would have been among the first of the main fleet to land there. Arthur Bowes Smyth, op. cit. pp. 63, 64, mentions Lt. Johnston's instruction to *'proceed on Supply to go with a detachment on shore at Port Jackson';* Also see Roberts, *'Marine Officer, Convict wife',* (2008) p. 19, for reference to Johnston's son Robert, retelling the story of his father wading ashore, and the officers and men laughing when, after stumbling, his hat floated across the water. See Mitchell Library: MSS6485, part 4, folder1 & 2, *'Items relating to Douglas Hope Johnston'.* Also, an article 'The First Hawkesbury Farmer' in *Windsor and Richmond Gazette,* 22 April, 1899, supports the story. See also an article: *'Lieutenant-colonel George Johnston'* in Manly Daily, 14th Aug, 1924: *'George Johnston was the first man to land both at Manly and at Sydney Cove, being ordered by the governor...'*

See Esther Abraham's listing as a convict on board the *Lady Penrhyn,* see, *'The journal of Arthur Bowes Smyth',* op. cit. p. 7 (listed as Esther Abram) George Johnston is also listed on the same ship as Lieutenant of the Marines. See Chapman, (1986).*1788: 'The People of the First Fleet',* pp. 21-23 for entries on Esther and her daughter, Roseanna.

For further detail on Esther Abraham's background, crime & sentence, see Roberts, op. cit. pp. 200-201. Also De Vries, (2009) *'Females on the Fatal Shore',* devotes a whole chapter to Esther and Roseanna, pp. 11- 41.

For Esther's appearance see her portrait painted in 1824 by Richard Read, when she was in her early fifties, in Roberts, (2008) *'Marine Officer, Convict wife',* p. 68.

The actual date of the beginning of George Johnston and Esther Abraham's lifelong love affair is unknown. Some historians have suggested that it began on board the *Lady Penrhyn,* others soon after disembarkation. George would certainly have met and spoken to Esther during their eight month voyage as part of his role was to supervise the109 convict women on the *Lady Penrhyn.* Johnston's first dwelling was on the east side of the cove near the governor's marque. His and Esther's first child together, George junior, was born in early 1790. They remained partners for life.

January 26th 1788, see Lt. King's journal, op. cit. p. 36, for reference to 'English colours displayed'. Collins, op. cit. p. 60, says 'a flag-staff had been purposely erected and an union jack displayed'. See, *'The Voyage of Governor Phillip to Botany Bay with an Account of the Establishment of the Colonies of Port Jackson and Norfolk Island'* entry for Jan 26th 1788.

6. Reflections

Collins' description of Sydney Cove; disembarking & clearing work, op. cit. pp. 59-60

Esther Abraham's city background, crime and sentence: see her listing of convicts in Chapman op cit. pp. 21-23. Also, Gillen, (1989) *'Founders of Australia: A Biographical Dictionary of the First Fleet'.* Also see, Roberts (2008) *'Marine Officer, Convict wife',* pp. 200-201.

Speculation on what the convicts had heard about their destination is based on newspaper articles such as, *General Evening Post,* November 9, 1786, Issue 8262: *'Botany bay scheme, a settlement in those regions of the South, the habitation of cannibals',* and from the gist of convict letters before they left England. See Tench, op cit. p.18. There were the inevitable stories of crew members who had been to places such as Asia & Africa, where large insects, reptiles & flesh eating animals existed. Several imagined sitings of dangerous creatures were reported in the early days of settlement. See Chapter 11, 'Strange appearances and disappearances' below. Speculation would have been rife as no white man had been beyond the coastline of New South Wales.

For details on Ann Inett and the children she left in England, see Gillen (1989) p. 188. See extensive research on Ann Inett's family history and transportation compiled by Edward Inett, (2010), *'Inett, What's in a name?,* Rock and District News, pp. 54-65 (originally published in 12 episodes in the Rock and District News, Worcestershire, England 2009).

For proof of seasickness and storms, see Bowes Smyth's journal, op. cit. p. 14 *'The women were very sick with motion of the ship.'* Also pp. 37-38. *'Heavy gales and great swell...many of the women received hurts and bruises from falls.' See also Lt. King's journal,* op. cit. pp. 25, 26, 29. Also see accounts of seasickness and high seas in the early weeks of the voyage, see Clark, *'The journal and letters of Ralph Clark 1787-1792',* pp. 12-14.

Details and punishment of women found with crew before the fleet sailed, see Bowes Smyth's journal, op. cit. p. 13, 14.
Female convict's punishment on board *Lady Penhryn,* see ibid. pp. 47, 48. For Bowes' comment: *'there was never a more abandoned set of wretches collected in one place',* p. 47.

Accounts of female convicts on the *Lady Penrhyn* : Elizabeth Needham, Elizabeth Hayward, Dorothy Handland, Ann Inett, Isabella Rawson and Esther Abrahams, see Gillen, (1989),

'The Founders of Australia', in alphabetical listings. Also see Chapman, (1986) '1788: The People of the First Fleet', (alphabetical listings): Robinson.

Isabella Rawson's story (also, Rosson), see Gillen, op. cit. p. 315. Also, see Chapman, op. cit. p.151. Birth of her baby, see Bowes Smyth, op. cit. p. 18.

For listings & details of all female convicts on board the Lady Penrhyn, see: 'The journal of Arthur Bowes Smyth: Surgeon, Lady Penrhyn 1787 – 1789', pp. 6-8. Most of the women were listed as domestic servants or factory workers; a few were needle-workers, hawkers or dealers (in second hand goods). One was listed as an artificial flower maker, one as a furrier and Elizabeth Hayward (the youngest female) was listed as a clog-maker. Esther Abrahams was listed as a milliner. Esther's address before transportation was in central London; her crime of stealing was allegedly in a shop in close proximity. See Roberts, op. cit. pp. 200-201.

For stormy weather and dangerous seas later in the voyage, see Lt. P.G. King's journal op. cit. entries for mid-November to early January, pp. 23-29. For thick fog in unchartered waters, see entries for December 4th - 6th, 1787, p. 27; for extreme coldness, see p. 29. For contrary winds and water reduction, see Bowes Smyth's journal, op. cit. p. 43.

On whales, see Lt. King's journal, op. cit. entries for Nov 28th and Dec 8th 1787, pp. 25, 27, 29; see Bowes Smyth's journal (op. cit.) p. 26, 'it was full as long as the ship', p. 43: 'three whales rose near ship...almost touched ship', p. 48, 51. Also, Clark, pp. 70, 81. For the dead whale mistaken for large rock, see Bowes (ibid) entry for Nov 27th, p. 45.

For storms and high seas in the last leg of the voyage, 'women washed from their berths' see Bowes Smyth's journal ibid. entries December 29th – January 10th. pp. 52-54. Women praying, see ibid. p. 55.

Lady Penrhyn conveyed 1 captain, 2 lieutenants, 2 sergeants, 3 corporals, 1 drummer and 35
privates, as well as over one hundred female convicts: see http://firstfleetfellowship.org.au.

7. Different eyes – different sights

For Ann Smith's listing on Lady Penrhyn, see Bowes Smyth's journal op. cit. p. 4-8; her refusal of clothing and threats of escape, see ibid. entry for February, pp. 66 and 72. Details of her conviction: see Gillen, op. cit. (alphabetical listing). Also Chapman, op. cit. p.165

The 'laughing jackass' or kookaburra was called Go-gan-ne-gine by the Aboriginal people: see Collins op. cit. p. 506.
The 'large white bird', a white cockatoo, referred to by the native people as Garraway: see Dawes' Notebook C, p. 24, Collins op. cit. p. 506, see mention in White's journal, pp. 53, 79.

For details on Susannah Homes, see Gillen, 'The Founders of Australia' (alphabetical listing) Also Chapman op. cit. p.106. For a newspaper account of the Holmes/Kable story, see London Chronicle, Dec 2-5 1786 (see online via the State Library of NSW: 17th & 18th century Burney Collection Newspapers) See also, Chapter 16. 'The Kable story', below for reference to their saga.

For Ralph Clark's impressions of Port Jackson and his changing opinions, shown in his letters, see *'The journal and letters of Ralph Clark 1787-1792'* entries for January 26th, 27th, 1788, p. 93 and February 1st, 7th, 10th 1788, pp. 95-96.

8. Issues and challenges

Collins' description of the cove and the clearing work, see his account op. cit. pp. 59, 60 Phillip's remarks on the encampment see *'The Voyage of Governor Phillip to Botany Bay'* p.42.

For reference to 'red gum', see White's journal, op. cit. p. 62 *'...an amazing quantity of an astringent red gum... This gum I have found very serviceable in an obstinate dysentery that raged at our first landing...'* See also Tench, op. cit. p. 71.
Reference to wild vegetables found around Sydney Cove, see Collin's account, op cit. p. 60.

See Tench's account of the initial going's-on at the settlement, op. cit. pp.43-44. The actions of the white visitors, seen through the eyes of black observers who were witnessing such activities for the first time, can only be imagined. However, Tench tells us that the natives began avoiding the settlement within a few days of its establishment. He was baffled: *'From what cause their distaste arose we never could trace'*, see p. 45. Collins, op. cit. p. 60, describes what the natives would have seen: the officers around the flag saluting the health of the King and *'success of the new colony'*.

For another account of the natives' growing reserve, see Bradley, op. cit.: Lt. William Bradley and John Hunter (both of *HMS Sirius*) surveyed Port Jackson from late January to 6th February 1788. Lt. Bradley wrote that initially the natives at various points around the harbour received them 'cordially' but were protective of their womenfolk. On January 29th he reported, *'these people mixed with ours & all hands danced together'*, (Transcript of a138067), although he adds: *'we could not persuade any of them to go away in the boat with us.'* (Transcript of a138069).

By the beginning of February the natives had become more reticent: February 2nd: *'... at daylight saw several canoes in the cove we were surveying, they all fled some out of of the cove & others up to a cove... We could not by any means get these people near us.'* (Transcript of a138074) 3rd February: *'As we proceeded up the harbour, the natives all fled in their canoes as far & as fast as they could'* (Transcript a138075). Although after this time they saw natives, it was generally at a distance: *'As we returned to the ship we saw natives in almost every part of the harbour in small parties.'* Transcript of a138076.

On returning to the settlement, Bradley learnt that the French sailors who were still repairing their ships in Botany Bay *'had been obliged to fire on the natives at Botany Bay to keep them quiet'* and that two native scouts who visited the Sydney camp on February 8th, could not be persuaded to stay, (Transcript a138081). Though natives were seen on the harbour and the outskirts of the settlement, *'they would not come nearer the camp.'* (Transcript a138082) See Southwell's journal in HRNSW, Vol. 2: *'...the inhabitants had ever since our arrival at Pt Jackson kept at so great a distance as never to be seen but by our boats in the survey of harbour by Capt. Hunter... or when hauling the seine...'* Southwell Papers M1538, SLNSW.

By 11th Feb. they would witness one of the white men tied up to a frame for a public flogging of 'one hundred and fifty lashes', see Collins, op. cit. p. 62. For an account of Lt. King visiting the French in Botany Bay, see King's journal entry for Feb 1st, op. cit. pp. 37-40.

Prior to the French leaving Botany Bay in March 1788, one of La Perouse's men visited Governor Phillip to request that their dispatches be forwarded to the French ambassador in London by the earliest returning transports to sail for Europe, see Collins, op. cit. p. 66. For details of La Peruse's expedition & time at Botany Bay, see Turbet (2011), pp. 21-25.

After leaving Botany Bay on 10th March 1788 and sailing northward into the Pacific Ocean, the French ships disappeared, never to be heard of again. When they did not arrive back in France by 1790 theories of their fate abounded; the most spectacular rumour was that they had been shipwrecked and eaten by cannibals. In 1826 items from the ships where retrieved on one of the Santa Cruz islands (now Solomon Islands) but no trace of the crew was found. It was not until 1964, that the French shipwrecks were found sunk off the Islands. See 'La Perouse' in Australian Dictionary of Biography online.
See: http://www.sl.nsw.gov.au/discover_collections/society_art/French/perouse/index.html.

9. A night of revelry

For an account of the 'night of revelry', see Arthur Bowes Smyth's journal, op. cit. p. 67, (6th February), and for Tench's comments on the episode see Tench, op. cit. p. 45. Karskens (2010) p. 313-315 disputes accounts in Hughes (1986), Flannery (1999) of an 'orgy' occurring on Feb 6[th,] 1788. She terms their portrayal as the 'legend of Sydney's foundational orgy'.

Fifty eight convicts were married by Rev Johnson in February 1788: see Cobley (1987) 'Sydney Cove 1788', pp. 67-84.
According to Schofield (1987), 12 of the 28 babies christened in 1788 were illegitimate and those were all fathered by sailors or marines, not by convict men.

For Lt. Clark's account of Elizabeth Pulley's behaviour & treatment on 'Friendship', see his journal (ibid) pp. 19, 22, 30, 32.

For more details on Elizabeth Pulley (or Pooley) & Anthony Rope, see Murray & White (1988) pp. 35-40. See also Chapman, op. cit. p.148 for Elizabeth Pulley (Pooley') and p.156, Anthony Rope. Also, Saunders (2002) The remarkable Story of Elizabeth Pulley, Local Studies Library, Penrith Library, NSW.

Note: Soon after their wedding day, Elizabeth and Anthony Rope had a brush with the law. Anthony, 'finding a dead goat on a rock' took it home where he & Elizabeth turned it into a delicious pie to share with friends as a wedding celebration. However, as Lt. Johnston's goat had been reported missing, rumours about the dish quickly circulated and the young couple was called to answer charges of stealing the livestock. Fortunately, Anthony's story was convincing and the charges were dropped.

10. The governor's speech

The attendee describing the governor's speech and the reading of his commission was Arthur Bowes Smyth; see his journal op cit. pp. 67-69. The governor's commission & speech,

(described by Tench as *'dull detail'*), see Tench, op. cit. pp. 46-51.
Phillip's official commission & instructions, see HRA Series 1, Vol.1 pp. 1 – 15.
Also, see Collins, op. cit. p. 61 for Phillip's *'encouragement to those who showed themselves worthy by good conduct'*, and William Bradley's account, op. cit. Transcript of a138080.

Also, Worgan, op. cit. pp. 74, 84-87 for the governor's warning & encouragement to convicts.

Details on Ruse and Wilson, see Chapman, op. cit. (alphabetical listings). Also Gillen, op. cit. Ruse, p. 318; Wilson, p. 388.
Ruse and Wilson's reaction to the governor's speech is based on each one's subsequent behavior and course in the colony (see note for Chapter 53 herein for each man's undertakings & progress). Their summation of the other convicts reactions is based on accounts of the officers. See Bowes Smyth's journal, op. cit. p.68: most convicts were *'very idle...not more than 200 out of 600 were at work'*. Collins, op. cit. p. 62, said many of the convicts deliberately *'lost'* or *'secreted'* their tools and *'that any sort of labour was with difficulty procured from them'*.

Regarding the issue of convict indent papers being left in England, see Collins, pp. 108-109. Also, HRA Series 1, Vol.1, p. 57.

Phillip's background before becoming Governor of NSW, see Parker (2009) *'Arthur Phillip: Australia's first Governor'*, pp. VII-XV & 1-10. Philip's letter to his sister see, *'Arthur to Rebecca Phillip'* 21 June 1756, Public Record Office, 30/8/53, in ibid. p. 8.

11. Strange appearances and disappearances

For the 'alligator' incidents, see Bowes Smyth, op. cit. entries for Feb 1788, pp. 73, 77.
For the 'tiger' sighting, see Worgan's account, op cit. p. 64.

Mention of the missing sailor, see Bowes Smyth, op cit. entry for Feb 19th 1788, pp. 76
(Bowes suspected the sailor had been murdered by the convicts.) For the sailor's return and an account of his ordeal, see Bowes Smyth, ibid. p 77.
For a description of the large snake brought into the camp, see Bowes Smyth, ibid, p 79.

12. Creatures, great and small

See *'The Voyage Of Governor Phillip to Botany Bay'* p. 62, for a list of imported animals brought to the colony. By May 1788 the colony had: 1 stallion, 3 mares, 2 bulls, 5 cows, 29 sheep, 19 goats, 49 hogs, 25 pigs, 5 rabbits, 18 turkeys, 29 geese, 35 ducks and 87 chickens. For Phillip's analogy of Noah's ark, see ibid. p. 35.

See also Reynolds (2006) *'The Other Side of the Frontier'*, University of New South Wales Press, for accounts of natives seeing cattle, horses, etc. for the first time, p. 17-18.

For a list of fruit trees procured at Rio and Cape Town, see Collins, op. cit. p. 47.
See also Bowes', op. cit. p. 53 mention of success of grape vines *'which flourish very much'*.

Landing livestock & planting imported fruit trees at Sydney Cove, see Collins, ibid, p. 61:
'Some ground having been prepared near his excellency's house on the East side, the plants

from Rio-de-Janeiro and the Cape of Good Hope were safely brought on shore...and we soon had the satisfaction of seeing the grape, the fig, the orange, the pear, and the apple, the delicious fruits of the Old, taking root and establishing themselves in our New World.'

For the loss of six sheep, two lambs, and one pig killed by lightning, see Collins, op. cit. p. 68.

13. A beating for a beating

For Phillip's directive regarding the shooting of any male found in the women's camp, see Bowes Smyth, op cit. p. 68.
For Elizabeth Needham's incident with the marine, his subsequent punishment and the officer's criticism of the governor's decision, see Bowes Smyth ibid. p. 70. See also Ralph Clark's journal, op. cit. entries for February 9th 1788, p. 96.

Elizabeth Needham's marriage to William Snailham on 14th February 1788, in Gillen, op. cit. pp. 262-263; also, Chapman op. cit. p.167. My assertion of Elizabeth Needham's resolve to 'show her worth' is based on her future success in the colony and her later respectable reputation, see details in Gillen, ibid. Also see, Barkley-Jack (2009) for her later success story.

The officers' discontent with Phillip's administration of punishment was asserted by Bowes Smyth, op cit. p. 74. Ross' difficult relationship with Phillip, see Clark's letter, op. cit. p. 268.

Ross' opinion was that most of the officers and marines wanted to return to Britain, see his correspondence to England (July 1788 to Colonial Secretary Stephens), in HRNSW ii:173: *'Every person ...who came out with a desire to remain in this country (is) now most earnestly wishing to get away from it.'* See Ross to Nepean (ibid) p.212.

For ongoing tension between Ross and Phillip, see correspondence from Phillip to England, cited in Cobley, *'Sydney Cove 1789 – 1790',* pp. 43-47 (Ross had complained that it was not part of the officer's duty to be part of the criminal court); pp. 134-137 (Ross had objected to the 'night watch' comprised of convicts.) See Phillip's letters to England in HRA Series 1 Vol. 1, p. 148-152.

For the need to use convicts in supervisory roles, see Collins, op. cit. pp.62, 78, 84. Also see, Tench, op. cit. p. 77.

14. A view from the ridge

Natives' 'admiration' for British implements & methods, (iron pots for boiling food): see Phillip, op cit. p 38, & Tench's observation, op. cit. p. 261, that the natives had 'never conceived the method of boiling food' until shown by the whites. Also, HRA Series 1 Vol. 1, p. 25.

Natives taking British tools: see Collins' account, op cit. p. 67: Feb 1788, they *'carried off a shovel, a spade, and a pick-axe'.*

Accounts of natives observing the British from a distance & away from the main settlement, see Bradley's journal, op. cit. p.43: March 1788: *'Several canoes passed down the harbour, one stopped to fish between the ship & the shore with 2 women in her, they remained 'til near sunset but would not come to the ship';* p. 44, April 1788: *'two natives landed on the point of the cove where the observatory is fixed, but could not be persuaded to go into camp'*; p. 48, *'On our return to Spring Cove, we observed a cave in which there was a man and a little girl; they were so intent upon the motions of our people on the beach, that they did not see us until we were close upon them'*

Native scouts' visit see Bradley, op. cit. p. 36: *'Two Natives came to the camp, the governor gave a hatchet & several other things but could not persuade them to stay.'* Also, see Collins, op cit. p. 66.

British bewilderment at the natives' avoidance of the settlement, see Tench, op. cit. p. 45. See Phillip's journal, op. cit. p. 63, regarding his frustration. Hindrance to his goal of amity with the natives was *'much regretted by Governor Phillip, as tending entirely to the frustration of the plan he had so much at heart, of conciliating the affections of the natives, and establishing a friendly intercourse with them.'* Also Phillip, ibid. p. 72: July 1788, *'the natives still avoided all intercourse with our settlement, whether from dislike or from contempt is not perfectly clear.'*

See a summary of the observable changes that took place in the first months at Sydney Cove (clearing, sawing, brick making, building an observatory, storehouses, hospital, enclosing farms and gardens, etc.) in Worgan, op. cit. p. 33.
See Collins op. cit. pp. 54-55 re: *'a detachment of marines parading with their arms'. Also,* a barrack (begun March '88) comprising four buildings with *'space in the centre for a parade'.*

The first execution took place in Feb 1788, with the hanging of Barrett: see Collins, ibid. p. 62. Bowes Smyth op. cit. p. 74-75, *'the prisoners were brought heavily ironed...the arm of a large tree...was fixed upon for a gallows...all the convicts were summoned to see the deserved end to their companion...the body hung an hour and was then buried in a grave dug very near the gallows.'* (Barrett was the only convict hung that day.)
White, op. cit. p. 47 mentions 'the fatal tree, where Barrett was launched into eternity'; Worgan, op. cit. p. 89, 90. See also Tench, op. cit. p. 50.
Record of 'lashes' inflicted in the first weeks of the settlement, see Collins, ibid. p. 62. Also Bowes Smyth, op. cit. p. 74.

Natives' code of 'retributive justice', see Collins, op. cit. pp.480-481;
Artist, J.H. Clark in a painting entitled: *'Foreign Field Sports'* (1814), depicted a native man holding a shield, facing the spears of his countrymen, in their method of punishment. For ritual combat, see White, op. cit. p.71, *'A champion from each party, armed with a spear and a shield, pressed forwards before the rest, and, as soon as a favourable opportunity offered (till which he advanced and retreated by turns), threw his spear, and then retired; when another immediately took his place, going through the same manoeuvres; and in this manner was the conflict carried on for more than two hours..'* See also Phillip, op. cit. p. 71.

Details of Dawes' observatory and his expectation of a comet in 1788, see Collins, op. cit., p. 66. Also, Tench, op. cit. p. 78.

For Phillip's contemplation of the settlement, 'order...arising from confusion', and tracing out of streets for the future town, see *'Voyage Of Governor Phillip to Botany Bay'*, op. cit. p.66.

15. Beyond the boundary

Tench's background: see Flannery's introduction to Tench's journal pp. 2-12. Also, see Australian Dictionary of Biography' online.
Tench's comments on Sydney's weather: see his journal, pp. 76, 235.

Natives fishing and their dexterity in their canoes, see Tench, ibid. p. 53. For his contemplation of the unexplored country & description of the known area, see ibid. pp. 70-72.

See Hunter's journal, op. cit. p. 34-39 for details of his harbour charting with Bradley and their interactions with natives.

Tench's eagerness to go exploring was demonstrated by his attendance on many excursions in his free time. He voiced his disappointment when unable to do so by his comment on being 'unluckily' invested with the command of Rose Hill *'which prevented me from being in the list of discoverers of the Hawkesbury'*, In the next sentence he added that later the same month, *'Stimulated, however, by a desire of acquiring a further knowledge of the country,'* he joined another excursion westward, ibid pp. 110-111.

For Tench's comments on convict's conduct during the voyage and release from fetters, see Tench, ibid. p. 20.
An account of Barrett's forgery is given in White's journal, 5th August 1788, ibid. pp. 21-22. No account of the incident was recorded by Tench.

The 'Charlotte Medal', a metal disc engraved on one side with an image of the 'Charlotte' transport and on the other details of the First Fleet voyage, is on display at the Australian National Maritime Museum, www.anmm.gov.au
See also: http://www.nma.gov.au/exhibitions/irish_in_australia/home

Barrett's crime of stealing food & his execution see, Clark's journal, op. cit. p. 102.
See Tench, pp. 49-50; White p. 47; Collins p. 62. Also see Bowes' journal, pp. 74-75.

Convicts, James Bloodworth and William Bryant both arrived on *'Charlotte'* and were under the supervision of Watkin Tench on that vessel. For details of convict, Bloodworth, see Gillen, op. cit. p. 39. Also Collins, op. cit. p. 156. See Bryant below.

For praise of Bloodworth's building ability and initiative, see Collins, op. cit. p. 156. See construction of dwellings with cabbage tree and plastered with clay (ibid.) p. 70; reference to scarcity of limestone, ibid. p.118. Reference to lime stone made from shells, see (ibid) p. 461; also Collin's Volume 2, p. 204; see White, op. cit. p. 49 for reference to lime and the building of the governor's house.

Misgivings about construction at Sydney, see Tench, op. cit. p.64: *'the incredulous among us ...declare that ten times our strength would not be able to finish it in as many years'.* See also, ibid. p.77 for Tench's description of the settlement and officers' *'little huts...thatched over'.* Also, see Ross' negative letters to England about the future of the colony (referenced above to HRNSW ii: 173, 212); see Clark, op cit. p. 274, in a letter dated July '88, to a friend, 'I was never so sick of anything in my life as I am of this settlement'. Also Clark's ibid. p. 264, '...by God I would not stay longer than I could help in this country'.

For details of William Bryant, see Gillen, (listed alphabetically); also Chapman, op. cit. p. 53; also Collins, op. cit., p. 94. Details of Mary Bryant, see Chapman, op. cit. p. 47 (listed as Mary Brand alias Broad); also see Gillen, (listed alphabetically)
John White's journal, op. cit. p. 31, mentions the birth of baby Charlotte taking place on the ship *Charlotte* on Sept 8th 1787.

16. The Kable's story

For an overview of the Kable's story, see Chapman (ibid) pp. 56, 57 (listed as Cable) and for Susannah, his wife, see Susannah Holmes, p.106. Gillen, op cit. p. 178 gives a slightly different version of events: However, I have chosen to use the account publicised in the *London Chronicle* of Dec 2-5, 1786. (see online State Library of NSW: 17th & 18th century Burney Collection Newspapers).

Henry Kable, had been chosen to act as overseer of the women's encampment.: see a newspaper account of Kable's letter (dated November 1788) to a family member, Dinah Cable: *London Chronicle*, 21-23 July 1789 issue ; in the same letter Henry details the extreme weather, strange animals, as well his success in growing turnips, cabbage and peas. He also mentions his contentment in his situation. Of Henry junior he says: 'Our little boy Harry is a promising little fellow...' See also, Holden, *'Orphans of history – the forgotten children of the first fleet'*,1999, Text, Publishing, p. 170.

Kables versus Duncan Sinclair regarding their missing goods, see White's journal account (p. 64) giving background and details of the court-case of *'the Norwich convicts who so much excited the public attention'*; see also Neal, D., *'The Rule of Law in a Penal Colony – Law and Power in Early New South Wales'*, 1991, CUP, for details of British law regarding convict rights during the colonial era. Note: the Kables, unlike other prosperous convicts, never returned to England.

17. Into the wild blue yonder

For Phillip's instructions for Norfolk Island, see, Collins p. 65; see, journal of P.G. King, entry of Feb 1st & Feb 7th; pp. 37, 40; also White's journal, p. 47 (entries, Feb 12th and 14th) also Hunter's, *'An Historical Journal of the Transactions at Port Jackson and Norfolk Island*, p. 42; also Tench, op. cit. p. 50; also George Barrington's, *'The History of New South Wales'* (accessed online through The Project Gutenberg) p. 52.

Phillip's Instructions for Norfolk Island to Philip Gidley King, Esq; Superintendent and Commandant of the Settlement of Norfolk Island, see Phillip's journal (Gutenberg online: p 46, 47). Also re Norfolk Island, see HRA series 1, Vol 1 p.13
'British East India Company's trade monopoly in Asia/Pacific:Cobley, *Sydney Cove 1788*, p. 61

King's background to the time of his taking control of Norfolk Island, see Jonathan King's (1981) *'Philip Gridley King: a biography of the third governor of New South Wales'*, pp. 2-35; For details on Ann Inett and her relationship with King, pp. 39, 40.

For Arthur Bowes Smyth's account of King's consultation regarding women recommended for the group to Norfolk Island, those who had 'uniformly behaved well during the whole of the voyage', see Bowes Smyth, op cit. p 65. His list included: Elizabeth Lee, Elizabeth Hipsely, Elizabeth Colly, Olivia Gascoin, Ann Inett & Ann Yates. (Yates opted to stay in Sydney.)

For Ann Inett's background, see Edward Inett, (2010), *'Inett, What's in a name?'*, Rock and District News, Chapter VI. pp. 54-65 (originally published in 12 episodes in the Rock and District News, Worcestershire, England, 2009) See also Chapman, op. cit. p. 106 (listed as Hinett). Also Gillen, op. cit., listed alphabetically.

King makes reference in his journal, op. cit. p. 177, to the birth of 'one male child', his son, Norfolk Inett-King, in January, 1789. Although his paternity was not directly acknowledged in the journal, King was openly recognised as the child's father throughout his life. Ann Inett and baby Norfolk returned to Sydney with King when he left Norfolk Island.

For Ann Smith's details and background, see Chapman op. cit.) p. 165. Also Gillen, *'The Founders of Australia'*, op. cit. listed alphabetically.

Regarding Ann Smith's disappearance, Bowes Smyth, op. cit. p. 72: *'This day Ann Smith (the woman who refused taking the slops on board from Mr. Miller the Commissary) eloped from the camp, as she often, when on board, declared she would as soon as she was landed'*. Also on Ann Smith and her disappearance, see Collins, op. cit. p. 409 and White, op. cit. p. 46. For the remains of a petticoat believed to have been Ann Smith's: Collins, ibid. p.120.

For the proposal of a town plan for Sydney and the intention of exploring further afield, see Tench, op. cit. p. 64.
Also see *'The Voyage of Governor Phillip to Botany Bay'*, Chapter XIII, p. 67.

18. Into an unknown wilderness

April 1788 expeditions, see John White's *'Journal of a Voyage to New South Wales'* April 15th – 27th 1788) (ebook, Project Gutenberg version), pp. 49 - 55. Note: The group made two journey's westward in April 1788; April 15th-18th, then another beginning April 22nd. 'See his entry for 16th April, 1788 for his comments on the natives' carvings.

See Tench, pp. 64, 70 re the governor's intentions for the 1788 expeditions westward. See Tench ibid. pp. 64 -65 for details of the governor's April 1788 excursion.

Tench's quote re natives' invisibility, ibid. p. 65. Other accounts demonstrate the natives' ability to remain undetected when it suited them: see White, op. cit. p. 51; see Clark, op. cit. p.109. See also Reynolds (2006) *'The Other Side of the Frontier'*, University of New South Wales Press, for accounts of natives' easy avoidance of white explorers, p. 30.

Governor Phillip's comments re the terrain of NSW: *'I believe no country can be more difficult to penetrate into than this is'*, cited in Barnard Eldershaw, (1972) *'Phillip of Australia'*, p. 280.

19. Friends and thieves

For an account of the Aborigines avoiding the white settlement, see Tench's Book One, p. 51

That some Aboriginal people adjusted their view, seeing the whites as 'not all the same', is supported in Collins, op. cit. p. 81 were good relationships were formed between individuals and groups though they still avoided the white camp.

William Dawes later developed close relationships with several Aboriginal people; he was deeply interested in their culture and kept detailed 'language notebooks' comparing English and the language of the Aboriginal people. Dawes recorded the original Aboriginal names of places and people, see Book C, page 52, 'Warran' for Sydney, Book C pp. 54-55,'Tarra' for Sydney Cove's western point; Book B, page 6 for 'Eora' meaning 'people'; Book C pp. 61-63 for Aboriginal personal names of men and women. See also Smith, op. cit. pp. 72-73. Admiration for the throwing stick, 'womara', by Hunter, op. cit. p. 34. Collins, op. cit. p. 479, referred to it as 'wo-mer-ra'. It is now known as 'woomera'.

According to Phillip's estimation, native inhabitants on his landing 1788 numbered about 1,500 natives in the area. When the settlers set up their camp there was almost twice that number of mouths to feed: *'Governor Phillip had calculated before, from the parties he had seen, that in Botany Bay, Port Jackson, Broken Bay, and all the intermediate country, the inhabitants could not exceed one thousand, five hundred.'* See HRA Series 1 Vol. 1, p. 29; also *'Voyage Of Governor Phillip'* (1789) p. 64.

For the account of song and dance enjoyed between convicts and Aborigines, see Collins Vol 1, p. 81. For co-operative interaction between black and white on the water away for the settlement see Collins, ibid, p. 67.

For thefts by convicts and sailors of Aboriginal equipment, see Collins, ibid. p. 67 ('note: fizgigs' were special fishing spears). See Collins, ibid. for an account of the natives forcibly taking a share of the fish caught by white fishermen, pp. 80-81. Phillip's comments on their response, see *'The Voyage Of Governor Phillip to Botany Bay and Norfolk* Island', pp. 72-73.

20. Frustration and progress
For the hanging of Bennet, see Collins, op. cit., p. 75.
For the initiative of Bloodworth, see Collins, pp. 75 & 156.
Regarding the brickworks, see Worgan, op. cit. pp. 39, 90, 103.
Laying of the foundation for Phillip's residence on May 15th, see Collins op. cit. pp. 75-76 .
Laziness of some convicts: Collins, p. 86, 92. Log bridge-building and stonecutters: pp. 86,109.

21. The rush-cutter incident
See Bradley's journal op. cit. entry for 30th May 1788 for his account of meeting the native man and children eating fruit.
Murder of two rush-cutters the same day & Phillip's subsequent pursuit of the issue: Collins, p. 77. Also, White op. cit. pp. 57-58.
Phillip's meeting with a large group of natives: *'Voyage of Governor Phillip to Botany Bay'*, p. 63.
Phillip's dispatch regarding the 'rush-cutter' incident, see HRA Series 1, Vol. p. 48-49.
For the Aborigine's customs & decrees on justice and reprisal, see Collins, (op. cit) Appendix VI-Customs & Manners, p. 480-481; Also Tench, op. cit. admired the natives' 'war operations' writing: *'Their ardent fearless character seeks fair and open combat only.'* See, p. 262.

22. Across the social divide

Details of June 4th celebrations & Phillip's mingling at the bonfire with convicts: see Worgan, op. cit. pp. 116-118; Also, White's journal op. cit. p. 60; Collins, op. cit. pp. 77-78; Tench op. cit. pp. 66-67.

For thefts the following day, see Worgan, ibid. p.119. Also: White's journal, op. cit. p. 61; Collins, op. cit. p.78.

For an account of the missing cattle, see Collins ibid. p. 79; Tench, p. 67.
Ross' correspondence to England (July 1788 to Colonial Secretary Stephens), in HRNSW ii: 173: See also Ross to Nepean ibid. p.212. Also, Cobley (1987) *Sydney Cove 1788*, p. 253. See Clarke's letter describing a kangaroo op. cit. p. 96, 98.

For the anonymous letter of a female convict, see Flannery, (editor), 1996, *The Birth of Sydney*, p.80. Also, in Bladen (ed) Historical Records of NSW, Vol II, pp. 746-747, 1893.

White's account of the court case involving Sinclair and Kable (written as Coble): see his journal entry for 8th July, p. 64.

Kable's letter to a family member, Dinah Cable (dated Nov 1788) stating the ease of his situation and his son 'as promising little fellow', see: *London Chronicle*, 21-23 July 1789 issue.

For convict rights in 18th century Britain, see Neal, (1991), *'The Rule of Law in a Penal Colony - Law and Power in Early New south Wales'*, *(Chapter 1, Great Changes)*, Cambridge University Press.
For an account of the marines' scam to steal provisions and their execution: Collins, pp. 97-98. Also see Lt. Newton Fowell's letter to his father July 1790, Letter 20 of *'The Sirius Letters - the complete letters of Newton Fowell 1786 – 1790'*, p. 112.

23. Across the racial divide

Details of dealings between black & white during July1788: White's account, op. cit. pp. 65-67.

24. Rose Hill

Hunter prepared Sirius for sail to Cape Town in September 1788; he left on October 1: see Hunter's journal, op. cit. p. 49.
Establishment of Rose Hill, see Tench, p. 92; Collins, pp. 88, 96; 'The Lump' see Collins p. 88.
For the Burramata people's displeasure at the settlement of Rose Hill, see Tench, p. 140.
See Aboriginal people's food gathering methods and tribal organisation, in Kohen (2009).
The Aborigines of Western Sydney, Darug Tribal Aboriginal Corporation. pp. 4-5
Collins' comments on treatment of Burramata people near Rose Hill, p. 96.
Rose Hill's cultivation & expansion, Collins, pp. 96, 100.

25. An opportunity not to be missed

See Tench, op. cit. p. 157-158 re Ruse' story and method of farming.
For Collins' account of Ruse and the governor's objective, see op. cit. pp. 122,169.

Note: 'An Historical Journal of the Transactions at Port Jackson & Norfolk Island' by Hunter, included accounts from Phillip's dispatches. See Phillip in Hunter, op. cit. p. 213.

Phillip's plan to seduce natives into the settlement: see Voyage Of Governor Phillip' op. cit. p. 73. British acknowledgment of the displacement of the Aboriginal families: Hunter op. cit. p. 220.

26. Kidnaps and adoptions

Johnston's character & appointment as Aid-de-Camp: see Bowes Smyth op. cit. p. 66, 69. For details of Arabanoo's capture & time in the settlement, see Tench (Bk 2), p. 95-108. Arabanoo's assumed belief that the white men intended to eat him: see Lt. Fowell's letter to his father July 1790, 'Sirius Letters - the complete letters of Newton Fowell 1786 – 1790', p. 114.

Hunter's impression of Arabanoo, see his journal op. cit. Chapter VI, p. 69.

Also see Tench re smallpox, the treatment and adoption of Nanberry & Boorong (also called Abaroo), p. 102-106.
See Tench, ibid. p.102 for an account of convicts' conflict with natives, their punishment and Arabanoo's reaction. Arabanoo's death & Tench's heartfelt regret, ibid. pp. 106-108. Smallpox affliction on the Aboriginal people, see Collins p. 488; Also, Phillip to Lord Sydney: HRNSW 2: 308.
Nanberry's adoption by John White, see Tench, op. cit. p. 105. Also, Collins, op. cit. p. 477. Boorong's adoption by Reverend and Mary Johnson, see Tench, op. cit. p. 106. Details of Mary Johnson: see Gillen, op. cit. p. 194; naming her daughter, Milba: Tench, op. cit. p. 265. Johnson's letter regarding Boorong, see Cobley, 'Sydney Cove: 1790', p. 69.

27. Further into the vast unknown

For the governors June 1789 excursion north-westward (along Hawkesbury River), see Hunter, op. cit. p. 71; for Hunter's account of finding the young Aboriginal woman, see p. 73; for report of yams and animal traps at the river, see p. 79.
Tench's journey westward from Rose Hill in June 1789: see Tench op. cit. pp. 111-113; Tench's notes on ducks frightened away by gunshot, on native, canoes, bird traps, notches cut into trees, see ibid. p. 111. River named 'Nepean', see p. 113.

Clark's journal, op. cit. p. 109: 'They could see me although I could see nothing of them...'

Dawes and Johnston's journey into the Blue Mountains in Dec 1789 to 'Mt Twiss', see Tench' op. cit., p. 116.
George Johnston's first son with Esther Abrahams, George Johnston Jnr, was born on 12th January, 1790.

See mention of Dawes 1789 expedition in Collins' op. cit. p. 119.

Tench included a map in his 'Complete Account of the Settlement of Port Jackson', 1793. See Cunningham (1996) 'Blue Mountains Rediscovered' for; details of Dawes trip, pp. 52-53; map of Dawes' journey, ibid. p.46. The river that Dawes believed flowed southward through the mountains, was later found and named Cox River.

The unidentified animal footprints seen by Dawes, see Collins op. cit. p. 119: Dawes reportedly saw '...the impressions of the cloven feet of an animal differing from other *cloven feet by the great width of the division in each. He was not fortunate enough to see the animal that had made them.'* The description doesn't fit any native Australian animal footprint; however an explanation may be that it was the footprint of a large kangaroo that appeared to be two segments of one foot, but was in fact the print of two feet close together.

28. 'A most unpleasant service'

See Bradley's account, op. cit. of the capture of Bennelong and Colbee, Transcript: a138182 Bradley's background, see Chapman op. cit. p. 46. Also see his listing in Australian Dictionary of Biography' online.
The captured natives' at Sydney Cove, see Tench, op. cit. pp. 117-119; Collins' account, see op. cit. p. 117.

Details of Jane Dundas, see Gillen, op. cit. p.110. Also Chapman, op. cit. p. 82.

29. Teachers and students

For Bennelong's property *Me-mel*, see Collins, op. cit. p. 490; on his demonstration on 'fire making' p. 485.
Bennelong's bestowing the title *Be-anna* on Phillip, see Tench, op cit. p. 119; also Collins, op. cit. Appendix 1, p. 453.
See Tench's admission on keeping Bennelong ignorant of the dire situation in the colony & keeping him supplied with an adequate food supply, op. cit. p. 125-126.
As a couple, Isabella Rawson & William Richardson, were in charge of the first specifically designated schoolhouse in Sydney beginning 1790. See Barcan (1965)' *A Short history of Education in New South Wales'*, p 25; Also, Cobley, (1983), '*Sydney Cove – Spread of settlement 1793-1795'*, p. 212: '*Richardson, together with his wife, began to teach a few children at Sydney about the year ninety'.(ie.1790).* See Gillen, op. cit. p. 315 for details on Isabella Rosson (Rawson); also Chapman op. cit. p.151. See details on William Richardson Chapman ibid. p. 154. Also, see Gillen, op. cit. p. 307.
Henry Kable mentioned in a letter that his son, little Henry attended school; see London Chronicle, 21-23 July 1789 issue.
In 1790, he would have been about four years old. On the 'Society for the Propagation of the Gospel' for financing education and sending books, see Cobley, '*Sydney Cove 1795-1800'*, p. 114. Also, Cobley, '*Sydney Cove – Spread of settlement 1793-1795'*, *Vol. IV*, p. 212.

30. Impatient for news

A description of the 'gloom and dejection' which 'overspread every countenance' in the colony, see Tench, op. cit. pp. 119-120.
White's letter, see Cobley, (1963) '*Sydney Cove 1789-1790'*, p 191.
Lieutenant Clarke's comment, see his journal,op. cit. p.113, diary entry for February 20th, 1790.
Collins' letter to his father, see Cobley, (1965) '*Sydney Cove 1791-1792'*, p. 129.
See Tench, op cit. pp. 120-121 for the governor's orders to prepare '*Sirius'* for a voyage to China to buy provisions.

31. Survival tactics

As a precaution against starvation Major Ross & 280 others were sent to Norfolk Island, March 1790: Collins, op cit. p. 125-127. See also Tench, p. 120-121; also Bradley's journal, op. cit., Transcript of a138188

John Hudson's details, see Gillen, op. cit. p. 181. Also Chapman, op. cit. p. 108. See also his details and living conditions for young chimney-sweeps in 18th century London, 'Orphans of history – the forgotten children of the first fleet' 1999 Text Publishing, pp. 12, 17, 24-41, 55-59.

For details of King & Inett's time together on Norfolk Island, see Jonathan King's (1981) 'Philip Gridley King: a biography of the third governor of New South Wales', Methuen Australia. pp. 38-42.

Ann Inett's time on Norfolk Is., see Inett, (2010) pp. 65-69. See Lt. P. G. King's journal for details of Norfolk's (his son's) birth & baptism (Jan 1789), op. cit. p. 177, 187.

32. Crucial decisions

Reduction of rations & conditions in the colony in 1790, see Tench, op. cit. pp. 120-122. Also, Collins, op. cit. pp. 127-128. For the governor's sharing of his own provisions, see Collins, ibid. p. 133; for the starving man, p. 134. Also Tench, p. 125.
For the anonymous soldier's letter, Cobley,(1963)'Sydney Cove 1789-1790', p. 184; also Flannery op. cit. p. 98, 99.
See a record of the attempted suicide of McManus in Cobley, ibid. p. 277.
See Chapman, op. cit. p. 129, for details of James McManus; James Bagley, see p. 31.
For Reverend Johnson's letter on dire conditions, see Cobley, ibid. pp. 167-169. On hearing news of the sinking of the Sirius, see Tench, op. cit. p. 121, 122.
Shipwreck of Sirius, see Collins op. cit. pp. 129-130. Lt. King's departure on Supply for England via Batavia, see ibid. p. 132.

33. The escape

Bennelong's escape, see Tench, op. cit. pp. 125-126. Southwell's account of the escape, see Cobley (1963) 'Sydney Cove 1789-1790', p. 194. See Hunter, op. cit. p.102. Also, Collins, op. cit. p. 136. Collins' concern that there was 'nothing to eat' in the colony, see ibid. p. 137.

34. Thoughts of freedom

John Wilson, on his sentence expiring, left the white settlement and lived with Aborigines, learning their language and taking on their lifestyle. The natives gave Wilson the name, Bun-bo-e. See Collins, op. cit. p.353: 'Wilson, a wild idle young man, who, his term of transportation being expired, preferred living among the natives.' Collins' opinion of Wilson was that: 'gratifying an idle wandering disposition was the sole object with Wilson in herding with these people... it was by no means improbable, that at some future time...he would join the blacks.' Natives' use of waist cords to alleviate hunger, see Tench, op. cit. p. 260: 'To alleviate the sensation of hunger, they tie a ligature tightly around the belly, as I have often seen our soldiers do from the same cause.'

Notes on an idyllic Aboriginal family scene: see Collins' journal, op. cit. Appendix VI, p. 485. Collins suspected that Wilson would side with the Aborigines when disputes arose with the whites, see ibid. p. 353.

35. Letters and questions

For the arrival of the *Lady Juliana* and news from home, see Tench, op. cit. p.126, 127; also Collins, op. cit. p.138.

For details of the fate of the *Guardian*, which had been sent from England with supplies, but had been prevented from reaching the colony by hitting an iceberg which caused her shipwreck, see Collins, ibid. pp.139 -140.

News from England, see Tench, op. cit. p.128.

36. The Second Fleet - 1790

For the arrival of Second Fleet ships (*Neptune, Surprise, & Scarborough*) from June, 1790, see Hunter, op. cit. p. 214.

See Flynn, (1993) *'The Second Fleet: Britain's Grim Convict Armada of 1790'* pp. 16-53 for background on the 'Second Fleet'.

Collin's account of the condition of convicts on board *Neptune, Surprise,* and *Scarborough,* see op. cit. pp. 143, 144. Reverend Johnson's letter with numbers of the dead, see Flannery, op. cit. pp. 100-102; also Cobley, *'Sydney Cove 1789-1790',* op. cit. p.264, 265. Rev. Johnson's account of dead bodies of convicts 'thrown into the harbour, and their dead bodies cast upon the shore, and were seen laying naked on the rocks around the harbour', ibid. p. 264.

Captain Hill's letter to a Mr Wathen on the appalling condition of convicts of the Second Fleet, see Cobley, ibid. pp. 250-252.

For accusations against Donald Trail & his prosecution, see, Collins, op. cit. pp. 149, 218.

Collins mentions Wentworth's medial qualifications and his embarking for Norfolk Island, ibid. p.149.

For further details of D'Arcy Wentworth, see his entry in Australian Dictionary of Biography online.

For further details of William Wentworth, son of D'Arcy and Catherine Crowley, see his entry in Australian Dictionary of Biography online. See ibid, for details of Catherine Crowley.

The later friendship between George Johnston Jnr (and younger brother Robert) and William Wentworth (son of D'Arcy Wentworth) is apparent through correspondence, cited in Roberts, op. cit. p. 114, 145-146. In March 1819 George Jnr expressed the concern and well wishes of 'the whole of the family' for Wentworth's return to good health. In the same correspondence George Jnr told WC Wentworth about his role in commissariat granaries in Jan 1819 saying his 'farming concerns are going as well as I can expect'. Wentworth Papers ML MSS A757 p.1 referred to in Roberts, p. 233.

William Wentworth went on to become a prominent statesman, reformer and famous explorer. George Johnston Jnr also engaged in exploration with his father and was appointed acting provost martial and later superintendent of government stock by

Gov. Macquarie. Although he died at the age of thirty in 1820, Macquarie had high praise for him.

Elizabeth Macarthur's voyage: see her letters to England in Clarke & Spender (editors, 1992) *'Life Lines - Australian women's letters and diaries 1788 to 1840'*, Allen and Unwin, p 21.

Further details of John & Elizabeth Macarthur's voyage, see Bickel, *'Australia's First Lady'*, Allen & Unwin, 1991, p.6 - 27
Also see King, *'Elizabeth Macarthur and Her World'*, Sydney University Press, 1980, pp.11-14. Also, Ellis, *'John Macarthur'*, (1955), pp. 15-26
See Elizabeth Macarthur's journal of Nov 1789 in *'Some Early Records of the Macarthurs of Camden'*, by Sibella Macarthur Onslow, (Project Gutenberg ebook No. 1302011h.html)

For Elizabeth Macarthur's first weeks in the colony and her friendship with Dawes, Tench and Worgan, see her letters to her friend Bridget Kingdon in England, dated March 1791, in Macarthur Papers (MP), held in the Mitchel Library Sydney. Also, Sibella Macarthur Onslow, op. cit. pp. 16-17.
Details of the 'whale incident' see Tench's journal, op. cit. p. 133. Also, Collins, op. cit. p. 149.

37. Mayhem at Manly

Natives feasting on the beached whale at Manly Cove, see Tench, op. cit. p. 134. Also Collins, op. cit. p. 151.
Details of the spearing of Phillip: see Tench's journal, pp. 136-140. Collins, pp. 152–153.
Waterhouse's first-hand account of the spearing: see copy held in the Mitchell Library: AW 109/2. His version of the incident is also relayed in Bradley's, *'A voyage to New South Wales - the journal of Lieutenant William Bradley RN of HMS Sirius*, facsimile copy, Ure Smith Pty Ltd, 1969, pp. 225-230.
Phillip's account: Chapter 17, *Transactions at Port Jackson* in Hunter, op. cit. pp. 217-218. Also Cobley, op. cit. pp. 279-284. See Elizabeth Macarthur's version of the event in her letter to England, HRNSW, Vol. 2 pp. 503-504.
See an in-depth analysis of Waterhouse's & Phillip's accounts in Clendinnen (2003) *'Dancing with Strangers'*, pp. 110-138.
Phillip's pondering on the incident; see Phillip in Hunter, op. cit. p.218; his decision for a peaceful resolution: ibid. p. 219. Also, HRA Series 1, Vol.1, p. 57.

38. Making Amends

The mid-harbour meeting between Dawes, Rev. Johnson and the native man from Burramatta, Maugoran (later learnt to be Boorong's father), see Tench, op. cit. p. 140.

Phillip's stated vision and intention for natives in *'Phillip's Views on the conduct of the Expedition & the Treatment of the Convicts'*, February 1787, HRNSW, Vol 1, Part 2, p. 53.
Effects of Rose Hill on Burramatta people, Ward, op. cit. pp 199 – 201.
Phillip's reinforcement of Rose Hill, Tench, op. cit. p. 140.
Boorong's relationship to Maugoran, see Hunter, op. cit. p. 220, 'Mau-go-ran, the father of the native girl who lived with the clergyman'.
Meetings with Bennelong on the north shore, Tench, op. cit. pp. 141-142; Barangaroo &

the 'petticoat incident' and her conversation with Boorong, see ibid. pp. 142-143. Return of stolen property, ibid. pp. 144-145.

Phillip's reunion with Bennelong at Manly, see Hunter, op. cit. p. 220;

Bennelong's return to the settlement, ibid p. 221. Tench, op. cit. p. 147. Collins, op. cit. p. 155.

Assurance that Bennelong could 'be his own master, and go and come when he pleased', see Hunter, op. cit. p. 221.

Bennelong showing his companions around the governor's house: Tench, op. cit. pp.148-150. Bennelong's avoidance of McEntire: ibid. p. 148.

Barangaroo's visit to Sydney settlement; description of her and her nose piercing, her nakedness, see Hunter, ibid. p. 224.

For reference to 'Berewolgal' (*men come from afar*) see Tench op. cit. p.266; Also Dawes Notebook C, p. 9: 'Berewal ': 'a great distance'; 'Berewalgal': 'the name given us by the natives'.

Bennelong takes up residence in the house built for him on the eastern point with Barangaroo and two adopted children, Hunter, op. cit. p. 223. Hunter and other officers were invited spectators at a native a dance at Bennelong's house, see Hunter, op. cit. pp.104-106. 'Barter' arrangements' commence between natives and whites, see Tench, op. cit. 146.

Tench on natives attending church, ibid. p. 251

Elizabeth Macarthur's reference to Daringa, see her letter of March 1791 to England, in HRNSW Vol.2, p. 504.

Also, see Macarthur Onslow, op. cit. p. 20. Also, Bickel, (1991), *'Australia's First lady'*, p. 45-46.

Description of the 'soft paperbark blanket, see Hunter, op. cit. p. 254.

The incident of Daringa's baby's finger & Surgeon White, see Hunter, ibid. p. 102 (the practice was referred to by the Eora as 'malgun', see Dawes' Notebook, op. cit., Book C, p. 23.

Language learning sessions outside Dawes' hut, see *'William Dawes' notebooks on the Aboriginal languages of Sydney 1790-1791'*, or see online at www.williamdawes.org. For examples, see Dawes' Book B, p. 8 & Book A, p. 26. See Karskens, (2010) p. 410-412. Barangaroo teasing Bennelong & Dawes, while he was shaving, see Dawes, Book A, p. 26. Dawes also visited the Eora: see Notebook A, p. 44. See also Turbet (2011), op. cit. pp. 60, 61.

Dawes' attempt at religious discussion with Boorong and her attendance at church, see Tench, op. cit. p. 251.

The 'candle snuffer' incident, see Tench, op. cit. 149. Pronunciation issues, ibid. (footnote). English pronunciation issues, ibid. pp. 266-267. Bennelong as go-between & his brick house at Bennelong Point, (site of Sydney Opera House), Tench, ibid. p. 160. On the Sydney native's language and its difficulties for the British, see Tench, op. cit. p. 265-267 *'The letter 'y' frequently follows 'd' in the same syllable. Thus the word which signifies a woman is 'dyin'; although the structure of our language requires us to spell it 'deein'.* Also on language exchange, see Smith, pp.72-74, 108-110. King, Philip Gidley,

'*A Sydney vocabulary 1790*', Smith, curator, State Library of New South Wales, Sydney
Pemulwuy, '*a leader of the tribe that resides about Botany Bay*' in disagreement with
Bennelong, see Hunter, op. cit. p. 222.
'Pemulwuy': 'man of the earth' is derived from 'pemul' meaning 'earth': see Collins, op. cit.
p. 500; Hunter, op. cit. p. 195.
Also, Kohen, (2005) ADB: http://adb.anu.edu.au/biography/pemulwuy-13147/text23797.

39. Pemulwuy

Turwood (or Tarwood) and four other convicts' escape by sea, see Collins, op. cit. p. 154.
For Pemulwuy's attack on McEntire (Macintire), see Collins, op. cit. pp. 158-159. Also
Tench, op. cit. pp. 164-165.

McEntire's confession and death see Tench ibid. pp. 165-166 (footnote).
Details on McEntire see Gillen, op. cit. p. 231. Also, Chapman (listed as McIntire), op. cit.
p.128.

40. Retaliation

Phillip's orders to Tench for a retaliatory expedition see Tench, op. cit. pp. 167-170.
Retaliatory action, see Collins, Ch. XI, Dec 1790, op. cit. p. 159.

41. Conflict and Bungles

Dawes' refusal to go on the punitive expedition, see Phillip's dispatch to England in HRA
Series 1, Vol. 1, pp. 289-292 & 293-294. Reference to Dawes as 'unofficerlike', ibid.
p. 291. Also see, Cobley,(1963) '*Sydney Cove 1789 -1790*', p.309, 13th Dec. Also see
Moore (1987) Ch. 17 for Phillip's dispute with Dawes.

Tench's account of his interaction with natives in the settlement before punitive expedition,
see Tench op. cit. p. 160.
For reference to Dawes' close friendship with Aboriginal people and in particular with
Pattye (Pattyegarang), see *Dawes' Notebooks,* op. cit. Books A, B, C, throughout. Book A
has entries from November 1790 – a month prior to the punitive expedition. Reference to
Dawes visiting the 'Eora', see his Book A, p. 44. Also, Karskens, op .cit. p. 397-398.
For maps of the routes taken on both expeditions, see Turbet, op. cit. pp. 55, 57.

Tenches' account of the punitive expeditions to Botany Bay, see Tench, op. cit. pp. 170-176.
Collin's comments on the purpose of the expedition see Collins op. cit. p. 159.

42. Growth and adjustment, Sydney – 1791

The short period of positivity was due in part to the colony being back on 'full ration' due
to provisions landed from a Dutch ship, *Waaksamhey,* see Collins, op. cit. p. 161. New
Year's Day, ibid. Grapes harvested, see Tench, op. cit. p. 179.
Reference to January 26th commemorating landing date, see Collins, op. cit. 162.
Summer heat & drought of 1790-91, see Tench, pp. 233-234. Also Elizabeth Macarthur's
comments on heat and storms, see her letter to Bridget Kingdon, Macarthur Papers (10),
held in the Mitchell Library.

Tanks cut into the fresh water stream, see Collins, op. cit. p. 192. Thefts from gardens, see Tench, op. cit. p. 184.

Punishment of convict thieves witnessed and abhorred by Aboriginal women, see Tench ibid.

43. Life and death

Bennelong's desire for his child to be born at the governor's house: see Hunter, op. cit. p. 254.

Birth of Bennelong & Barangaroo's baby, Dilboong: see Collins, op. cit. p. 467- 468.

Dilboong, meaning 'small bird', see: Collins, Vol. 2. p. 117.

Barangaroo's death & funeral rites see Collins Vol. 1, op. cit. pp. 453, 493, 495-496.

Attendance of Phillip, Collins & John White at Barangaroo's funeral, see bid. pp. 495-496.

Aboriginal custom of not using the name of a deceased person, ibid. p. 496.

Barangaroo and Bennelong's relationship see, Hunter, op. cit. p. 223-224, 227-229; Tench op. cit. pp. 147, 149.

Dilboong's death & funeral, see Collins Vol 1, op. cit. pp. 483, 495.

For Collins' discussion with Bennelong on life and death, see his journal, ibid. p. 455.

44. Forward planning

Phillip's physical pain, mentioned as early as April, 1788 by surgeon White, op. cit. pp. 53, 55. Also, see Phillip's letter of April 1790: HRA, Series 1, Vol. p. 17. Phillip's request to return to England: Cobley, 'Sydney Cove 1790', op. cit. pp. 187-188.

Also HRA, Series 1, Vol. 1, p. 262. Phillip's dispatches on the state of the colony & request to resign: HRA, pp. 272-279, 295.

Phillip's announcement to quit the colony England due to ill-health, see Collins, op. cit. p. 231.

Plots of ground allotted to convicts, see Tench, op. cit. p. 184.

By Dec 1791, there were 1,628 British settlers living at Rose Hill; see Tench, ibid. pp. 225-226. At Sydney there were 1,259.

For figures of the vast areas of land cleared for farming at Rose Hill & surrounding districts by the end of 1791, see Collins, op. cit. p. 191. Also see land cultivated & buildings erected, Tench, op. cit. pp. 210-224.

In May 1792, the people of the 'wood tribes' of whom Pemulwuy was leader, were involved in attacks on corn crops at Parramatta. Natives were shot, with subsequent reprisal attacks following; see Collins p. 209.

Phillip in Hunter, op. cit, p. 220: 'wherever our colonists fix themselves, the natives are obliged to leave that part of the country'.

45. New Territory

The April 1791 expedition westward with Colbee and Ballooderry was recorded by Tench, a participant in the events, see his journal, op. cit. pp. 185 -198.

Compass mentioned as 'naa-moro', literally 'to see the way' ibid. p.189; navigation methods, see footnote, pp. 186-187.

'Cooee', ibid. p. 188, 'Budyeeree', p.189; 'goninpatta' p. 190 (footnote); Rosehill as a place of plenty, see pp. 192, 198.

For mention of the *'koradji'* or 'Caradyee', meaning 'doctor of renown' see ibid, p. 197. See also Dawes' Notebook C, p. 5: 'Carrahdy – a person skilled in healing wounds'. Hunter's journal, op. cit. pp. 241-247, verifies Tench's account of the same journey.

For confusion about the Hawkesbury/Nepean Rivers, see ibid. p. 246.

For meeting with Yellomundee (also Yellomundi) & Tench's assessment of *'unabated friendship and good humour'* see Tench (op. cit) p. 197 Details of the May, 1791 trip of Tench & Dawes, see Tench op.cit. pp.199-201.

Kohen, op. cit. referred to the people of the Hawesbury area as Darug, however this has recently been disputed by Dr Geoff Ford who in his 2012 thesis, claims they were Darkinung; see also his 'Darkinung Recognition' Thesis, 2010.

For Tench & Dawes' last expedition in the colony in July 1791, see his journal, ibid. pp. 201-202. Confirmation of Hawkesbury & Nepean Rivers being the same, ibid. p. 199.

46. Great Escapes

Bryant's background: see Collins, op. cit. p. 94. Also Gillen, op. cit. (listed alphabetically); Chapman, op. cit. p. 53.
Bryants' escape, with a list of accomplices is described in Collins, ibid, pp. 165, 167-168; Also Tench, op. cit. pp. 180 -181 for an account of their voyage to Timor. James Martin, one of the survivors, later wrote 'Memorandums' giving details of the voyage (reproduced with introduction and notes by Victor Crittenden, 1991). See Martin's reference to the distress of Mary and 'the two little babies', ibid. p. 5. Details of the escape, ordeals and account of survivors, see Erickson, C. (2004) *'The girl from Botany Bay'.* Also Hirst (2013) *'Great convict escapes in colonial Australia'*, pp. 6-26.

John Easty's quote: see his journal entry March 1791 SLNSW Call no. DLSPENCER 374

Reference to 'Chinese travellers', see Tench, op. cit. pp. 208-209, 211; entry for Nov. 1791. Siting of 'fifty skeletons' by John Wilson, see Collins' *Account,* Vol. 2, op. cit. p.64.
The *forty-four men and nine women 'seeking China'* is reported in Collins Vol 1, op. cit. p. 196; also see, p. 189.
Levell, D, (2008) *'Tour to Hell'*, UQP, provides many more examples of convict escapes.

For the expectation of *Gorgon's* arrival in Sept. 1791, see Collins, ibid. pp.142 &177; for Gorgon's arrival, see p.184.

47. Family matters

Johnston & Esther's return to Sydney. Johnston's use of 'Hetty' for Esther Abrahams, see extracts from Johnston's diary, May 1791, p. 75, Diary No. 2, MMS6485, Folder 2, Mitchell Library, Sydney. Also, De Vries, op. cit. p. 29.
De Vries' (2009) devotes a whole chapter to Esther & Roseanna, pp. 11- 41.
Johnston's reference to *HMS Gorgon's* arrival to Ralph Clark, see Clark's *'Journal and letters'*, op. cit. p. 296.
Johnston refers to Esther as 'Hetty' and 'Hett' in his diary where he also recorded births (and stillbirths) of his children, and their annual birthdays. See diary entry referring to

baby George, 12 Jan, 1791: *'The boy is a year old!'* p. 60, Diary No. 2, MMS6485, Folder 2, Mitchell Library. Referring to son Robert on 9 March, 1794: *'Robert is 12months old today'*, ibid. p.158. Also, De Vries, op. cit. pp. 29-30.

Regarding the influx of native families into Sydney, see Hunter, op. cit, p.102, 104, 221; also, Elizabeth Macarthur's letter (March 1791), *'the natives visit us every day...A great many take up their abode entirely among us'*: Macarthur Papers 10, Mitchel Library, Sydney.

See Tench's reference to continued contact with natives from Oct 1790: Tench, op. cit. p. 150.

48. Arrivals and departures

Arrival of the ships of the Third Fleet, the *Queen* & the *Active*, with unhealthy convicts, see Collins, Vol 1, op. cit. p. 185.

For sale of goods from the ships, see Collins ibid. p. 186. Also, see Collins' letter to his father, in Cobley (1965), *Sydney Cove 1791-1792.*
Incentives for convicts to settle: Collins, op. cit. pp. 177-178. Also, Tench, op. cit. p. 206.

Arrival of *Gorgon*, see Collins, ibid. p.184; the dinner party at Government house, ibid. p. 187
Elizabeth Macarthur's opinion of the new Mrs King & Mrs Parker, see her letters to England in HRNSW Vol. 2. p. 507.

Lt. King, Paterson and their wives sailed for Norfolk Island on *Atlantic*, see Collins op. cit. p. 187. Also, Clark, op. cit. p. 221.

Anna Josepha King & Elizabeth Paterson were highly regarded in the colony; in Matthew Flinders' words: 'Two better or more agreeable women than Mrs King and Mrs Patterson are not easily found.' He described them as everyone's 'choicest friends', from Flinders papers, cited in Bassett, (1940).

Mrs Parker's observations: see her publication *'Voyage around the world on the Gorgon'* pp. 73-92, quoted in Barnard Eldershaw, op. cit. pp. 203-204.

Lt. King's commission as Lieutenant Governor of Norfolk Island, see Clark, op. cit. p. 223. Details of Jane Dundas, see Gillen, op. cit. p.110. Also Chapman, op. cit. p. 82.
See Ann Innet's story in Gillen (listed alphabetically). Also, Inett, op. cit. pp. 54-69.

See details of Richard John Robinson in Flynn, op. cit. pp. 503-505.

49. Nanberry and Ballooderry

Nanberry, see Tench, op. cit. pp. 104-105, 136, 163; as an informant to his countrymen, Hunter, op. cit. p. 254.
Incident of Ballooderry's canoe: Tench, op. cit. p. 203-204; Collins, op. cit, p. 175; Hunter, op. cit. Chapter XXII June 1791 to September 1791, p. 249-250, 254.

For the growing issue between Ballooderry & Governor Phillip, see (ibid) pp. 252-254; Collins, op. cit. p. 182; for Bennelong's intervention and Ballooderry's illness, see Hunter, p.264; Collins, p. 493.

Details of Ballooderry's funeral, see Collins, op. cit. p. 493; Maugoran, ibid. p. 491. Also, Smith, (2001), op. cit. p. 124-126.

50. Maugoran's family

Maugoran, father of Boorong & Ballooderry, see Hunter, op. cit. p. 220 & Collins, op. cit. p. 491. Displeasure of natives from Parramatta, Tench, op. cit. p.140.

Ballooderry's trade initiative & demolished canoe, see Hunter, op. cit. p. 249-250. Maugoran's wound treated by Dr. White, see Hunter, op. cit. p. 220.

Boorong wish to leave white settlement to marry: Hunter, ibid. p. 219, 222, 225, 231.

Maugoran's assumed independence, see Phillip in Hunter, op. cit. p. 221 *'he could be his own master, and go and come when he pleased'* (referring to Bennelong but equally applied to all natives in Sydney).

Boorong's role as go-between, see Collins Vol. 1, op. cit. p. 153.

51. More goodbyes

Gorgon departed Sydney 18th December, 1791: Tench, op. cit. p. 226.
Captain Hunter & George Worgan left Sydney in March 1791, on Waaksamheyd.

Elizabeth Macarthur's friendship with Dawes, Tench & Worgan: see her letter to England, March 1791: Macarthur Papers (MP), Mitchel Library Sydney. Also, HRNSW Vol. 2, pp. 498.

Elizabeth's complaint about lack of suitable female company, see her letter to Bridget Kingdon, March 1791, ibid.

Elizabeth Macarthur described Mrs King as 'possessed of a great share of good nature and frankness' in her letter to England, see Macarthur Papers, A2906, Mitchell Library, Sydney. See also, HRNSW Vol. 2, p. 507.

Tench's elation at *Gorgon's* arrival to take them home, see op. cit. p. 209-210. His admission of 'affection' for his Aboriginal friends, see ibid. p. 267. His departing account of Rose Hill: ibid, pp. 210-226; his account of George Barrington, p. 224; his comments on Matthew Everingham, p. 220.

For a full account of George Barrington's life, see Rickard (ed. 2001) *'George Barrington's Voyage to Botany Bay'*. Barrington's speech to a London jury, in September, 1790: see Rickard ibid. pp. 27, 59.

Everingham's account of life in the colony, see Ross (ed.1985) *'The Everingham Letterbook'* Closing words of Tench's journal: op. cit. p. 273-274.

For reference to Dawes' close friendship with Aboriginal people and in particular with Pattye (Pattyegarang), see *William Dawes' Notebooks,* op. cit. Notebooks A, B, C, throughout.

Dawes' conversation with Pattye about the black men's anger, see *William Dawes' Notebooks,* ibid. Notebook B, p. 34, also online at www.williamdawes.org
Also, Jakelin, (1992) *The Sydney Language Notebooks and responses to language contact in early colonial NSW,* originally in *Australian Journal of Linguistics,* 1992, pp.12, 145-170.

52. A time of transition

Collin's despondency at Gorgon's and Supply's departure, see Collins' journal, op. cit. pp. 193-194. For events following in early 1792, thefts, absconders, etc., see ibid. 194-201. Phillip's resignation acknowledged by Lord Dundas in a letter received in October, 1792, by the ship Reliance. See HRA, series 1, Vol. 1, pp. 353–355.

Phillip's announcement about his departure, 'excited no small degree of concern in the settlement', Collins, op. cit. p. 231.

Major Grose arrived in Sydney, 14th Feb, 1792; to take command when Phillip left: Collins, ibid. p. 201.

For backgrounds on Susannah Kable & Esther Abrahams see Gillen, (alphabetical listings). For Elizabeth Macarthur, see Australian Dictionary of Biography online. Also her account of her voyage on Scarborough, see her letter to England, in Clarke & Spender (editors, 1992) op. cit. p 21.

By the end of 1792, Susannah Kable's son, Henry was about 6 years old; Esther Abrahams' daughter, Roseanna was about five, and Elizabeth Macarthur's son, Edward was about three.

For crawling insects & maggots, see Clark, op. cit. pp. 95-96. Summer heat & storms, see Tench, pp.182, 233-234. Also Clark on terrifying storms, ibid, p. 96. See Elizabeth Macarthur's comments on heat and storms, in her letter to Bridget Kingdon, Macarthur Papers (10), Mitchell Library.

For the future trials of Henry Kable, George Johnston and John Macarthur, see their entries in 'Australian Dictionary of Biography' online. (Also the sequel to this book: Kable is arrested by Governor Bligh; Johnston faces charges for his involvement in deposing Bligh; Macarthur is in trouble over the same and other incidents.)

Susannah Kable's (Holmes) story, see Gillen, (alphabetical listing). Chapman, op. cit. pp.106 -7 By the end of 1792, Susannah Kable already had two colonial born children under the age of three, as well as their English born son, Henry. Her daughter, Diana was born in Sydney in December 1788; a son, Enoch in April 1791. In mid-1793 she would give birth to another boy, James: see Gillen, op. cit. p. 178. Susannah eventually bore eleven children by Henry Kable and lived to 1825, aged sixty-three.

Henry Kable, by 1792, had been appointed as a constable and night watchman, as well as receiving a free pardon; see his entry in 'Australian Dictionary of Biography' by Hainsworth, online: www.abd.anu.edu.au

Henry Kable mentioned in a letter that his son, 'little Harry' attended school; see London Chronicle, 21-23 July 1789 issue.

Esther Abrahams' story, see Chapman, op. cit. pp. 21-23. Her first son to George Johnston was born in Jan 1791; a second son Robert was born in March 1793. Esther gave birth to a stillborn baby girl (mentioned in George's diary) in March 1792. Esther eventually had eight children with George Johnston, in addition to her English born daughter, Roseanna.

Johnston's promotion as commander of a company of NSW Corps, see Collins, ibid. p. 246.

He was among the cartel of officers who chartered Captain Raven's *Britannia* to buy 'such articles as would tend to the comfort of themselves and the soldiers of the corps' see Collins, ibid. p.227.

Extracts from George Johnston's diary show him to be a dedicated father recording the birthdates and ages of each of his children. See, MSS 6485 Folder 2, Mitchell Library.

Johnston moved into the newly completed barracks at the end of 1792 : 'One barrack being now completed,...it was occupied by Captain George Johnston, a party-wall having been thrown down adapting the building to the accommodation of one instead of two officers', see Collins, op. cit. p. 242. This may have been adapted as family quarters as Robert was born at newly built barracks in March 1793. In July, 1793, Johnston wrote in his diary about his son, then two and a half: 'George's clothes caught fire in the evening and if I had not been present he must have been burnt to death.' See Johnston's diary p.142, ML MSS 6485, Folder 2.

Three months after the departure of Phillip, George Johnston (and Esther) took possession of a hundred acre land grant a few kilometres south-west of Sydney, naming it 'Annandale'. It would eventually grow to an estate the size of a village. Now it is a suburb of modern Sydney.

Esther was referred to in newspaper article, *'Johnstons of Annandale'*, Sydney Morning Herald 28 April 1931*: 'through evil and through good report remained a faithful wife and companion'.*

Elizabeth Macarthur's fear of thunderstorms and adjustments to the climate, see her letter to Bridget Kingston Macarthur papers, 10 (March 1791) &12 (November 1791), Mitchell Library, Sydney. Also her opinion of her adopted land and its prospects, see ibid. Also Macarthur's letters to friends & family regarding the colony: HRNSW Vol. 2, pp. 494-499.

Macarthur's daughter Elizabeth, was born Feb 1793 (named in remembrance of their baby who lived only an hour on the voyage to the colony): see Bickel, op. cit. p. 53. Also, see Ellis, op. cit. p. 59. Note: some references put baby Elizabeth's birth as 1792, however, in letter Elizabeth Macarthur states that her daughter was *'able to walk by one hand'* at ten months old at the end of 1793. Macarthur papers, extracts from letters A2908 Mitchell Library.

Macarthur's appointment as 'Inspector of public works' in early 1793, see HRA 1, Vol. 1, 416. Also, see Collins p. 249: *'The lieutenant governor...deputed his trust to lieutenant John Macarthur; the superintendents, storekeepers, overseers, and convicts at the two settlements, being placed under his immediate inspection.':*

Macarthur's circumstances and prospects in the colony in late 1792, see Bickel op. cit., pp. 42, 47, 51-53; See also, King, (1981) *'Elizabeth Macarthur and her world'*, pp. 18-19, 71.

53. Pondering the known and the unknown

For details of progress in Sydney in the latter half of 1792, see Collins op. cit. pp. 210-244. 'Parramatta' had officially replaced the name for Rose Hill in June 1791, Tench. op. cit. p. 203. Reference to the market, hospital & town hall at Parramatta, see Collins op. cit. p. 205.

Members of the NSW Corps remaining in the colony as were 59 privates, 3 corporals & 1 drummer: Tench, op. cit. p. 210.

Phillip's donation of sheep and goats to settlers, see Collins, op. cit. p. 238.
Added incentives of tools, grain & stock and reported success, see ibid. p. 237.

Phillip's recommendation for Johnston's promotion to Captain-lieutenant, see HRA, Series 1 Vol. 1 pp. 392, 446.
The formation of NSW Corps from marines under the command of Captain Johnston (47 men enlisted), see Collins, ibid. p. 246.

Appointment of Major Francis Grose as Lieutenant Governor, see Collins, ibid. p.202.

Charter of Captain Raven's *Britannia* by Macarthur & other officers to buy '*such articles as would tend to the comfort of themselves and the soldiers of the corps*' see Collins, ibid. p.227.

Capt. Raven lodging in Esther Abrahams' dwelling, see Cobley, '*Sydney Cove 1791-1792*', (1965), pp. 321-322, 359.

Major Grose's trust in Macarthur & the latter's influence & promotion: Collins, ibid. 249, 264. James Bloodworth's commendation, see Collins, ibid. p. 156.

Isabella Rosson (Rawson) & William Richardson, ran the first specifically designated schoolhouse in Sydney, see Barcan (1965) p 25. Also, Cobley, (1983), *Sydney Cove - 1793-1795*, p. 212: '*Richardson, together with his wife, began to teach a few children at Sydney about the year ninety'(ie.1790)*. Henry Kable's son attending school; see London Chronicle, 21-23 July 1789 issue.

Henry & Susannah Kable learnt to write in NSW: see Gillen op. cit. pp. 561, 564, 567.

James Ruse and his wife Elizabeth, see Collins, op. cit. p. 219, 237.
Also see Tench, op. cit. pp. 157-158, 223.

John Wilson, on his sentence expiring, left the white settlement and lived with Aborigines, learning their language and taking on their lifestyle. They gave Wilson the name, Bun-bo-e. See Collins, op. cit. p. 353.' Collins' opinion of Wilson was that: '*gratifying an idle wandering disposition was the sole object with Wilson in herding with these people... it was by no means improbable, that at some future time...he would join the blacks.*'

Bryants' fate in Timor: Collins op. cit. pp. 213–214. Details & list of accomplices to the escape: Collins, ibid. pp. 165, 167-168. See Tench, op. cit. pp. 180 -181, for their voyage to Timor. Also see James Martin's,' Memorandums' for details of the voyage (reproduced with introduction and notes by Crittenden,1991). See Erickson, C. (2004) '*The girl from Botany Bay*', for full details of the escape.

The escape was reported in the Dublin Chronicle, July 21st, 1792, which wrote that it '*was perhaps, the most hazardous and wonderful effort ever made by nine persons (for two were infants) to regain their liberty*', in Currey, C (1983), p. 38.

Dorothy Handland left Sydney for England aboard *Kitty* in 1793; see Collins, Vol. 1 Chapter 21. Also, Gillen op. cit. p. 159.
Men dragging brick carts, see Collins, op. cit. pp. 198, 251, 263. Working hours for convicts, see Ward, op. cit. p. 205.

Native children's ball game: Collins, op. cit. p. 468.

Resentment of some Aboriginal people toward white settlers, see Collins, op. cit. p. 161. Elizabeth Macarthur's reference to Daringa, see letter to Bridget Kingdon: HRNSW Vol.2, p. 504. Also, Bickel op. cit. p. 45-46.

Boorong's departure from the white settlement to marry: Hunter, ibid. pp. 219, 222, 225, 231. Nanberry's adoption by John White, see Tench, op. cit. p. 105. Also Collins, op. cit. p. 477.

Nanberry & Boorong living between two cultures, see Hunter, pp. 219, 222, 225, 231, 254. Collins: op. cit. pp. 467, 477, 487, 488. Tench, op. cit. p. 163 (footnote). Nanberry & Boorong's role as go-betweens: Collins Vol. 1, op. cit. p. 153. Tench: op. cit., pp. 134, 141.

'Berewolgal' (*men come from afar*): Tench, op. cit. p. 266; Dawes book C, p. 9: Berewalgal: the name given us by the natives'.

Departure of Phillip on *Atlantic* with Bennelong & Yem-mer-ra-wan-ne, see Collins, Vol 1. op. cit. p.238: *'With the governor there embarked, voluntarily and cheerfully, two natives of this country, Bennillong and Yem-mer-ra-wan-ne, two men who were much attached to his person; and who withstood at the moment of their departure the united distress of their wives, and the dismal lamentations of their friends, to accompany him to England, a place that they well knew was at a great distance from them.'*

★

Bibliography

Abbreviations:

ADB   Australian Dictionary of Biography
HRA   Historical Records of Australia
HRNSW   Historical Records of News South Wales
ML   Mitchell Library, Sydney

Primary sources – published, unpublished and archival material

Anon., Letter from a female convict at Port Jackson, November 1788, in HRNSW, Vol 2, pp. 746-747, F. Bladen (ed.) Government printer Sydney, 1893.

Atkins, Richard, *Journal 1791- 1810*, transcript held at Mitchell Library, MSS 737.

Bowes Smythe, A., *The Journal of Arthur Bowes Smyth: Surgeon, Lady Penrhyn 1787 - 1789*, Sydney, Australian Documents Library Pty Ltd, 1979.

Bradley, William, *A Voyage to New South Wales, December 1787 - 1792*, Facsimile reproduction, Trustees of the Public Library of NSW,1969; available online through The State Library of NSW website: www.sl.nsw.gov.au

Clark, Ralph, *The Journal and Letters of Lt. Ralph Clark, 1787 - 1792*, Sydney, Australian Documents Library Pty Ltd, 1981.

Collins, David, *An account of the English Colony in New South Wales, Volume 1 (of 2) facsimile edition Libraries Board of Australia, 1971; first published by T. Cadell Jun. & W. Davies, London, 1798.*

Collins, David, *An account of the English Colony in New South Wales, Volume 2 (of 2) facsimile edition Libraries Board of Australia, 1971; first published by T. Cadell Jun. & W. Davies, London, 1798.*

Dawes, W., Williams *Dawes Notebooks on the Aboriginal Language of Sydney, 1790-1791,* Hans Rausing Endangered Language Project & School of Oriental and African Studies, London, 2009.

Easty, Private J, *Memorandum of the/transactions of a Voyage from England to Botany Bay, 1787-1793: A First Fleet Journal by John Easty, Private Marine, Trustees of the Public Library of New South Wales, Sydney 1965;* available online through the State Library of NSW website: www.sl.nsw.gov.au

Everingham, Matthew, *The Everingham Letterbook* (edited & intro. by Valerie Ross, Anvil Press in Assoc. with The Royal Australian Historical Society, 1985

Fowell, Newton., (Nance Irvine, editor.)*The Sirius Letters: The complete letters of Newton Fowell 1786 - 1790',* The Fairfax Library, 1988.

Historical Records of Australia, Vol. 1, collected & published by the Library Committee of the Commonwealth Parliament, 1914-1925. J.F. Watson (ed.) Now available online <http://trove.nla.gov.au/work/17995589>

Historical Records of New South Wales, Government Printer, Sydney, 1892-1901, F. Bladen (ed.) Now available online <http://trove.nla.gov.au/work/478037>

Hunter, John, *An Historical Journal of Events at Sydney and at Sea 1787 – 1792*, copy published by Angus & Robertson, Sydney 1968. Available online as: *An historical journal of the transactions at Port Jackson & Norfolk Island with the discoveries which have been made in New South Wales & in the southern ocean, since the publication of* Phillip's voyage, compiled from official papers; including journals of Governor Phillip & King, & of Lieut. Ball; and the voyages from the first Sailing of the Sirius in 1787, to the Return of that Ship's Company to England in 1792. Online <http://www.gutenberg.org/files/15662/15662-h/15662-h.htm>

Johnson, Reverend Richard, *Letters from the Rev. Richard Johnson to Henry Fricker, 30 May 1787-10 August 1797*, ML, Safe 1/121.

Johnston, George., Extracts from the diary of George Johnston, Douglas Hope Johnston Papers, 1789 – 1951, ML MSS 6485, Part 1, Folder 2.

King, Lt. Philip Gidley, *The Journal of Philip Gidley King: Lieutenant, R.N. 1787 - 1790*, Australian Documents Library Pty Ltd, Sydney, 1980.

Macarthur, Elizabeth., journal of her voyage to New South Wales, Nov 1789 in *Some Early Records of the Macarthurs of Camden*, edited by Sibella Macarthur Onslow, Angus and Robertson, 1914. Also Project Gutenberg ebook No. 1302011h.html. See also Macarthur Family Papers (MP), held in the Mitchel Library, State Library of New South Wales, Sydney.

Macarthur, Elizabeth., letters to Miss Kingdon, 1790 - 1794, in *'Some Early Records of the Macarthurs of Camden'*, edited by Sibella Macarthur Onslow, Angus and Robertson, 1914. See Macarthur Papers (MP), held in the Mitchel Library Sydney. Also: Project Gutenberg ebook No. 1302011h.html.

Martin, James, *Memorandoms* (manuscript discovered in 1937 among the Bentham Papers, University of London Library.) Published in 1991 as: *Escape from Botany Bay, 1791: being Memorandoms*, with introduction & notes by Victor Crittenden, Mulini Press, Canberra.

New South Wales Legislative Council Proceedings, *'Minutes of Evidence taken before the Select Committee on the Aborigines.'* See, 8 Sept 1845: (information by Mahroot alias the Boatswain), Government Printing Office, Sydney, 1845.

Nicol, J, *The life and Adventures of John Nicol, mariner*, (edited & introduced by Tim Flannery) Text, Melbourne, 2012.

Phillip, Arthur, *The Voyage of Arthur Phillip to Botany Bay*, John Stockland, London, 1789. Available online: http://gutenberg.net.au/ebooks/e00101.html

Southwell, D, *Daniel Southwell - Papers M1538, (1783-1793)* State Library of NSW, Sydney.

Tench, Watkin, *A Narrative of the Expedition to Botany Bay*, 1789 reproduced in *1788* (introduced & edited by Tim Flannery) Text Publishing, Melbourne, 1996.

Tench, Watkin, *A Complete Account of the Settlement at Port Jackson*, 1793. Reproduced in *1788* (intro. & edited by Tim Flannery) Text, Melbourne, 1996.

Waterhouse, Henry, Waterhouse's first-hand account of the spearing: see copy held in the Mitchell Library: AW 109/2.

Worgan, George, *Journal of a First Fleet Surgeon,* The William Dixon Foundation, Library Council of New South Wales, Sydney, 1978.

Books, journals and printed works

Australian Dictionary of Biography, Vol. 1 - 18, Australian National University, Canberra, 1966 – 2012. Online http://trove.nla.gov.au/version/33452370

Barcan, A, *A Short History of Education in New South Wales*, Martindale Press, Sydney, 1965.

Barkley-Jack, J., *Hawkesbury settlement revealed: a new look at Australia's third mainland settlement*, Rosenberg, Kenthurst, 2009.

Barnard, M, *Macquarie's World*, Angus & Robertson Pty Ltd, Sydney, 1971.

Barnard Eldershaw, M, *Phillip of Australia: An Account of the Settlement of Sydney Cove 1788-92,* Discovery Press, Penrith, 1972.

Bassett, M, *The Governors Lady*, Oxford University Press, London, 1940.

Bateson, C, *The Convict Ships: 1787- 1868,* Library of Aust. History, Sydney, 1983.

Bertie, C. *The Story of Sydney*, Shakespeare Head Press, 1933.

Berzins, B, *The Coming of Strangers, Life in Australia 1788 - 1822*, William Collins Pty Ltd, Sydney, 1988.

Bickel, Lennard, *Australia's First Lady: the story of Elizabeth Macarthur*, Allen & Unwin, 1991.

Bowes Smythe, A., *The Journal of Arthur Bowes Smyth: Surgeon, Lady Penrhyn 1787 - 1789*, Sydney, Australian Documents Library Pty Ltd, 1979.

Broome, R., *Aboriginal Australians: black response to white dominance*, Allen & Unwin, 1982.

Chapman, Don, *1788: The People of the First Fleet, Sydney*, Doubleday Australia Pty Ltd, 1986.

Clark, Manning, A Short History of Australia, Mentor Books, New York, 1963.

Clark, Ralph, *The Journal and Letters of Lt. Ralph Clark, 1787 - 1792*, Sydney, Australian Documents Library Pty Ltd, 1981.

Clarke, P. & Spender D, (eds.) *Life Lines - Australian women's letters and diaries 1788 to 1840*, Allen & Unwin, 1992.

Clendinnen, I, *Dancing with Strangers*, Text Publishing, Melbourne, 2003.

Clune, F, *Rascal, Ruffians & Rebels of Early Australia*, Angus & Robertson, Sydney, 1978.

Cobley, J, *Sydney Cove 1789, 1790* Angus & Robertson, Sydney, 1963.

Cobley, J, *Sydney Cove 1791-1792*, Angus & Robertson, Sydney, 1965.

Cobley, J, *The Crimes of the First Fleet Convicts*, Angus & Robertson, Sydney, 1982.

Cobley, J, *Sydney Cove 1788*, Angus & Robertson, Sydney, 1987.

Collins, David, *An account of the English Colony in New South Wales, Volume 1 (of 2) (Illustrated edition)*, The Echo Library, Middlesex, 2008.

Collins, David, *An account of the English Colony in New South Wales, Volume 2 (of 2) (Illustrated edition)*, The Echo Library, Middlesex, 2008.

Connor, J, *The Australian Frontier Wars 1788 - 1838*, UNSW, Sydney, 2005.

Cunningham, C, *The Blue Mountains Rediscovered - Beyond the Myths of Early Australian Exploration,* Kangaroo Press, Sydney, 1996.

Curry, Charles. H, *The Transportation, Escape and Pardoning of Mary Bryant*, Sydney, Halstead Press, 1983.

Daniels, K, *Convict women*, Allen & Unwin, Sydney, 1998.

Dawes, W., Williams *Dawes Notebooks on the Aboriginal Language of Sydney, 1790-1791,* Hans Rausing Endangered Language Project & School of Oriental and African Studies, London, 2009.

de Vries, Susanna, *Historic Sydney,* Pandanus Press, Brisbane, 2003.

de Vries, Susanna, *Females on the Fatal Shore, Australia's Brave Pioneers*, Pirgos Press, Brisbane, 2009.

Elder, B, *Blood on the Wattle, Massacres and Maltreatment of Aboriginal Australians since 1788*, New Holland Publishers, Sydney, 2003.

Ellis, M.H, *John Macarthur*, Angus & Robertson, Sydney, 1955.

Erickson, Carolly, *The girl from Botany Bay,* Pan Macmillan Australia, 2004.

Flannery, Tim, (ed.) *The birth of Sydney,* Text Publishing, Melbourne, 1999.

Flynn, M, *The Second Fleet: Britain's grim convict Armarda 1790*, Library of Australian History, Sydney, 1993.

Foster, David, & Duffy, Michael, *Crossing the Blue Mountains, Journeys Through Two Centuries*, Sydney, Duffy & Snellgrove, 1997.

Fowell, Newton., (Nance Irvine, ed.)*The Sirius Letters: The complete letters of Newton Fowell 1786 - 1790'*, The Fairfax Library, 1988.

Fraser, B, (ed.) *The Macquarie book of Events, Macquarie Library,* Sydney, 1983.

Frost, A, *Arthur Phillip: His Voyaging,* Oxford University Press, Melbourne, 1987.

Gillen, M, The Founders of Australia- A Biographical Dictionary of the First Fleet, Library of Australian History, Sydney, 1989.

Frost, A, *Botany Bay Mirages Illusions of Australia's Convict Beginnings,* Melbourne University Press, Melbourne, 1994.

Hainsworth, D, *Builders and Adventurers: The Traders and the Emergence of the Colony 1788-1821*, Cassell, Melbourne, 1968.

Hill, D, *1788: The Brutal Truth of the First Fleet*, William Heinemann, Sydney, 2008

Hirst, J, *Convict Society and its Enemies: A History of Early New South Wales*, Allen & Unwin, 1983.

Hirst, W, *Great convict escapes in colonial Australia*, Kangaroo Press, Sydney, 2003

Holden, Robert, *Orphans of History: the forgotten children of the First Fleet*, Text Publishing, Melbourne, 1999.

Howell, John, *John Nicol, mariner, Life and Adventures 1776 – 1801*, Text Publishing, Melbourne, 1997.

Hughes, Robert, *The Fatal Shore*, Vintage, London, 2003.

Inett. E., *Inett – What's in a Name?* Rock & District, Worcestershire, 2009.

Irvine, N, *Mary Reiby: Molly Incognita, Emancipist Extrordinaire, A biography 1777-1855*, Sydney, Library of Australian History – Publishers, 1987.

Irvine, Nancy (editor) *The Sirius Letters - the complete letters of Newton Fowell 1786 – 1790*, The Fairfax Library, 1988.

Jakelin, Troy, *The Sydney Language Notebooks and responses to language contact in early colonial NSW,* originally printed in *Australian Journal of Linguistics* 1992, 12, 145-170.

Karskens, G, *The Rocks: Life in Early Sydney*, Melbourne University Press, 1997.

Karskens, G, *The Colony: A History of early Sydney*, Sydney, Allen & Unwin, Sydney, 2010.

Kenealley, T, *The Commonwealth of Thieves*, Random House, Sydney, 2005.

Kenealley, T, *Australians Origins to Eureka*, Allen & Unwin, Sydney, 2009.

King, H, *Elizabeth Macarthur and Her World*, Sydney University Press, 1980.

King, H, *Colonial Expatriates, Edward and John Macarthur Junior*, Kangaroo Press Pty Ltd, Sydney, 1989.

King, Lt. Philip Gidley, *The Journal of Philip Gidley King: Lieutenant, R.N. 1787 - 1790*, Australian Documents Library Pty Ltd, Sydney, 1980.

Kohen, J, *The Darug and their neighbours – The traditional Aboriginal owners of the Sydney region'*, Darug Tribal Aboriginal Corporation, 1993.

Kohen, J, *Pemulwuy,* Australian Dictionary of Biography, National Centre of Biography, Australian National University, Canberra. 2005. <http://adb.anu.edu.au/biography/pemulwuy-13147/text23797>

Kohen, J, *The Aborigines of Western Sydney,* Darug Tribal Aboriginal Corporation., 2009.

Levell, David, *Tour to Hell, Convict Australia's Great Escape Myths*, Brisbane, University of Queensland Press, 2008.

Liston, Carol, The Darawal and Gandangara in colonial New South Wales 1788 - 1830,*Aboriginal History,* Vol 12,1988.

Mackaness, George, *Admiral Arthur Phillip: Founder of New South Wales, 1738-1814*, Angus and Robertson, Sydney, 1937.

Martin, James,*Memorandoms (Escape from Botany Bay, 1791: being Memorandoms,* introduction & notes by Victor Crittenden, Mulini Press, Canberra, 1991.

Mitchell, B, *The Australian Story and its Background,* Cheshire Publishing Pty Ltd, Melbourne, 1968.

Moore, John, *The First Fleet Marines 1786 – 1792,* University of Queensland Press, Brisbane, 1987.

Murray, R., & White, K., *Dharug & Dungaree, The History of Penrith and St Marys to 1860*, Melbourne, Hargreen Publishing Company, 1988.

Neal, David, *The Rule of Law in a Penal Colony - Law and Power in Early New South Wales, (Chapter 1, Great Changes),* Cambridge University Press, 1991.

Nicol, J, *The life and Adventures of John Nicol, mariner,* (edited & introduced by Tim Flannery) Text, Melbourne, 2012.

Parker, D, *Arthur Phillip: Australia's first Governor,* Woodslane Press, Sydney, 2009.

Perry, T. M, *Australia's First Frontier: The Spread of settlement in New South Wales,* Melbourne, Melbourne University Press, 1963.

Rees, S, *The Floating Brothel: The Extraordinary Story of the Lady Juliana and its Cargo of Female Convicts Bound for Botany Bay*, Hodder, Sydney, 2001.

Reynolds, H., *The Other Side of the Frontier – Aboriginal resistance to the European invasion of Australia*, University of New South Wales Press, 2006.

Richards, Joanna Armour, *Blaxland-Wentworth-Lawson, 1813*, Hobart, Blubber Head Press, 1979.

Rickard, S, (ed) *George Barrington's Voyage to Botany Bay,* Leicester University Press, 2001.

Roberts, Alan, *Marine Officer, Convict Wife, The Johnstons of Annandale*, Sydney, Annandale Urban Research Association, 2008.

Robinson, P., *The Hatch and Brood of Time,* Oxford University Press, 1985.

Robinson, P., *The Women of Botany Bay*, Macquarie Library, 1988.

Ross. V., (ed.) *The Everingham Letterbook*, Anvil Press in Association with The Royal Australian Historical Society, Wamberal, 1985.

Ryan, R. J, The Second Fleet Convicts, Star Printery, Sydney 1982.

Saunders, J.B, *The remarkable Story of Elizabeth Pulley*, Local Studies Library, Penrith City Library, NSW, 2002.

Schofield, Ann, *Signposts of Change: a chronology of Australian history and world events*, Aird Books, Melbourne, 1987.

Smith, Babette, *Australia's Birthstain: the startling legacy of the convict era*, Allen & Unwin, Sydney, 2008.

Smith, V. K, *Bennelong: The Coming in of the Eora Sydney Cove 1788 - 1792* Kangaroo Press, 2001.

Smith, K, V, *Wallumedegal: An Aboriginal History of Ryde*, City of Ryde, 2005.

Smith, K, V, *Eora: A Sydney Vocabulary, 1790*, State Library of New South Wales, Sydney, 2006.

Smith, K, V, *Mari Nawi: Aboriginal Odysseys*, Rosenberg, Kenthurst, 2010

Tench, Watkin, *Watkin Tench, 1788* (edited by Tim Flannery) Text Publishing, Melbourne, 1996.

Turbet, P, *The Aborigines of the Sydney District*, Kangaroo Press, Sydney, 2001.

Turbet, P, *The First Frontier: The occupation of the Sydney Region 1788-1816*, Rosenberg Publishing, Kenthurst, 2011.

Van Sommers, Tess, & Emanuel, Cedric, *Early Sydney Sketchbook*, Royal Australian Historical Society, Sydney, 1983.

Ward, Russel, *Finding Australia, The History of Australia to 1821*, Heinemann Educational Australia, Melbourne, 1987.

Willey, K., *When the sky fell Down*, William Collins Pty Ltd., Sydney, 1979.

Worgan, George, *Sydney Cove Journal January - July 1788*, (edited by Currey) The Banks Society.

Newspapers

Dublin Chronicle, 1792

London Chronicle, 1786, 1789

Manly Daily, 1924

Sydney Gazette, 1827

Sydney Morning Herald, 1931

Windsor and Richmond Gazette, 1899

Online resources

Australian Dictionary of Biography http://adb.online.anu.edu.au/

Botany Bay Medallion: http://botanybaymedallion.com/?page_id=15

Colonial Secretary's Papers, 1788-1825:
http://www.records.nsw.au/indexes/colsec/default.htm

National Library of Australia: archives, images, historic newspapers, maps etc.
http://trove.nla.gov.au

Newspaper archives (Search using 'periodicals only')
http://library.sl.nsw.gov.au/search/

Notebooks of William Dawes on the Aboriginal language of Sydney:
http://www.williamdawes.org/

Online resources relating to early Australian History:
http://gutenberg.net.au/aust-history.html
http://gutenberg.net.au/first-fleet.html

Proceedings of the Old Bailey: http://www.oldbaileyonline.org/

Sir Joseph Banks papers relating to Australia:
http://www.sl.nsw.gov.au/banks/

State records of New South Wales: http://www.records.nsw.au

State library of New south Wales: http://www.sl.nsw.gov.au

Pictures

Governor Arthur Phillip: National Library of Australia: Ref. an9846228

David Collins: Mitchell Library, State Library of NSW: DON d1_12261

Captain John Hunter: Mitchell Library, State Library of NSW

Lieutenant-Colonel Philip Gidley King: Mitchell Library, State Library of NSW

Rev. Richard Johnson: Mitchell Library, State Library NSW (artist, Richard Read)

George Johnston: Mitchell Library, State Library NSW (artist, Robert Dighton)

Watkin Tench: Mitchell Library, State Library of NSW: FM 1-2115

Bennelong, in British clothes: Mitchell Library, State Library of NSW

Elizabeth Macarthur: Dixon Library, State Library of NSW (artist unknown)

John Macarthur: Mitchell Library, State Library of NSW

Lieutenant William Paterson: Mitchell Library, State Library NSW

Frenchman, La Pérouse: Mitchell Library, State Library of NSW

'First Fleet in Sydney Cove', Frank Allen

'Lady Penrhyn', Frank Allen

Index

Aboriginal
  childbirth, 176, 200
  children's games, 259
  dance & song (as celebration/
    storytelling), 2, 78, 129, 148,
    179,270, 276, 284, 291
  familial responsibility, 202
  fire-making, 131
  fishing, 60, 98, 231, 268
  food and food sources, 85, 98, 101,
    109-10, 118, 122, 161, 205
  hereditary property, 131
  justice & retribution, 87-8, 101,
    112, 172, 199, 280, 284
  language/s, 178-9, 212
  'malgun', 177, 291
  medicine and healing, 32, 212-13,
    233
  ornamentation, 5, 9, 176
  rock art, 75
  tooth extraction, 5, 262, 271, 273
  weapons, 9-10, 79, 80, 87, 97, 107,
    126, 164-7, 169, 182, 271, 280
Abrahams, Esther, xiv, 18, 20-4, 26,
  71-2, 106, 123-4, 133, 137-8, 156,
  223-4, 240, 249-51, 255, 268,
  273-5, 286, 294, 297-9
Alexander (ship), xiv, 67, 69, 92
animals (and birds), 25, 28-9, 44-6,
  47-8, 91, 121-2, 124, 197, 275, 278
Arabanoo, xv, 109-17, 125, 127, 129,
  224, 241, 286
Araboo (see Boorong)
Atlantic (ship), 263-4, 295, 300

Bagley, James, 144, 288
Ballooderry, xv, 206, 208-10, 214,
  230-6, 261, 293, 295-6

Barangaroo, xv, 172-7, 199-202, 237,
  263, 290-1, 293
Barrett, Thomas, xiv, 56, 61-2, 280-1
Barrington, George, 241-3, 282, 296, 307
Bennelong, xv, 127-32, 146-8, 161-6,
  168-9, 172-9, 186, 195, 200-3,
  214, 232-4, 237, 241, 260-3,
  265-6, 269-70, 272, 287, 290-3,
  296, 300, 308-9
Bennelong Point, 179, 265, 291
Bennett, James, 82
Berewalgal (people from afar), 173,
  205, 263, 291, 300
Bloodworth, James, xiv, 63-4, 83, 255,
  267, 281, 284, 299
Blue Mountains, vii, 74, 118, 123, 206,
  266, 286, 304-5
Boorong, xv, 115-7, 127, 154, 170-3,
  177, 234, 236-7, 261-2, 286, 291,
  296, 300
Borrowdale (ship), xiv
Botany Bay, xii, xvii, xviii, 1, 3, 6, 8,
  11, 13-5, 18-9, 26, 34-5, 65-6,
  70, 86-7, 97, 112, 118, 124, 165,
  180-3, 184-5, 189, 191, 208, 241,
  269, 270-4, 276-8, 280, 283-4, 292,
  294, 296, 299, 301-3, 305-7, 309
Bowes Smyth, Arthur, xiv, 22-3, 36-7,
  39, 51, 71, 273-5, 277-81, 283,
  286, 301, 303
Bradley, William, xiv, 60, 85, 87, 125,
  126-8, 276, 280-1, 290, 301
Britannia (ship and see also Raven,
  Captain), 254-5, 298-9
Bryant, Mary (nee Mary Broad), xiv,
  64-5, 143, 217-8, 220, 258, 282,
  294, 299, 304
Bryant, William, xiv, 64-5, 143, 217-20,
  257-8, 281-2, 294, 299

Burramatta (see also Parramatta and Rose Hill), 101-2, 104, 116, 170, 236, 290

cabbage tree palm, 63, 96, 281-2
Cadigal (also spelt Gadigal, 15, 209, 272
Charlotte (transport ship), xiv, 28, 61, 67, 281-2
Charlotte Medal, 62, 281
'Chinese travellers', 222, 247, 281, 294
Clark, Ralph, xiv, 29-30, 38, 51, 91, 135, 227, 272, 274-7, 281, 283, 294-5, 297, 301, 304
Colbee, xv, 127-8, 161-2, 164-6, 176, 183, 186, 190, 198, 206, 208-14, 234, 241, 260, 262, 272, 287, 293
Collins, David, xiv, 20, 22, 31, 39, 42, 54, 74, 82, 88, 94-5, 102, 112, 114, 118, 131, 135, 142, 153, 162-4, 167-8, 193, 196, 202-3, 206, 219, 222, 225, 231, 234-5, 239, 247-8, 253, 260, 262, 268, 270-301, 304, 309

Daringa (Colbee's wife), xv, 176, 198-9, 260, 272, 291, 300
Dawes Point (see 'Tara')
Dawes, William, xiv, xv, 57, 59, 77-8, 109, 123-4, 141, 158, 170, 177-8, 188-9, 194, 206, 208, 215-6, 226, 239, 245-6, 251, 272-3, 275, 280, 284, 286, 290-2, 294, 296, 300-1, 304, 309
Dilboong (Bennelong's baby daughter), 200, 202, 293
Dundas, Jane, xiv, 129, 229, 287, 295

education, 132-3, 228, 256, 287
Eora (people), x, xv, 78, 180, 187-8, 203, 245, 284, 291-2, 308
Everingham, Matthew, xiv, 244, 296, 301, 307
Executions, 56, 62, 82, 84, 95, 169, 199, 280-1, 285

First Fleet, vii- xii, xiv, xvi-xviii, 13, 38, 43, 52, 59, 66, 100, 133-4, 152, 223, 226, 228, 247, 259, 267, 273-5, 281, 301, 303-5, 307, 309
Fishburn (ship), xiv
Friendship (ship), xiv, 29, 38, 67, 277

Gadigal (see Cadigal)
'galgalla' (see also 'smallpox'), 171, 237
Golden Grove (ship), xiv
Gorgon (HMS), 222-3, 226-8, 239-41, 246-7, 294-7
Government House, 142, 200, 230-1, 265-7, 295
Grose, Francis, 248, 251, 254-5, 297, 299
Guardian (ship), 152, 289

Handland, Dorothy, xiv, 23, 259, 274, 299
Hawkesbury River, 118, 121, 211, 214-5, 273, 281, 286, 294, 303
Hayward, Elizabeth, xiv, 23, 274-5
Holmes, Susannah (see Kable)
Hunter, John, xiv, 60, 100, 111, 118, 120, 134, 176-7, 201, 232, 237, 239, 268, 270-2, 276, 281, 284-6, 288-96, 300, 302, 309

Inett, Ann, xiv, 21, 71-2, 138, 144-5, 228-9, 274, 282-3, 288, 295, 305

Johnson, Mary, xiv, 115-6, 158, 236-7, 240, 262, 286
Johnson, Reverend Richard, xiv, 38, 65, 69, 92, 115-6, 133, 142-3, 158, 170, 172, 188, 223, 236-7, 256, 261, 268, 277, 286, 288-90, 302, 309
Johnston, George, xiv, 17-9, 22, 26, 41, 71, 74, 86, 106, 113, 118, 123-4, 137, 156, 223-4, 239-40, 250, 254-5, 268, 273-4, 277, 286, 289, 294, 297-9, 302, 307, 309

Kable, Henry, xiv, 65-9, 92-4, 256, 275, 282, 285, 287, 297, 299

Kable, Susannah (nee Holmes) 29, 65-8, 92-4, 249-50, 256, 275, 282, 297, 299

King, Anna Josepha, 227, 240, 295

King, Philip Gidley, xiv, 3, 25, 34-5, 70-2, 136-8, 144-5, 227-9, 239-40, 268, 271, 274-5, 277, 282-3, 288, 290-1, 295, 302, 306, 309

Koradji, (man of special power), xv, 115, 212, 233, 236, 295

La Pérouse, 34, 70, 269, 272, 277, 309

Lady Juliana (ship), 151, 153, 289, 307

Lady Penrhyn (transport ship), xiv, 21, 23-4, 26-7, 36, 50, 71-2, 132, 137, 250, 273-5, 301, 303, 309

language learning & exchange (see pronunciation issues), 2, 7, 10, 78, 98-99, 110, 111, 114-15, 119, 129, 162-3, 166, 177, 178, 203, 215, 208-9, 210-11, 245, 272, 284, 291, 293, 296, 306, 309

Macarthur, Elizabeth, 156-9, 176, 197, 227-8, 230, 239-40, 247, 249, 251, 260, 269, 290-2, 295-8, 300, 302-3, 306, 309

Macarthur, John, 156-7, 159, 229, 254-5, 269, 290, 297-9, 302, 305, 309

Manly Cove, 11, 161-9, 273, 290-1

Martin, James, 220, 294, 299, 302, 306

Maugoran, xv, 170-1, 235-7, 261, 290, 296

McEntire, John, xiv, xv, 175, 181-4, 186, 194, 205, 291-2

Nanberry, xv, 114, 116-7, 127, 154, 161-2, 172, 177, 230-7, 261-2, 286, 295, 300

Needham, Elizabeth, xiv, 23, 50-1, 274, 279

Nepean River, 121, 123, 211, 215, 286, 294

Neptune (ship), 153, 157, 257, 289

New South Wales Corps, 154, 156, 161, 194, 248-51

Norfolk Island, 70-3, 135-8, 141-2, 144-5, 155, 181, 187, 223-4, 227-9, 239, 270, 272, 274, 282-4, 286, 288-9, 295, 302

Parker, Captain and Mrs, 227-8, 295

Parramatta (see also Rose Hill and Burramatta), 102, 197, 205, 227, 231, 236, 246, 252, 256, 260-1, 272, 293, 296, 298

Paterson, Elizabeth, 228, 239, 295

Paterson, William, 227-8, 239, 269, 295, 309

Pattyegarang, (also Pattye) xv, 177, 245-6, 292, 296

Pemulwuy, xv, 180-3, 190, 195, 205, 260, 292-3, 306

Phillip, Arthur, ix, xiv, xvii, 4-5, 11-3, 15, 19, 22, 24, 30, 32, 34, 36, 39, 42-4, 47-8, 51-2, 54, 57, 61, 64, 70, 72-4, 79-80, 86, 88, 90, 100, 102-4, 112-3, 117, 120, 130, 132, 136, 142, 161-170, 175, 181, 183-4, 193, 201, 202, 204, 206, 214, 227, 229, 230-5, 237, 239, 248-68, 272, 274, 276-80, 282-7, 290-3, 295-300, 302-3, 305-7, 309

Pinchgut (island), 89

Port Jackson, xii, 11, 15, 29, 113, 241, 265-6, 270, 272-4, 276, 282, 284, 286, 290, 301-3

'Port Jackson painter'', (see also Thomas Watling), 265-6

Prince of Wales (ship), xiv

pronunciation issues, 178-9, 212

Pulley, Elizabeth, xiv, 38, 277, 307

Raven, Captain (see also *Britannia*), 254-5, 298-9

Rawson, Isabella, xiv, 23, 132, 274-5, 287, 299

Reliance (ship), 297

Religion and beliefs, 177-8, 202-3, 270-81, 293

Richardson, William, xiv, 132, 256, 287, 299

Robinson, Richard, 229,295

Rope, Anthony, xiv, 38, 243-4, 277

Rose Hill (see also Parramatta and Burramatta), 76, 100-4, 118, 121, 134, 158, 170-1, 181, 184, 206-8, 210, 213-4, 221-2, 236, 241, 243, 252, 281, 285-6, 290, 293, 296, 298

Ross, Robert, xiv, 51-2, 63, 91, 123, 136, 279, 281, 285, 288, 296

Ruse, James, xiv, 17, 40-2, 103-4, 257-8, 273, (farming techniques, 278), 285, 299

Scarborough (ship), xiv, 153, 157, 229, 249, 289, 297

Scurvy, 29, 32

Second Fleet, 152-61, 181, 218, 224, 249, 289, 305, 307

Sinclair, Duncan, xiv, 92, 280

Sirius (HMS), xiv, 60, 91, 100, 111, 128, 134-6, 139, 141-2, 151, 181, 271, 276, 285-8, 290, 301-2, 305-6

Smallpox, xv, 114, 116-7, 127, 171, 230, 234, 236, 261, 286

Smilax glyciphylla ('sweet tea'), 218

Smith, Ann, xiv, 27-8, 72-3, 273, 283

Supply (HMS), xiv, 3, 25, 71, 91, 99, 100, 136, 138-9, 141, 145, 247, 273, 288, 297

Surprise (ship), 153-4, 289

Sydney Cove, vii, ix-x, xiii, 13-5, 17-20, 22, 35, 44, 53, 55, 63-4, 67-8, 70-1, 73-4, 77-9, 86, 100-1, 103, 107, 111, 114, 116, 127, 131, 134, 137, 139, 143-4, 147, 153, 155, 157, 177, 179, 249, 252, 256,

265-7, 271-4, 276-80, 282, 284-9, 292-3, 295, 299, 303-4, 308-9

Tank Stream, 198, 266

'Tara' (Dawes Point) 78, 109, 239

Tench, Watkin, xiv, xvii, 6, 8, 14, 33, 37, 59, 61-2, 64, 67, 74-5, 90, 106-11, 113-4, 116-7, 120-1, 129, 132, 139, 141-2, 146, 150-152, 159-61, 171-2, 175, 177-9, 183, 185-6, 188-92, 196-8, 201, 204, 206-17, 221, 226, 232, 239-41, 243-6, 253, 257-8, 269-72, 274, 276-300, 303, 308-9

Third Fleet, 225, 295

Thomas Watling (see also 'Port Jackson painter'), 265

Waaksamheyd (ship), 218, 239, 296

Wangal, 15, 272

Warran (Sydney Cove), x, 13, 17, 78, 272-3, 284

Waterhouse, William, xiv, 162-8, 290, 303

Wentworth, D'Arcy, 155-6, 289, 307

whales, 25, 159-60, 161-2, 274, 290

White, John (Chief Surgeon), xiv, xv, xviii, 8-10, 32, 62, 74-5, 86, 92, 96-8, 113-4, 127, 135, 154, 161, 177, 200, 202, 206, 230, 232, 236, 239, 261-2, 265, 270-1, 275-6, 280-87, 291, 293, 296, 300

Wilson, John (convict), xiv, 40-1, 148-9, 258, 278, 288-9, 294, 299

Worgan, George, xiv, 3-5, 44, 89-90, 158, 239, 271, 278, 280, 284-5, 290, 296, 303, 308

Yellomundee (Yarramundi), xv, 211-13, 294

Yemmerrawanne, xv, 265

'Stories of life at Sydney Cove'

A young reader edition of 'Across Great Divides'

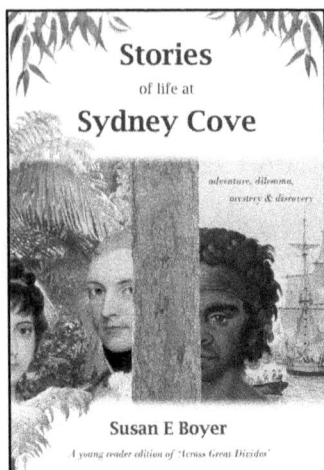

'Stories of Life at Sydney Cove' is a gripping narrative that weaves together the everyday experiences of convicts, soldiers and Aboriginal people with the events of history. These true stories are told through the words of those who really lived at Sydney Cove in 1788, and are so intriguing they read like fiction.

The stories begin with the voyage of the First Fleet when thirteen year old convicts, John Hudson and Elizabeth Hayward, are sent to a mysterious land at the end of the world. They have no idea of what life holds for them. At Sydney Cove there are no roads, no fences, no buildings ... just wilderness.

All the stories relate to the people and actual events as recorded in journals, letters and official reports of the First Fleet.

Later when Indigenous children Nanberry and Boorong come to live with the white strangers, they see life through different eyes. The mystery of a new world had begun and the lives of all involved would never be the same again.

'Stories of Life at Sydney Cove', is for readers aged 10+.

Australian history - Fiction - RRP $18.95
ISBN 9781877074493

Available online at **www.birrongbooks.com** and all good book stores

Go to www.birrongbooks.com for Australian curriculum notes and free teacher resources.

Susan Boyer is available for library and school visits to talk about the stories in her books.

© birrongbooks

www.ingramcontent.com/pod-product-compliance
Lightning Source LLC
Chambersburg PA
CBHW070340090426
42733CB00009B/1238